Veterans For Lunch Bunch

**A BOOK OF SHORT WWII & VIETNAM
WAR STORIES AND VARIED EXPERIENCES
RECOUNTED BY HIGHLY-DECORATED
VETERANS**

Publish Authority

All rights reserved. No part of this book may be reproduced in any form or by any electronic or mechanical means, including information storage and retrieval systems, without written permission from the publisher. The exception would be in the case of brief quotations embodied in critical articles or reviews and pages where permission is specifically granted by the publisher. For permission requests, solicit the publisher via the address below.

Copyright© 2024 by Veterans For Lunch Bunch

Veterans For Lunch Bunch: A Book of Short WWII & Vietnam War Stories and Varied Experiences Recounted by Highly-Decorated Veterans
ISBN 978-1-954000-70-4 (Hardback)
ISBN 978-1-954000-71-1 (eBook)

All events, locales, conversations, and observations in this book are from the individual author's memories of them and from their perspectives. Although every precaution has been taken to verify the accuracy of the information contained herein, the editor and publisher assume no responsibility for any errors or omissions. No liability is assumed for damages that may result from the use of information contained within.

Editor: Terrence "T.D." Jorgensen
Cover design: Terrence "T.D." Jorgensen
Interior design: Teresa Evans

Published 2024, by Publish Authority
300 Colonial Center Parkway, Suite 100
Roswell, GA 30076-4892 USA
PublishAuthority.com

First Edition. Printed in the United States of America

Veterans For Lunch Bunch

These individual war stories herein, were composed by each Veteran themselves, describing memories they recalled of their time in service to our great country, and were a combination of heroic acts of unselfish patriotism by some, as well as an array of semi-humorous anecdotes and unusual experience(s) each had while serving in Vietnam, OR . . . in places they will never admit to having been in. They were never there. They do NOT exist, and never have.

All of these wonderful stories were also proofread, edited, and enhanced with graphics and photo images by our Veterans-For-Lunch-Bunch Coordinator – T.D. Jorgensen.

We hope all who read these military experiences by our Veterans, will appreciate them, and thank a Veteran for insuring we're all STILL speaking English, and not German, or Russian, today.

We also want to send out a HUGE *THANK YOU* to all of our Veterans, who donated their hard-earned American Dollar$ during these difficult fiscal times in our Republic. You ARE *The Greatest*, just like "The Greatest Generation" of World War II.

Thanks, also go out to Billy Davis, who offered to pay for all of this `Album` project, but we didn't need to go there. Our Veterans answered the calling for donations, and then some. We thank them all.

And lastly, I want to thank Hal Burke for assisting me in obtaining several Veterans' stories, who were somewhat reluctant to submit their individual story. You did a great job, Hal, and I so appreciated your help.

Warmest Veteran regards,

T.D Jorgensen

    Bruce   Mike   Jack   Rick

Years ago, **Rick McDowell** and I would meet up for lunch at the *Saigon Cafe* in Woodstock. We settled on Mondays with a meeting time of 1230-hrs. in order to miss the lunch hour rush. That meant we could secure a table and not feel rushed. So, one day after several months of this routine, my friend **Mike Lichter** from church joined in the conversation and asked if he could join the two of us. Of course, we said, *"Yes!"* and he spontaneously invited **Jack Kowall** ... and, after a few weeks went by Brad Wright was invited, so word spread and our numbers increased to about 12 regulars ... every week, someone new would show up and our numbers of *Luncheonaires* grew.

In the growth, I wanted to keep the group together as Veterans, without the exclusive club atmosphere. No rules other than to be civil with one another, and feel free to chat amongst ourselves without constraints of any kind.

Time is not much of a friend to us older guys, especially not Mike & Rick, as both passed on to their final reward, but the numbers slowly grew until I had to give up coordinating the group, due to my increasing health concerns.

But who should I pass the reigns to? They were all my friends. Then He walked into church one Sunday and the message was clear. I needed someone who was computer savvy, friendly, well organized, and had a beautiful wife, who would support our military circle of friends.

So, I asked T.D. Jorgensen if he would consider being *RingMaster* to a bunch of *stray cats*.

I begged, pleaded, and promised him that I would support him. Time has been our friend, and NOW we have about **45-50,** and sometimes **85** Veterans, who show up for our weekly luncheon. I am proud of the strides that this group has taken, and the leadership of T.D. Keep in mind, this is NOT a club, but a gathering of Veterans with a common set of values -- *We Love America*... the home of the Brave.

Respectfully submitted,

Bruce Publicover
United States Army Security Agency 1963-67
319th USASA Bn, Rothwesten, West Germany 1964-66
371st RRU (ASA) 1st Air Cav 1966-67 RVN

Our Greatest Generation

We owe our gratitude and admiration to the many members of our Armed Forces, who fought so courageously, and with such bravery, so as to win the battles of WWII, and eventually culminated with the Unconditional Surrenders of the evil Axis of Germany, Italy, and Japan, to the United States of America and her Allies.

We're so very proud to be able to call these WWII Veterans, our Friends. They make us PROUD to have also served when our Nation called upon us during our own era's battles.

These gentle and humble souls are our "Greatest Generation," and it is our honor to recognize them in this book.

Left: Hilbert "Hibby" Margol -Age-100 (WWII Infantryman in Europe),

Center-Top: -T.D. Jorgensen (Vietnam Veteran/Aviator),

Center-Bottom Left: Russell Vaudrey - Age-101 (WWII Army Air Corps Crewmember /Pacific Theater),

Center-Bottom Right: Charlie Duncan - Age-104 (WWII Infantryman zn Europe),

Far-Right: Miles Willis - age-97 (WWII U.S. Navy/Pacific Theater).

Table of Contents

LAST NAME:	FIRST NAME:	PAGES:
Aloia	Dennis	10
Bevich	John	11-13
Brown	Bill	14-20
Brown	Johnny	21-22
Bruss	John	23-24
Burke	Hal	25-26
Cape	Chuck	27-28
Chellino	Edward	29-30
Cochran	Ted	31-32
Davis	Billy	33-37
Drew	Ernie	38-40
Driscoll	Jack	41-42
Dunn	Bo	43-45
Fletcher	Terrence	46-50
Forsberg	Philip	51-61
Foster	Tom	62-64
Frankle	John	65-66
Futral	Ronnie	67-69
Goddard	Bruce	70-71
Goddard	Dick	72-74
Hale	Fred	75-76
Hambrick	David	77-80
Harper	Bill	81-84
Heflin	Al	85-86
Hollingshed	Harold	87-90
Jacobs	Richard	91-93
Jorgensen	T.D.	94-98

LAST NAME:	FIRST NAME:	PAGES:
Judkins	Cliff	99-105
Kotler	Mike	106-108
Kowall	Jack	109-110
Landin	Bob	111-113
Lantz	Roy	114-115
Lester	P. Dickson	116-118
Liposky	Richard `Doc`	119-121
Lula	John	122-123
Maloney	Mark	124-126
Margol	Hilbert	127-129
Martin	Ben	130-131
McCabe	Mike	132-134
Murphy	George	135-136
Nelson	George	137-140
Pfister	Robert	141-143
Pillar	Pete	144-145
Publicover	Bruce	146-147
Redding	Edward	148-149
Rogers	Jim	150-153
Smith	Robin	154-157
Snider	Bob	158-160
Tran	Duc	161-163
Vasquez	Gus	164-168
Vaudrey	Russell	169-173
Willis	Miles	174-176
Woods	Edward	177-182
Wright	Richard	183-187

Veterans For Lunch Bunch

Our largest gathering of Veterans is when our group meets at The Cowan Historic Mill in Acworth, thanks to our patriotic friend Kevin Marcy, who treats us to lunch 3-times each year. *THANKS*, Kevin! 😊

Above: Many of our *Veterans-For-Lunch-Bunch* group are also active, dues-paying members of the **G.V.V.A.** (*Georgia Vietnam Veterans Alliance*), and meet at the American Legion Post #29 in Marietta, the 3rd Thursday of each month, at 1800-hrs. **At right**, our Veterans enjoy camaraderie & good chow at alternating restaurants, each week.

Veterans For Lunch Bunch

Above: **Jake-the-Snake** and **Jack Driscoll** enjoy the Wings at '**Hooters**' Bar & Grille in Kennesaw. BOTH of these gentlemen are **USAF Pilots**. Coincidence?

Top right: **Harold Hollingshed** presents to **Kevin Marcy** the gift from our Veterans' group. *Below* Harold & Kevin is **Philip** `*Spike*` **Forsberg**, presenting the V.A.'s Disability Compensation Qualification-process, to our Veterans' group.

Below-Center: Our Veterans pay homage to WWII Veteran **Russell Vaudrey**, who turned **101** on July 10th, 2022. With Russell are **Bill Harper** & **Randy Scamihorn**.

Veterans For Lunch Bunch

Above, *and* **below:** Dining at `Tomatoes Country Buffet` in KENNESAW, GEORGIA.

ABOVE: At `Twin Peaks,` and below -- *THANKS* to *Ed Woods* for his informative speech on *National Cemetery benefits*.

BELOW: **John Drew** thanks **Kevin Marcy** with **G.V.V.A.** cap and applause. **Miles Willis** & **Tom Foster** enjoy some memories.

DENNIS ALOIA

U.S. Navy 1960 – 1966
Cell: 678-772-4097
DenBar500@Yahoo.com

MY MILITARY EXPERIENCE

I joined the U.S. Navy when I turned 17-years of age. A very big adventure for an inner-city kid from Chicago, who had never left the neighborhood, or seen the ocean.

1961 WELCOME TO THE GATOR NAVY

My 1st assignment in 1961 was to Admiral Eugene Fluckey's staff aboard the USS Mt. McKinley AGC-7, at Norfolk, VA. ADM Fluckey had been awarded the Medal of Honor in WWII as Commander of the USS Barb, a highly decorated submarine in the Pacific Ocean. The Mt. McKinley was an Amphibious Command Ship. We carried U.S. Marines and conducted landings in the Caribbean Sea and South Atlantic Ocean. Great memories of Liberty in Puerto Rico, The Virgin Islands, and Ft. Lauderdale, Florida.

1962

A banner year. Now, I was part of the ship's Company aboard the USS Taconic AGC-17, a sister ship of the USS Mt. McKinley. Leaving the U.S. in January we started a 9-month deployment to the Mediterranean Sea. I was a loader on a 40-MM gun mount. After landing Marines in Suda Bay, Crete, Sardinia, and Corsica, we visited various ports in Italy. I celebrated my 18th birthday in Genoa, Italy. It was that day while docked, while the Captain was ashore, that the cruise ship Leonardo DaVinci struck our ship, while coming into port. The collision Alarm was sounded aboard ship, and our illustrious Executive Officer Lieutenant Grafton appeared on the Bridge in his underwear, while the cruise ship passengers applauded.

(Continued ☞)

We all thought Grafton was related to Captain Bligh, so he got his just due. Port visits to Spain, Greece, France, and amphibious landing practices followed, then it was back to the U.S.A. in September.

13-DAYS OF OCTOBER

The Cuban Missile Crisis occurred while I was aboard ship in Philadelphia. I remember President Kennedy announcing a Naval Blockade of Cuba. The next day, any ship in an East Coast Port that could float was out to sea. We anticipated an Amphibious Landing on mainland Cuba and were prepared. After a tense 13-days, the Russian ships and submarines turned around, and left Cuba with their missiles.

1963

I was proud to serve for a short time aboard the USS Prichett DD561 in Long Beach, California. We searched for a downed airplane off the California Coast and conducted anti-submarine and anti-aircraft training.

Upon returning, I entered Reserve Status until 1966, when I was honorably discharged.

I am very proud of my U.S. Naval Service to this great country.

John Bevich
USAF
Cell: 678-849-3062
TJMB6484@Yahoo.com

My Military Experience(s)

I left Allentown, PA, March 1965, leaving behind my $1.00 an hour delivery job, and my '55 Chevy Bel Air coupe with a 289-HP engine & Hurst floor shifter, for the U. S. Air Force. After Basic Training, it was off to Sheppard AFB for aircraft Turbo-Prop Maintenance School. Firstassignment -- Charleston AFB, SC, where our C-130E aircraft were in support of the 1965 Dominican Republic Civil War (Guerra Civil Dominicana).

So, I sold that '55 Chevy and had to hitch-hike a time or two in and around Charleston, until my new assigned roommate revealed he had a '57 Chevy, so that ended my hitch-hiking era. Next, it was Nov. '66, and we were off to Ching Chuan Kang (CCK) Air Base in Taiwan, formerly known as Formosa. (for geography checkers.☺ It was a 13-month assignment with 45 days out on missions to Vietnam 1967. In December 1967, I was assigned to Detachment #1, 314 TCW (USAF SOG- later designated it as the 15th Special Operation Squadron) at Nha Trang, RVN. We arrived the day before Christmas, and, of course, office staff personnel got the day off, so I processed in on the next work day. We were a Special Ops Squadron, so we had separate quarters (with state side toilets) next to the Flight Line with our 4-assigned MC-130 Combat Talons aircraft. The following is a Synopsis of the aircraft I was assigned to, on my third day in the Squadron, as we waited for MC-130 #64-0547 to return in the early morning hours of 30 December. The following specifics of the mission were written by USAF Colonel (Retired) John Gargus Mission Planner. The Detachment flew Covert & Clandestine Missions for Military Advisor Command Studies & Observation Group based in Saigon, RVN.

On 12/30/67, one Combat Talon MC-130 with 11-crew members failed to return from its combat mission over North Vietnam. It was a night mission, whose departure was timed to haveleaflets reach Hanoi area at daylight. The first part flown at high altitude from Nha Trang to acheckpoint in the Laotian Plain Of Jars. At that point, the aircraft descended into a terrainfollowing flight profile, flying at 1,000 ft above the ground, and at standard 230-Knot groundspeed (265mph). The altitude and frequent changes of heading over mountainous terrainpermitted the aircraft to penetrate into North Vietnam's Red River Valley without being detectedby enemy's early warning radars. Once there, the aircraft accelerated to its maximum airspeed and executed a rapid climb to 31,000 feet, their assigned leaflet drop altitude. It's climb and drop tracks were flight planned just outside of the lethal ranges of known surface to air missiles (SAM5) and anti-aircraft artillery (AAA), exposing it only to a possible encounter with a MiG Interceptor.

However, the planned avoidance of early detection, rapid climb to high altitude, with a short leaflet drop time, followed by an equally rapid descent to the terrain following altitude, insured that the enemy didn't have enough time to alert, launch and direct a MiG towards our MC-130 aircraft. After the drop, the aircraft proceeded westward through mountains into Black River Valley. There at 04:30 over a prominent river bend, the aircraft made its last progress report. The aircraft turned southward, and its crew was preparing for the diversionary cargo drop in the vicinity of Highway 6 east of Dien Bien Phu the cargo was intended to be discovered by the North Vietnamese, and its contents were to lead them to believe that a Commando Team was operating in that area. Unfortunately, the aircraft never reached its intended drop zone.

Almost 25 years later, in October 1992, local villagers led a joint recovery team to an aircraft crash site which confirmed to be that of the MC-130. The site was located on a steep mountain rise about seven and a half minutes of flight time from its last Reporting Point. Site examination confirmed that the destruction of the aircraft was total and instantaneous. The site was visited again one year later in October 1993 when the excavation and retrieval of the aircrew remains was complete.

Thanks to the Internet, I found my Squadron Reunion Group and attended my first reunion @ Ft Walton Beach, Florida, in 2013. I didn't run into anyone I knew, but did meet the guy that took my place, who I missed in Vietnam due to my credit time, the previous year. However,

on a trip to Hurlburt Field, I did me and my ol` friend MC-130 #64-0567 (replacement for #64-0547)which was on static display at the Air Force Base Memorial Park. After 46-years, we both survived that ol` crazy Asian War.

I did meet **Colonel Gargus** at our reunion in 2015. [**Note:** *he was the Navigator on one of the Combat Talon aircraft on the Son Tay raid POW rescue attempt on November 21, 1970, in North Vietnam. [He had a book published in 2010 about The Son Tay Raid, by The Texas A&M University Press]*.

In 2016, I had another one of life's surprises. The Reunion Committee decided to honor our 50- year founding of "**Project Stray Goose**" (*Squadron Logo Maynard the Duck*) and sponsored anall-expense trip to Kadena Air Base on Okinawa Island in Japan -- the location of a Pacific CombatTalon Squadron. I was one of 10 selected. The Committee and Colonel Hess ... ***I thank you.*** (Others were 50-year members; I was a mere 49-year member). Apparently, Close enough in Air Force specs. 😊

The trip was great meeting, and socializing with the younger people was fun, and to hear their attitudes for the missions, and the dedication of their country was much the same as our own generation many, many years ago. We did a few toasts to all in attendance, and to our fallen brothers.

They had Squadron Bar, with a lot of memorabilia. I must have had ESP, because I took along a South Vietnam Tiger uniform hat that I had traded for, or picked up somewhere back when, so I autographed the hat, and wrote the years in-country to add to their collection.

And finally, at our reunions we always end them with a meeting and prayer at the Black Granite Memorial erected at the Hurlburt Field to honor all our fallen heroes. And I say, "May God rest their souls." Amen!

I'LL BE HOME FOR CHRISTMAS

I received the following Christmas email message from Bill Brown, a brother from Vietnam who served as a combat photographer. A Christmas card sent through the mail by family and friends is thoughtful and traditional, but Bill's heartfelt message was something special that needs to be shared. Veterans of all wars understand its significance. The story is in his own words:

BILL BROWN

U.S. Army
404-281-8239
WBrown6@Bellsouth.net

MY VIETNAM EXPERIENCE

I'll be home for Christmas,

You can count on me.

There'll be snow, and mistletoe,

And presents beneath the tree.

Christmas Eve will find me,

Where the love lights gleam.

I'll be home for Christmas,

If only in my dreams.

Bill and his guitar out in the boondocks

It was Christmas of 1967. I was in Vietnam surrounded by the members of my platoon, some fellow officers, and a few Donut Dollies. I had an old guitar that my platoon had given me. It was just a guitar body with no strings, tuning knobs or hardware when they gave it to me. But I had written home to Mom and Dad, and asked for a set of strings and the hardware to attach to the guitar.

We sat around the Photo Lab in Lai Khe, had a few drinks and sang some Christmas songs as well as other songs that reminded us of home. Lai Khe was 1st Division Headquarters at that time.

We had moved 1st Division HQ from Di-An just before Christmas. I was a platoon leader for a communication platoon while we were in Di-An, and my platoon and I spent a lot of time in the field. And now I was a platoon leader of a platoon of Combat Photographers and lab technicians. At least we were in the relative safety of the base camp this Christmas Eve, and not out in the field somewhere in Vietnam.

Of course, little did we know what lay ahead a month and a few days from this Christmas Eve. There would be fireworks of an unwelcome kind celebrating a different holiday. Mortar rounds and 122mm rockets, AK-47 and other small arms fire as the Viet Cong began what would be known as the Tet Offensive of 1968, the most intense fighting of the entire war.

All we knew was that it was Christmas Eve, and we were a long way from home and family and friends. And while our hearts ached, we were comforted by the Christmas music, the memories it stirred, and the camaraderie we shared in our little group so far from home.

Back in the U.S. in a small South Georgia town, was a young blond-headed girl I had met just before going on active-duty in 1966. After graduation from college, I had about six weeks before I was to report for active-duty. My home church in Albany, Georgia, asked me to drive a group of teenagers to a church camp in St. Petersburg, Florida. I was to stay at the church camp for the entire week, and I was referred to as a Counselor, although I was really just a glorified driver. This blonde-headed teenage girl was one of the campers. I found out she lived in Waynesboro, GA. My first active-duty assignment was at Fort Gordon, GA, and as it happens, Waynesboro is right along the way from Albany to Fort Gordon.

So, I stopped by to see her, and met her parents. I'm sure they were glad to see me leave.

Bill at Ft Benning before deployment

After all, I was a college graduate, and she was still in high school. A year later, I'm in Vietnam. I didn't have any Christmas cards, but I was a pretty good artist.

I drew a picture of a soldier, head and shoulders, in jungle fatigues and steel pot. Of

course, I put my name on the name tag. I took a photograph of the drawing, developed it in the photo lab, printed it on good paper, cut it out, and sent her a home-made Christmas card. That's the first she knew that I was in Vietnam. After that, we exchanged a few letters till I came home.

Soon after I came home from Vietnam in August of 1968, I went to see her. She was a little older now, and the age difference didn't seem as important as it had two years or more earlier. She was a college girl, away from home, and spreading her wings. That was the beginning of an on-and-off courtship that lasted another five or so years until we were married. I've shared every Christmas with her for the past forty-nine years, and I have no regrets.

Now, 50-years after that Christmas in Vietnam, I'm here at this Vietnam Veterans Christmas party sharing music, good food, and good times with other Vietnam veterans and their loved ones. We have so much to be thankful for. We survived the Vietnam War, we're home, and it is Christmas time.

So, thank you for your service, welcome home, and may God bless you, your family and friends, and the United States of America.

MERRY CHRISTMAS

Bill Brown   Vietnam '67, '68

1st Infantrry Division   Platoon Leader

NOTE: I asked Bill to jot down a few comments on his missions and/or assignments while in Nam. His response is restrained, even modest, considering he and his men went into combat with cameras instead of weapons. The following is his reply in his own words:

When I was a platoon leader for the Communications Platoon, we spent a lot of time in the field at various remote locations. We'd set up a VHF radio link back to 1st Division HQ to support operations from that location for several weeks.

That involved setting up a "fly swatter" antenna, which could be seen from quite a distance and made a good target. We'd fill sandbags to put around the radio truck and protect it, dig foxholes for ourselves, run wire to field phones, which we provided to the Infantry Commander and other key personnel he selected, and then maintain our VHF radio link, and protect the NDP perimeter. In addition to our concern about that antenna giving away our position, we were often reminded that the enemy was near because patrols operating out of our position would bring in captured enemy POWs from time to time.

Later as Platoon Leader for the Combat Photographers, we built the photo lab in Lai Khe with the help of the Engineers. I'd assign one or two photographers to go with the Infantry on various missions. They'd photograph the mission and bring the film back to the photo lab where we'd develop it and provide prints to *Army Intelligence* for analysis, as well as sending some pictures to various military publications to be included in their articles. On those missions, the Combat Photographers were exposed to the same dangers as the troops they were with. That included actual combat, fire fights, and the ever-present possibility of a Viet Cong ambush.

Other missions included going up in a Huey to photograph areas that we had just hit the night before with an artillery barrage, to assess the damage we had imposed on the enemy, or areas where there was suspected enemy activity. Sometimes our assignment was taking pictures from hidden locations of Vietnamese who were suspected of being spies. We also had more enjoyable assignments like photographing Change of Command ceremonies and events like the Bob Hope Show when it came to our area.

Note: Of 200 American military combat photographers sent to Vietnam, 2 were KIA (killed in action). One hundred thirty-five War Correspondents and Photographers of all nationalities lost their lives in Vietnam from the 1950's French involvement, to the Fall of Saigon in 1975. One who fell while on a Marine patrol in 1965 was Dickey Chapelle, the first female Combat Photographer and War Correspondent to die in a war. She also covered the Marines on Iwo Jima during

MY THOUGHTS

And that's the way it was … 10,000 miles from home, in a strange land of invisible enemies and crippling Rules of Engagement. It was a Christmas and New Year's Eve celebrated as best we could depending on where we were, who we were with, and how safe we felt to celebrate the birth of Christ and another year of war.

A month after Bill's 1967 impromptu Christmas party, the Viet Cong and North Vietnamese Army hit us with everything they had, including the kitchen sink. The goal of their infamous 1968 Tet Offensive was to win the war, to defeat America and her allies, and to push us all out of Vietnam. When the guns fell silent, we were still standing tall among a totally defeated and mostly dead enemy. Had we pushed back in a counter-offensive, as a military should have, then we would have been home for Christmas in 1968. Instead, Washington, D.C., decided to keep our hands tied behind our backs, and kept 'negotiating' for an 'honorable withdrawal,' which came to fruition five long years later

WWII and combat in Korea.

Nevertheless, Bill's 1967 Christmas would be the last Christmas for almost 4,000 American boys, who lost their lives during the 1968 Tet Offensive. Plus, 1968 proved to be the costliest year of the war for Americans killed in action: 16,592. The cost of victory in human lives does not assuage the broken hearts and spirits of loved ones on the home front. But, to waste young lives for limited results in a limited war with obviously limited intelligence among our political hierarchy in Washington, D.C., is borderline homicide. NFL players are instructed to 'win' on a football field; the same objective should be granted American soldiers on a battlefield.

This Christmas and New Year's, the warriors of the United States military are still deployed thousands of miles from home. Communication has improved with modern technology, but not the loneliness of a Christmas spent in Iraq or Afghanistan or even South Korea, Syria, or numerous other Ports-Of-Call categorized as in Harm's Way. Remember them. Pray for them. And, support them. They've earned it, and they need it.

Merry Christmas, and Hoorah!

JOHNNY BROWN
U.S. Air Force
770-608-6380
1JMBrown@Comcast.net

My Military Experiences

JOHNNY BROWN'S AIR FORCE STORY

I grew up dreaming of being an Air Force Pilot. In college, I immersed myself in AFROTC, even securing a highly-desired ROTC scholarship for my last two years. I had tested high in the Pilot Aptitude Test, which qualified me for the FIP Program my senior year. This was a program where the Air Force paid for a Private Pilot Course, so as to insure those slated for USAF UPT (Undergraduate Pilot Training) had the skills necessary to assure a high probability of success in the UPT course. In the mid-1960's, it cost $250,000 just to get a person trained to receive their wings.

I breezed through FIP and graduated from college in January 1966. I was commissioned immediately afterward, with orders to UPT for March 1966, Class 67-F at Craig AFB in Selma, Alabama. I entered that class, and received my wings in March of 1967. Because of the very limited mix of aircraft available for our particular class, I had a choice of backseat in the F-4 (in reality, an almost navigator-like position with limited flying) or Co-pilot in the B-52. For many reasons, I chose the B-52, and it was off to more training at Castle AFB, California.

I finished my BUFF Training in the summer of 1967, and then was assigned to Robins AFB, Georgia. I was assigned as a rookie Co-pilot as part of a 6-man B-52G crew, consisting of an Aircraft Commander, Co-pilot, Radar Navigator (known as Bombardier in earlier days), Navigator, Electronic Warfare Officer, and Gunner. We were Crew R-13 and quickly jelled into a great crew; one of the best at Robins AFB. We scored high in ORI's and became lead crew E-13. In late '68, we were selected to go to Southeast Asia as a part of Arc Light, a six-month tour where B-52's bombed South Vietnam, Laos and some in Cambodia (although we officially were never there), in support of our ground troops versus the Viet Cong & NVA. We flew a rotation out of Andersen AFB, Guam, (a 14-hour, round-trip flight, with 1 - 2 air refuelings), Kadena AFB, Okinawa, (8-hours, round-trip flight, with 1-air refueling), and U-Tapao RTNB in Thailand (3-4 hours round-trip flight, with no refueling). It was a busy time for the B-52, and we got all the flying time we wanted. Most of our missions were in South Vietnam. The bad guys shot 57mm AAA at us but couldn't hit us because of our altitude. SAM's (Surface-to-Air Missiles) were not yet in use. Crew E-13 returned to Robins AFB in June of '69, and became Select crew S-13, as all six of us were now instructors. Our Crew was disbanded in November of '69, and I was selected for upgrade to Aircraft Commander. I was also transferred to Westover AFB, Massachusetts, in January '70, as the U.S. Air Force needed more Aircraft Commanders, because Westover AFB was a Super-Wing with two Squadrons of B-52D Black Belly Arc Light cadre aircraft.

At Westover AFB, my new Lead Crew departed for another Arc Light tour in March of '70, but this time I was the Aircraft Commander and was now in the left seat. When we got into the Andersen/Kadena/U-Tapao rotation, the missions were much more demanding, in that 100mm AAA could now reach our bombing altitude, SAM's were now in place and North Vietnamese fighter aircraft were a threat to the B-52's. We spent more time out of U-Tapao and most missions sent us to heavily-defended areas on the Ho Chi Minh Trail and Laos. The Nixon Vietnamization of the war was well underway, as the ground war was winding down and B-52's were used more strategically against North Vietnamese incursion, as opposed to supporting our ground troops against the Viet Cong. The number of secondary explosions caused by our bombs was staggering, compared to my first Arc Light tour. Pipelines, ammunition dumps and trucks were richer targets than open fields and forests. We returned to Westover AFB in September of 1970.

Back at Westover AFB, I upgraded to Instructor Pilot and settled into the rigors of the Strategic Air Command (S.A.C.). Back to ORI's, low-level simulated nuclear bombing missions, and the normal Stateside SAC stuff. My crew were all-Instructor, and were Select Crew S-02, as well as a Standard-Evaluation Crew (Stan-Eval). We were as good as you can get.

In late 1971, for several reasons, I left SAC and Active Duty to join the Air National Guard and finally became a Fighter Pilot. I will save that story for another time. I will also save all my "I Was There" B-52 flying stories for another time. It was always my dream to be an Air Force Pilot. I was truly able to live my dream.

JOHN BRUSS
USAF
Cell: 678-689-8989
John_B1966@comcast.net

My Military Experiences

I was born in Union City, Indiana, April 10, 1948 – *"Yes I'm an old guy!"*

I grew up in that same small town of about 9,000 people, which is 50% in Indiana and 50% in Ohio.

I grew up as one of *"those ONLY children,"* however, I did have 2- older cousins (*guys*), and our backyards came together, so it was almost like having 2-older brothers without all the drama. One set of grandparents lived 5-houses down the street, while the others lives about 10-blocks away.

After graduating from High School in 1966, I was working for the local Chevrolet dealer, and in the summer of '67, I realized that since I wasn't in College, I would soon get drafted. **My plan was to join the Air Force to stay out of Vietnam**, (*my Dad was an Army-Air Corps guy in WWII*), so I enlisted under the *"90-day Delayed Enlistment Program"* and on September 7, 1967 I left for Basic Training at Lackland AFB, San Antonio, Texas.

Following Basic Training, I was sent to Chanute AFB, in Rantoul, Illinois, for Aircraft Electrical Maintenance training. After completing my training at Chanute, I was sent to my 1st Permanent Duty Station at Luke AFB, in Phoenix, Arizona, where I was only stationed at Luke from Feb – June 12th, when I was called to report to the Commander's Office. I was given notice that I had been *selected* for Overseas Duty – **Vietnam!!** *"OH Crap."* So, I went home for 2-weeks before shipping out for Vietnam.

When I arrived at McCord AFB, in Washington State, as I was walking around the boarding area, I ran into my short-time Luke AFB roommate, who had gone home on leave before shipping out, and ended up getting 60-days Free Leave, due to revised Orders. As it turned out, we flew into Cam Rahn Bay A.B. on the same plane, and we were the only 2-guys from our plane to be assigned to the 315th Air Commando Wing (*A.C.W.*) at Phan Rang A.B.

I was stationed at Phan Rang AB, just South of Cam Rahn Bay, with the 315th A.C.W., as an Aircraft Electrical Repairman (*AFSC-42350*) from June 1968 – July 1969. Once I got to Vietnam, I figured out that I wanted to be awake when the mortars and rockets started hitting the base, so I volunteered for the night shift (*7PM – 7AM*), which also gave me the opportunity to fly as an Assistant Loadmaster whenever they needed help. It also gave me *free time* to go into Thap Cham, which I did frequently when the base was open, and the town wasn't *Off Limits*.

One of my flights took me along with two other guys on a Recovery Mission down into the Delta. We had a downed C-123 at a Special Forces Camp in the middle of God only knows where. We had to cannibalize all the salvageable parts off the C-123 aircraft that we could, before the bird was to be blown up ... which we did, in what was supposed to be a 2-3 day trip actually took us 5-days to get back out of the camp, and back to Phan Rang.

I had the opportunity to help out a little on doing repairs on their Hueys and Gunships, while we were stuck there. Back at Phan Rang we dodged mortars almost nightly, and I took my R & R in Sidney in April, celebrating my 21st birthday there. I rotated back to the world in early July of 1969.

Following my tour in Vietnam, I was stationed in the Mojave Desert of California at Edwards AFB with the 6515th Field Maintenance Squadron working on numerous types of airplanes; F-4, SR-71, U-2, T-38, C-5A, F-104's, *etc*. While at Edwards, I was selected to go TDY to Luke AFB in Arizona to attend specialized training on the A-7D aircraft.

I was honorably discharged from U.S. Air Force on Nov. 4, 1971, and following the Air Force, I worked 5-years at *Lockheed-Martin* on the L-1011 project at the Palmdale, CA, plant as an Electrical Installer until promoted out to the Flight Test/Delivery crew. After 3-years at Lockheed, I got laid-off, at which time I joined *North American-Rockwell* on the B-1 project until it was shut down due to funding problems.

Following my lay-off from the B-1 project, I eventually moved my wife and son back to my hometown in Indiana, where I landed a job with a truck body manufacturer, contracted to build the bodies for General Motors. I spent a little over 20-years with them, starting out as a draftsman, then client service/relations, salesperson, and national Sales Mgr. before leaving.

I joined the **VFW Post 5262** in 2018 and assumed the position of Service Officer in 2019, and I am also the current *Finance Officer* for **American Legion Post 45** here in Canton, and actively involved in the *Cherokee County Homeless Veteran Program*. I am also a member of the **Georgia Vietnam Veterans Alliance**, one of the founders of the Canton *First United Methodist Church Veterans Group*, and a member of the *Vietnam Veterans-For-Lunch-Bunch*.

~ The End ~

HAROLD "HAL" T. BURKE
U.S. Navy, 1961-1967
Personnelman (E-4)
Cell: 708-387-7779
Hal@VictoryAndValorMemories.com

My Military Experiences

As a young boy growing up in Cicero, IL, in the mid 1950's, my favorite TV program every Sunday evening was to watch the 1954 Emmy award-winning, *"Victory At Sea,"* 26 half-hour segments of the documentary. The documentary was conceived by Henry Solomon, a former Navy Lieutenant Commander during WWII, who was a research assistant to historian Samuel Eliot Morrison. Morrison was writing the 15-volume of United States Naval Operations in WWII. Solomon learned of a large amount of film that the warring Navies had compiled and formed a research team that reviewed over 60 million feet of wartime film, which was edited down to about 61,000 feet for broadcast in the, *"Victory At Sea"* series.

Little did I know as a young boy fascinated with, *"Victory At Sea,"* that my life's journey would take me on an amazing adventure of discovery about *"The Greatest Generation."*

After graduating from Riverside Brookfield High School in 1960, I enlisted in the U.S. Navy in January 1961 on my 18th-birthday. During my enlistment, I had the honor of serving aboard the WWII Fletcher Class Destroyer **USS The Sullivans DD-537** (*named for the five Sullivan Brothers KIA aboard the Light Cruiser* **USS Juneau CL-52** *during the Battle of Guadalcanal on 13 Nov 1942*). Highlight of my time on *The Sullivans* was our cruise to the Azores, Lisbon, Portugal, and Palma De Mallorca, Spain.

Shore Patrol duty in Lisbon,   **Palma De Mallorca, Spain**

I also served on the destroyer **USS Prichett DD-561**, and the aircraft carrier **USS Lake Champlain CVA-39**.

Upon completion of my active-duty following the Cuban Missile Crisis (*13 Days of October 1962*), I used my V.A. benefits to attend, and graduate from, *Morton College*. And, in 1972 I received my Bachelor of Science in Commerce Degree from *DePaul University*, Chicago, IL. I received my Honorable Service Discharge from the Navy in 1967.

A 45-year career in Sales & Marketing developing new products and business for Fortune 500 corporations and suppliers to national retail drug, grocery, and mass merchandisers, culminated in 2016. In retirement, my new mission is to share inspirational and motivational presentations of historical military campaigns, and fallen heroes' legacies with students, civic, social, and corporate events.

I've written several articles for military publications and in the process of writing a book about the historical and fascinating connection between the five Sullivan Brothers and Alfred Eisenstaedt's iconic '*Life Magazine*' *V-J Day 14 August 1945* photograph of **George "The Kissing Sailor" Mendonsa** in New York City's Times Square. QM1 George Mendonsa was the helmsman of **USS The Sullivans DD-537** during WWII, and I had the honor of visiting with George over eight years, as he shared his incredible story of survival at sea. Sadly, George passed away in 2019.

THE 5-SULLIVAN BROTHERS

Below, L-R: George Mendonsa, and Hal Burke.

Above: *Hal told several of us fellow Veterans that when he last visited George Mendonsa and his wife, that Mrs. Mendonsa once quietly blurted out, "Well, you never kissed ME like THAT before, George!"*

We all got a good laugh out of that comment! Interestingly, George's future wife was behind him in the photo, watching George kiss the Dental Assistant in Times Square. Apparently, George was applying for the job as his wife's future husband? SOLD AMERICAN!

CHUCK CAPE

USA – 196th Infantry

Cell: 407-697-4637

ChuckCape747@hotmail.com

My Military Experience

I was draftee into the U.S. Army following graduation from Utah State University with a Bachelor's Degree in Wildlife Biology. I passed my physical with flying colors and was soon heading to my Basic Training at Ft. Campbell, KY.

Next, was my bus trip south to Ft. Polk, LA. for A.I.T. – Advanced Infantry Training. I then enrolled in NCO (*Non-Commissioned Officers*) School at Ft. Benning, GA. I graduated with flying colors (*again*) as an E-5 rank of Sergeant, as a Mortar Squad Leader, MOS of 11-C.

I then was assigned to what I call my "*on-the-job-training*" at Ft. Lewis, Washington, where I was an acting Platoon Sergeant for a group of A.I.T. Recruits for 8-weeks. After a short "*home leave*" I was on my way to South Vietnam. This was in September of 1970.

I arrived in Cam Ranh Bay for processing and shortly thereafter received my orders to join the AMERICAL DIVISION, based in Chu Lai, on Vietnam's northern coast in **I**-Corps. I received a couple of weeks of "*Jungle Training*" before receiving my orders to join Company C, 4/31 Battalion, 196th Light Infantry Brigade unit out in the beautiful and scenic jungle confines of South Vietnam in **I**-Corps.

I had been with my unit out in the jungle for about 30 days when the monsoon started. It continued, and continued raining (*often horizontally*), day and night, for **18-STRAIGHT DAYS!** I thought I, *and we*, were going to either drown, or starve, to death.

They could not get helicopters out to us to replenish our needs. We lost power on a couple of our batteries and were running out of food. The creeks became raging rivers, forming lakes, and moving us to higher ground. I might add here, I was not a good swimmer, so I was more concerned than most of my fellow Brothers.

At one point, we were stranded on the last sliver of bare ground with nowhere to go but to swim across a raging river. Our Captain selected our strongest swimmer to swim across the river to get to higher ground. We tied a rope around him and off he went. He got about halfway across the river and could go no further, so we pulled him back to us. He came out of the water covered head to foot with the largest leeches I have ever seen! *Somehow, miraculously,* we found a way to survive what I later learned was the worst monsoon in Vietnam in the past 30+ years! My thought was, *"Welcome to Vietnam, Chuck!"*

I failed to mention when I arrived in Vietnam, that they told me they had no need for Mortar squad leaders, but they had **VACANCIES TO FILL** in the position of Infantry Squad Leaders. So, I was given the famous "**M-16**," and I was sent out to the Bush to join my new found Squad. What a BUMMER! I was hoping to be a squad leader, but of a mortar squad.

I was in *THE BUSH* for about eight months, where we spent much of our time in what was called *"HAPPY VALLEY"* up in **I**-Corp. We operated off of two firebases – Firebase *"WEST"*, and Firebase *"SIBERIA"*. Our enemy in my time in Vietnam was all Viet Cong. We rarely fought against the uniformed NVA. I am pleased, and proud, to say that I did not lose one of my guys in my squad, and none were wounded **!** We did lose a radio man to a sniper firing in Happy Valley. His name is on the Vietnam Wall in Washington, D.C.

At about eight months in-country my Captain Robert Milner came to me saying he found I had taken some typing classes in High School and wanted to see if I was interested in becoming his company clerk when our unit moved up to Da Nang to take over security at the base there after the Marine Division was sent home. I said, *"When do I start?"* I never thought my typing in high school would come in handy someday!!!

I thought I would be much "safer as a company clerk In Da Nang, than being out in *The Bush,* but I soon learned that the enemy liked to send in a flurry of rockets and mortar rounds onto the base almost on a daily basis! I was very concerned that one of these in-coming rockets had my name on it! But, again, and again, The Good Lord protected me, and in September 1971 I left Vietnam, and was able to get a short, *"early out"* of the Army and to return in one-piece to my home in Wisconsin.

~ The End ~

My Military Experiences

I served in the U.S.A.F. from May 1959 till May 1979. I entered service as an Aviation Cadet with 3-months of Pre-Flight at Lackland AFB, Texas, and 9-Months of Flight Training at Harlingen AFB, Texas, in the T-29. Upon graduation, I was commissioned a 2nd Lieutenant, U.S.A.F. Reserves.

I went on to Electronic Warfare Officer (EWO) Training at Keesler AFB, Mississippi. My first operational assignment was with the Strategic Air Command's (S.A.C.) 301st Bomb Wing at Lockbourne AFB, Ohio. They had EB-47E's and my crew station was in the Phase-V capsule in the Bomb Bay with another EWO.

We had 2-Wings of the EB-47's, over 100 aircraft, plus 2-Squadrons of Refueling Tankers. We would routinely fly to Greeham Common RAFB, in the United Kingdom, to sit alert and we would often participate in Higher Headquarters missions that would normally have 30 EB-47's. Our crew was to fly in on one of these missions and when we showed up for the mission Briefing, we were told to go home and pack a bag, because they were going to disperse the aircraft.

I got a call to report to the Base, and when I got there, all but the Alert Aircraft where gone. This was due to the *Cuban Missile Crisis*. Our crew got on a C-47 and flew up to Syracuse, N.Y., where we had a dozen or so aircraft positioned. Fortunately, Russia decided to remove it's missiles from Cuba.

From there, I went to Mather AFB, California, as an EWO Instructor in the 3537th EW Training Squadron as a SAC exchange officer. The Squadron had C-54's and later T-29's. After 3-years with the 3537th, I returned to S.A.C. with a B-52 assignment.

Three months of B-52 school at Castle AFB, Merced, California, then on to the 34th Bomb Squadron at Wright – Patterson AFB in Fairborn, Ohio.

The 34th had B-52H's. After 6-months, my crew was sent ARC Light. Again B-52 training at Castle AFB, then on to Anderson AFB, Guam. We also flew missions from Kadena AB, Okinawa, and U-Tapao Royal Thai Navy Base, Thailand, for a total of 47 Combat missions.

Soon after returning to Wright-Patterson, I received Orders to report to the 9th Strategic Reconnaissance Wing at Beale AFB, California, home of the SR-71. The SR would cruise above 80,000 feet at **Mach-3+**; that's 3-times the speed of sound.

I was one of 3-EWO's assigned to the Deputy Commander for Operations. We had an Operational Location (OL8) at Kadena AB, Okinawa. I spent 3-years with the unit, much of it at the OL. I was, subsequently, assigned to the Strategic Reconnaissance Center at HQ SAC, (*Offutt AFB, Nebraska*), where I spent 6-years planning SR-71 missions.

As an additional duty, I was on the briefing team that would brief our 2-Star General and our 4-Star General, Commander-In-Chief, Strategic Air Command. At one of those 4-Star Briefings in 1976, the General said, *"You, (meaning SRC), should do something for the Bi-Centennial."* Well it just so happened that the year before we had planned to set new speed and altitude records with the SR-71, but were stopped by the State Department, because we (*the US*) were doing a *Handshake-In- Space* event with the Russians, and they held the speed and altitude record with the MiG-25. I said, *"General, do we have a deal for you!"* We went on to set new speed and altitude records that the SR-71 still holds, today.

I retired in 1979, a Master Navigator with over 3,000 hours of flying time, and Acting Branch Chief for SR Operations, HQ S.A.C.

S.A.C.'s B-47 w/ JATO. (*Jet Assisted Take Off*)

TedCochran1962@gmail.com
Home: 770-720-4451
Cell: 404-394-0788

Air Crewman Wings
Air Medal
Naval Unit Commendation Vietnam
Service Medal
Big Look Spook
100% VA Disability Compensation
(due to Agent Orange)

TED COCHRAN'S VIETNAM EXPERIENCE

My draft number came up sometime in the fall of 1965. I visited the local Navy recruiter to explore my options and joined the Navy under the Junior College program. I reported to the facility in Atlanta on Ponce de Leon Ave. the morning of November 3rd and departed for boot camp in San Diego that afternoon at paygrade E3 (*Seaman Apprentice*)

Orders after boot camp sent me to the 38 week Tactical Russian School at DLIWC (*Defense Language School West Coast*) Monterrey, California. At some point during school, probably a couple of months, my Top Secret Crypto clearance came through and I got a visit from a Chief Petty Officer who advised that the Navy needed my talents elsewhere. My new orders were to O Branch Crypto School at Navradsta, Skaggs Island, California. There were nine seamen in my 16-week class. We graduated in October of 1966 and I received orders to Navcomstaphil in the Philippines where I was assigned to a watch section in the Crypto Communications Center. I passed the test for CTO3 and was promoted.

My oldest daughter was born in February of 1967 and I put in a request to go home to see my wife and child. An officer came to the CommCenter later to review my request. He said that the arrangements had been made, but I would have to attend a school in California prior to going to Georgia. The name of the school was SERE. I had never heard of the school, and he explained *"Survival, Evasion, Resistance, and Escape."* I asked why I needed to attend this school. The answer was that I would subsequently go to Vietnam, did I need to think about it. I replied no and arrived at North Island, CA, in May of 1967 for the training.

Our class was transported to Warner Springs, California, for the practical part and my life changed. I could write a book about sensory deprivation, being put in small boxes, no sleep, being interrogated, etc. You learn who you are and what you are willing to die for. Our instructors were prisoners of war in Korea.

Got to VQ-1 Det Bravo Danang mid July 1967. We were attached to Marine Air Group 11. Our assigned barracks were at the base of Marble Mountain. We flew ops on EC121 "Willy Victors" and I was now a **"Big Look Spook."** (*"A species of carefully selected and highly trained members of the U.S. Navy and Marine Corps who do things they can never talk about for people they do not know with little recognition from those they have served."-Anonymous*)

We flew low-level reconnaissance (*non-pressurized*) and provided classified intelligence to the flights that originated from the carriers and the base in Danang. I visited the museum at Cory Field in Pensacola a while back and some of the crypto equipment I operated is still classified so I will tread lightly even though it has been over 50 years ago.

My space on the plane was once the forward head and was about 3 feet by 3 feet. I operated a voice crypto system and a teletype crypto system. I communicated one-way with the pilots. We had radar, Morse, and voice interceptors on the flight. We kept up with the location of all aircraft over North Viet Nam. We were AWACS; Before AWACS. We monitored the SAM missile sites and alerted our people when they were being aimed at so they could take evasive action.

The Comm Officer would come into my space, relay into my right ear the critical information, I would further relay the info by voice crypto to the flights and by teletype to the net, Carrier on Yankee Station, net control at NavComStaphil. I have to include the following: My space and the galley were separated by a curtain. During a very critical moment, the plane pitched to the port resulting in me leaning and on tip toes with the officer against my back. We did not cease operating. When the plane then rolled starboard, we both went through the curtain. The officer's butt hit the edge of a griddle, catapulting frying chicken. The plane pitched again; we went right back through the curtain all this in a manner of seconds and completed our warning. I believe we had peanut butter sandwiches for lunch.

In mid-July, rocket/mortar attack destroyed the barracks, unit was relocated to Camp Tien Sha at the foot of Monkey Mountain. The original barracks were rebuilt, and the unit moved back.

The last duty station was CINCPACFLT at Pearl Harbor, I was CTO2 by this time and was in charge of a watch section in Admiral Hyland's Crypto Communications Center.

On a more personal note, one of our planes was shot down by 2 North Korean MiG's over the Sea of Japan on April 15th, 1969. All 31 on board were lost. Only two bodies were recovered.

I met Cal at a pick-up basketball game at NavComStaphil. He was from South Carolina and an "*O brancher*" like me. We became best friends. Cal and I went TAD'd together to VQ-1 Det Bravo

DaNang. We flew with the plane and most of the crew that later got shot down. Cal and I both were serving in Hawaii at the time of the disaster, Cal at Wahiawa, I was at CINCPACFLT and living with my wife in Pearl Harbor. Cheryl gave birth to our second daughter at Tripler Army Hospital on April 15th, the day of the shoot down. Cal was her "*God Father.*" When we found out about the shoot down, Cal said he wished he was on the flight. I didn't hesitate, I told Cal I was thankful I wasn't. To shorten this up, after the service, would occasionally get a call from Cal usually drunk still talking about the friends that were killed. Cal's kidney failure and liver disease killed him. Each year during Kennesaw State's Memorial Day Ceremony, my workplace for 30 years, from the podium, I would call the names of four of our friends. I added Cal's name to that list after his death, because I think that in his mind, he went down with the crew.

My time in the Navy was a Blessing. The Good Lord afforded me the opportunity to get to know who I was, and to more appreciate life, and most importantly to get closer to Him. *However*, I was one of many Vietnam era Veterans exposed to the dreaded **Agent Orange**, and my exposure resulted in 25+ years later numerous health conditions that were ultimately awarded a Disability Compensation by the V.A., at the **100%** level. Service to the country has its hazards at times.

BILLY DAVIS
My Military Experiences

Billy Davis served four years in the U.S. Navy and two years in the Navy Reserves from 1963 to 1969, two of which were in Vietnam. Davis earned the National Defense Service Medal, The Vietnam Campaign Medal with Device (1960–), The Vietnam Service Medal (*with two Bronze Stars*) and the Navy Unit Commendation Ribbon and Letters of Commendations.

How the Military Changed My Life:

As America became increasingly divided over the Vietnam War, Billy decided to enlist and serve his country. Billy joined the U.S. Navy and served two tours in Vietnam. He joined, because all of his friends were coming back in body bags.

There was a Horrendous Fire aboard Billy's ship -- the USS Kitty Hawk (CV-63), where he watched in horror as two of his friends burned to death. Billy was also part of the cleanup. He would never forget that event, and the problems it caused, then, and thereafter.

Looking back on his time in The Navy, Billy now understands that his major contributions in life started after Military contributions in life started after Military.

Using the G.I. Bill, Billy attended The Universities of Tennessee and Indiana, South Carolina, and graduated Hyles-Anderson College in Hammond, Indiana.

While in schools Billy took on blue-collar jobs, working in construction, where he developed his skills in business.

Billy takes great pride in having operated over 50 successful companies over the past 5-decades, in fields from land development, vacation resorts, marinas, medical research facilities, Property Sales, Textile Industry, Manufacturing, Airline, Finances, Heavy Equipment and the occasional building development.

His major property developments were in purchasing parcels of land and developing them into single-family homes. Billy would joint-venture with builders to complete these neighborhood properties.

Military Service

Allegiance	United States of American
Branch/Service	United States Navy Honorable Discharge 3rd June 1969
Years of service	1963 - 1969
	Fallon, Nevada (1963 - 1964)
	Flight Training Exercises
	Naval Air Station Chase Field, Beeville, Texas
	(1965-1965)
	Air Station Training
	Uss Kitty Hawk (CV-63),
	(1965 - 1967) - Aircraft Carrier Training
Battles/Wars	Vietnam Two Tours
Awards	The Vietnam Service Medal with two Bronze Stars
	• National Defense Service Medal
	• The Vietnam Campaign Medal, with Service (1960)
	• The Navy Unit Commendation Ribon
	• Letters of Commendations

BILLY'S LIFE MILESTONE EVENTS

Saving the life of a man, whose heart had stopped beating at a casino in 1998.

In 1984, The Development of **The Arizona Vietnam Memorial.**

By 1989, Billy had taken his company public, and then purchased a Brokerage Firm in Boston, MA, to raise funds to acquire Resorts in Georgia, Alabama, Kentucky, North and South Carolina and Nassau, The Bahamas, and other Property Developments, in a separate Company owed, managed, and controlled by a friend.

* Between 1995 and 1996, Billy was indicted -- US Government *VS*. Billy Davis. But that's another story that will take longer to tell and needs to be told *in-person*. It was a great thing that happened. It not only brought Billy down to just nickels and pennies, *BUT* it also changed Billy's life, and the lives of many others, including Veterans, who are/were in a needy situation in their lives.

Billy had to start over from scratch and Billie J. Davis (Billy W. Davis's wife of over 59 years) was always there to help.

And yet, and on Valentine's Day, February 14, 2008, Billy and Billie founded a *Charitable Education Scholarship Fund*, mostly for students in The Bahamas attending college outside of their own country. A Scholarship Fund with a **$5 million** gift for gifted students within the Commonwealth of The Bahamas was established in February of 2008.

In 2016, the Davis Family placed their parents' assets into a Trust, modeled after the Trust of ***Arthur Vining Davis*** (*May 30, 1867 – November 17, 1962*).

Back to the Navy... while Billy was stationed in Beeville, Texas, in 1964, Arizona U.S. Senator **Barry Goldwater** was about halfway up the courthouse steps, allowing him to see most all of those who had come. Some, *if not all*, of the people were there to hear what this Arizona Statesman had to say. Senator Goldwater, known as *Mr. Conservative*, was making his bid for U.S. President. From that day forward, Billy believed in the fiscal side of Government involvement in the lives of its citizens and their businesses.

But back then, the lesson and the words of Mr. Goldwater stayed with Billy until one day in 1982, he and Billie would visit the home of the Senator near Wriggly Mansion in North Phoenix. Billie would become good friends with Betty Goldwater. And, that great Senator would become Billy's mentor in politics for a number of years.

The Navy and the things that the military taught Billy, has been the guiding force from which Billy would draw on, to build a giant business that would reach around the world, and would touch the lives of many, and would last for decades.

Billy and Billie placed around $3 Billion in assets into that Irreversible & Irrevocable Trust, to be used and given away for their family and many other designated entities and managed by very professional Trustees. Billy and Billie have raised their children to remember from where they came, and to not go flashy, but remain as they were when this all started - in other words … *Jeans are acceptable.*

Billy Davis grew up in Tennessee. His mother took on the role of a single-parent, after his father died when Billy was only eleven. Billy was the eldest son and helped his mom through the difficult years by working and contributing to the family finances. In Junior High School, Billy met the love of his life, **Billie Jo (Poe) Johnson**. The two were married right out of high school, and have been happily married for 59-years, and have three adult children, and five grandchildren. Billie's father (a Poe) died shortly after Billie's mom got pregnant, and her stepfather (a Johnson), who raised Billie, was also a Veteran, and served with Audie Murphy during WWII in Germany.

Billy was encouraged to, and successfully ran, for Arizona State Senator. In 1983, Billy was invited to travel to The Bahamas for a Tax Seminar on the island of Eleuthera, an island on which his ancestral family had roots. Billy stayed at former family-owned Rock Sound Club. After this trip to The Bahamas, Billy and his family fell in love with this island nation, its people, and its beauty. The Davis Family began to place their roots down by investing in land and building homes for themselves there.

Billy was recruited to the Republican Party by Senator Barry Goldwater in 1964. Since then, he has been involved with the party in many different positions. He served two terms in the Arizona State Senate from 1983 to 1987 for the 19th District in Phoenix, Arizona. In 2016, he made an unsuccessful bid for the Georgia District-11 Congressional Seat.

During his career, Billy has owned or started numerous small businesses. He has worked as a consultant to companies in the United States and Internationally. He has built relationships with political and business leader's local, state, federal and/or Governments. Business and political involvement has allowed him to visit most of Europe and many of the former Soviet Bloc Countries. He has arranged business endeavors with several Pacific Rim and Southeast Asian Countries, traveled throughout Central and several South American Countries, and throughout the Caribbean. He has also worked with several Asian countries through SEABIC "Southeast Asian Business Information Center". He has served as Corporate Representative to a number of Countries and Conventions including Medica, the world's largest medical convention in Düsseldorf, Germany.

As a self-made businessman, Billy is committed to offering ways and means of educating Small Business owners for a better use of the Internet and Software for profiting their businesses. He saved and restored many bankrupt companies in his long business career including several resorts, a clothing manufacturing company, a brokerage firm, a major land development company, a cruise ship company, a national glass and metal company, machine equipment and Aircraft Company, an Airline and a Cruise line.

[The Arizona Vietnam Memorial](#)

As a Vietnam Veteran, Senator Billy Davis spent over two years raising money and serving on committees to erect the **Arizona Vietnam Memorial** at the **State Capital** in Phoenix, Arizona, upon which there is an engraved plaque on display, honoring the 12 who spearheaded this project. Senator Davis was one of the twelve members to take the Arizona Vietnam Memorial from an idea to reality, at the State Capital in Phoenix. **General William Westmoreland** was with Senator Billy Davis at the *Dedication* of The Arizona Vietnam Veterans Memorial on

November 9, 1985.

Senator Davis did a Filibuster in the Senate until the Senate Leadership promised to hold a Special Session to address allowing a new hospital to be constructed in Sun City West, Arizona. The Senator persuaded former N.Y. Yankee Hall-of-Famer **Mickey Mantle** to come and help lobby for the building of the ***Del Webb Memorial Hospital***. Mantle and Del Webb (*team owner*) were both part of the New York Yankees. Senator Davis served on the committees to build the Del Webb Memorial Hospital. Time and growth of greater Phoenix has proved out that the hospital has been greatly beneficial to the Sun Cities and West Phoenix.

Special Invitations:

The President of the Arizona Senate sent Senator Davis on a *Good Will Mission* to the Republic of China, Taiwan. Senator Davis and numbers of other State and Federal representatives met with a host of Political Members of Government, while in Taiwan, such as **Raymond R.M. Tai**, (*Deputy Director-General Executive Yuan Taipei, Taiwan*), **Lu, Kuang Pu** (*Secretary General Kaohsiung, Taiwan*), **Kao Yu-jen**, (*Speaker of the House Provincial Assembly*), **Raymond R.M. Tai** (*Deputy Director-General Executive Yuan Taipei, Taiwan*), **Governor Chuang-Huan Chiu**, (*Taiwan Provincial Government, Republic of China*), The United States Representatives who traveled all over the country.

Billy was chosen to visit The Republic of China (*Taiwan*), meeting with many Heads of Government. He made visits to mainland China and other Pacific Rim and Asian Countries, including Japan. He has aided business development in the Pacific Rim Countries; searching out those companies that would come to America.

- Chosen in 1989 to represent business development to the country of Paraguay with other business and political leaders.
- Worked on several State and National Political Campaigns. He has personally been associated with, and worked with, many public individuals.
- Worked with medical institutions to a number of Countries, Conventions including Medica, the world's largest medical convention in **Düsseldorf, Germany**.
- Worked with several Asian countries through **SEABIC** (*"Southeast Asian Business Information Center"*).
- Business and political involvement has allowed Billy Davis to visit most of Europe, and many of the former Soviet Bloc Countries. He has arranged business endeavors with several Pacific Rim and Southeast Asian Countries. He has traveled throughout Central and several South American Countries. He has traveled to, and boated throughout, the Caribbean.
- Billy has owned 17-Aircraft, and several yachts.

SPECIAL ASSIGNMENTS

Billy was invited to several African Countries, meeting with Heads of State and Tribal Chieftains. He worked with the transition of the Republic of Togo from a *Dictatorial* Government to *Democratic* Free Elections at the request of former Togolese President **Gnassingbe Eyadema**, a Vietnamese friend, who served in `Nam` during the French-Indo-China War, before America arrived there.

- Traveling throughout the country of Togo, West Africa, and other West Africa nations (Liberia), Billy has visited Presidential Palaces and spent nights in The Bush. Billy met with President Gnassingbe Eyadema a number of times and with Prime Minister Joseph Koukou Koffigoh. He also held meetings with Tribal Chief's and with Gnassingbe Eyadema, the first elected President of Togo under Democratic free Elections. Under President Gnassingbe Eyadema, Lomé, Togo, is a Free-Trade Zone. Country. Industrial Minister Payadowa Boukpessi and held a Press Conference. Billy Davis was invited to attend the Inauguration of President

Human Rights Activist - Good Will Trips

- Billy has traveled world-wide in endeavors as a "***Human Rights Activist***," to the Republic of Togo, West Africa, and Congo, West Africa, Uzbekistan, and prior to 9/11 -- Venezuela and Costa Rico.
- In Togo, Billy was invited to help initiate their new voting system and *"The Rights of the People,"* which allowed him to spend weeks throughout the country working one-on-one with the tribes' and people's needs.
- With his own money, Billy has traveled to, and visited prisons in the U.S.A., as well as in other countries. Believing that families are punished along with the parent who is incarcerated, Billy and his attorneys have been able to right the wrongs to incarcerated persons, whose *"Sentencing Guidelines"* were too severe, and the severity of the sentence did not match the crime. Being able to rehabilitate the parents can remove the family from the support of the Government, and many of those attorneys are still employed by Billy to continue those efforts.

The Davis Family Foundation

- The Davis Family has been involved in numerous charity projects and has worked with organizations providing help for people in need. They have sent children to colleges, (with one recent graduate from Emory) and donated many material things to the citizens, and given money where needed. Multiple Hurricane victims in The Bahamas and Haiti have received supplies and money from The Davis Family.
- In 1999, the Davis Family founded their Davis Family Foundation, which is now providing Scholarships for gifted students within the Commonwealth of The Bahamas.
- **Hurricane ravaged Caribbean Countries, including those hitting the U.S.A. - On Going:**
- **Medical Supplies for Clinics.** - Fully Supplied Ambulance to Abaco Island. - Annual Christmas for Children after Hurricanes have hit. - Suppling Computers for damaged schools in The Caribbean. - Fresh Water Wells for elderly and others.
- **"Hurricane Floyd devastated Abaco Island on September 14, 1999"** - The Davis Family caused a fully-equipped ambulance to be donated by AMR of Marietta, Georgia, to the island of Abaco, The Bahamas, after Hurricane Floyd devastated the island on September 14, 1999. The Davis family and their friends donated medical supplies, clothing, and even computers, for the schools and the people of Abaco Island, Bahamas.
- Following – *"Hurricane Ike devastated Turks and Caicos and Inagua Bahamas"* – Billy, on behalf of the Davis Family, carried needed supplies to Grand Turk Island (Turks and Caicos) and Inagua, Bahamas, on September 7, 2008.

Multiple other Hurricane Victims have received supplies and money from The Davis Family. Medical Supplies were sent by ***The Davis Family*** to Haiti, following the devastation of the Earthquake of January 12, 2010.

The Davis Family is currently working with the ***Benevolent and Protective Order of Elks (Elks Lodges)*** in the donation of **$20 million** for the benefit of the ***American Military Veterans and First Responders.*** Wonderful things are in-store for the ELKS project.

**Ernest R. Drew, III
Lt. Col. USAF-Ret.**

MY USAF EXPERIENCE
ErnieDrew1942@Gmail.com

U.S.A.F. Fighter Pilot
1965 - 1985

My dream of being a fighter pilot began when I was in the 6th grade and my dad took me to see the USAF Thunderbirds put on an airshow in the F100 Super Sabre over Battle Creek Michigan airport. Our little airport was not long enough for the Thunderbirds to take off, so they departed from another airport. We were just standing there waiting for them to arrive when they flew right over our heads with the afterburners in full power. I thought it was the most beautiful and exciting thing I had ever seen. I turned to my dad and said right then, *"Someday I am going to fly that airplane."* I could tell by the expression on his face that he doubted that statement.

When I graduated high school, I applied for a Congressional appointment to the Air Force Academy. I received the appointment and went to Selfridge Air Force Base for my physical, which I failed because I had asthma. I enrolled in Battle Creek Community College and after my freshmen year I again applied for a Congressional appointment and again received it and again failed my physical because I had asthma. Giving up on my dream I went to Michigan State University to get a degree in teaching speech and debate.

While student teaching in Grand Rapids, I received a call from a recruiter who asked me if I wanted to join the Air Force and become a pilot. I said, *"Yes and that was what I always wanted to do but could not because I had asthma."* He replied, *"Come down and see me,"* which I did the next day.

When I got to his office we talked for a while and then he asked me how they knew I had asthma. *"Because they asked me, and I said yes,"* I responded. He said, *"Say no"*. I said, *"You mean lie???"* He said, *"Yes let's practice"*. He then asked me several times if I had asthma, and I replied, *"No"* with increasing confidence. I signed a third application and went back to Selfridge Air Force base for the physical. When asked if I had asthma, I answered, ***"No!"***

Several weeks later I received a letter from the Air Force in the mail telling me I had been accepted into the *navigator* training program. At that point, I called the recruiter and after making several disparaging comments about his tutelage, he calmly instructed me to reply in writing that I wanted to be a pilot. So, once again, I did exactly as he coached me to do! Within a few weeks, the Air Force responded, *"Your pilot training class is 66-H at Craig Air Force Base in Selma, Alabama."* I was thrilled and after finishing Officer Training School (*3 months in beautiful San Antonio, Texas*), I headed off to Selma, Alabama. Remember, this was the summer of 1965; Selma was not the garden spot of America at that time.

After several weeks of academics, it was time for my first flight in the T-37 (*affectionately called, "The Tweet"*). I remember the first time my instructor released the brakes and started down the runway, my thought was, maybe I had made a mistake trying this. However, when we lifted off, I was sure I was where I wanted to be. I managed to get thru the T-37 phase with fairly good results. That was despite navigating to the Mont- gomery airport instead of Craig AFB on my navigation check ride.

After telling tower I was on initial to land, they responded telling me repeatedly, *"We don't see you."* My check pilot finally asked, *"What side of the highway is Craig on?"* I confidently replied, *"The left"*. He asked, *"What side of the highway is this airport on?"* I thought on the right. At that point I realized my error and proceeded to Craig AFB and landed. From there, on to the

T-33 Advanced Phase of pilot training. We were the last class to fly the T-33. (*After 1966, all advanced pilot training took place in the Supersonic T-38.*) I finished 33 training without a hitch.

When my class neared graduation our assignment selections were disbursed. They were all back seat F-4's with just a few instructor assignments. The *last* thing I wanted to do was sit in the back seat of an F-4 - remember I had no desire to be a navigator. I had managed to finish high enough in the class standings that I was, **"Instructor-Qualified."** So, I selected T-37 Instructor assignment and stayed at Craig AFB.

After three years at Craig AFB as an Instructor Pilot, I finally got my dream and went to Luke AFB to learn to fly the F-100's. From there, it was on to **Survival School** in Washington state, and then to **Jungle Survival** in the Philippines. My final destination was Phan Rang Air Base in Viet Nam for a year of flying and fighting for freedom. Although we never won that fight, the soldiers and airmen that were there, represented the United States bravely and did their best to preserve freedom for the South Vietnamese. I have not regretted for one minute what we tried to do there.

The rest of my career was rather unexciting. From Viet Nam, I went to England AFB in Louisiana to teach Vietnamese pilots how to fly the A-37. I really enjoyed that. They were very eager to get back to their country and defend their freedom. I felt that being in the U.S. showed them what real freedom was and encouraged them to fight harder. My hope is that at least some of them got a chance to return to freedom after the Communist took their country.

After Louisiana, I was assigned to Wiesbaden AB in Germany. My stepmother was born and raised in Wiesbaden and had come to the U.S. after the War. I was eager to go and meet her family. While in Germany, I had a classified job that required a special high-level NATO clearance. The investigation showed that my stepmother was a member of *Hitler's Youth Movement* during the war. When the FBI questioned her, she said she had two choices, either join or get shot. NATO figured that she made the right choice and gave me the clearance anyway.

After that tour, I returned to the U.S. to fly the A-10, my favorite airplane of all time. During that time, I was transferred to the Tactical Air Command (TAC) Inspector General team for a couple of years. Then, because of my experience and knowledge of Air Warfare, I was sent to Korea to be an Air Liaison Officer (ALO) with the 2nd Armored Division.

It was my time working with the Army that taught me how lucky I was to be in the Air Force. At least we slept in comfortable beds, instead of on the ground in some bug-infested dump. Really…. on deployment one time the Brigade Commander had us bivouac in a garbage dump saying, *"No one would think of looking for us here"*. I also learned how much the South Koreans liked and appreciated the American military for helping them defeat the North Korean/Chinese communists. Many of those that were around at that time have since passed. Sadly, the young folks now believe the lie that we are preventing the reunification with the North and South Korea.

Following my Korean tour, it was back to the Texas town of Del Rio to spend my last two years as a Section Commander at Laughlin AFB teaching new pilots to fly the T-38, until I retired in 1985.

A-10/WartHog

JACK DRISCOLL
USAF *Captain*
B-52 Pilot
Cell: 404-580- 8811
B52Jack@Yahoo.com

It all began for me when I read a book in 5th Grade, on *"How to fly an Airplane."* I didn't worry about being a lawyer, or a Doctor. All I wanted to do was become a pilot. What better way than to be paid to learn how to fly.

So, in my Freshman Year in college, I visited the U.S. Air Force Recruiter and told him I wanted to be a pilot. His response was, *"Come back when you're a Senior."* Senior Year came, and I started all the necessary Tests, plus Physical Exam, which resulted in being, *"Qualified!"*

One glitch, the day I graduated, my 1-A Draft Status was in-the-mail. The Air Force Recruiter got a 2-week Deferment after I was ordered to report for Induction on August 3, 1966, so I Enlisted in the Air Force on August 19, 1966.

Three months of **O.T.S.** (*Officer Training School*), then one solid year of **U.P.T.** (*Undergraduate Pilot Training*).

Now begins my `Career` in the United State Air Force (**U.S.A.F.**). My assignment began as a Co-Pilot in the B-52 Stratofortress, assigned to the 306th Bomb Wing, 367th Bomb Squadron, at McCoy AFB, Orlando, Florida (June 1968).

By September 1968, I found myself deployed to fly *"ArcLight"* Missions out of Guam (*Anderson AFB*), Okinawa (*Kadena Air Base*), and Utapao Royal Thai Naval Base, Thailand.

After two 6-month deployments, I finished with 139 completed Missions, plus two aborts. That brings me to the *Aborted Missions* – **one** on the Takeoff Roll when we failed to make the *Acceleration Check*, and the **other**, an *Airborne Emergency* after Takeoff, both in Thailand.

It was my Takeoff that day. We experienced Runaway, Nose-Down Trim, as we broke ground. I accomplished the Takeoff, and we continued the Mission.

However, after we climbed through 15,000 feet, there occurred several thumps and shutters. The bombs were falling off the racks, and onto the closed Bomb Bay Doors. I immediately called an Emergency and we headed for the Ocean (*The Bay Of Thailand*).

The doors eventually ripped away and the bombs fell harmlessly into the water. After about 5-6 hours of burning fuel, we reached a light enough Gross Weight to land the plane.

The cause was a broken *pneumatic duct* in the Bomb Bay, beside the bombs (*Fire in the Bomb Bay*).

The Airplane trim and the bomb release system were affected. We landed with half of the bombs.

After landing, I put in for the *"Medal of Honor,"* but all we got was, *"Crew-of-the-Month!"*

A third Tour found me at DaNang Air Base in South Vietnam. I had applied for a **"Date of Separation"** (**D.o.S.**) shortly before that last assignment.

I flew the **EC-47** out of DaNang, until my hitch was up in December (**1971**).

Let me say this . . . I came home without a scratch, having flown over **150**-Missions. I certainly admire my fellow *"Veterans-For-Lunch-Bunch"* friends, some of whom received **2-3 Purple Hearts**.

I'm glad to have served my country and am certainly proud of my time in the Service, and the time spent with my colleagues at our local lunches on Mondays.

B-52 Stratofortress

EC-47

EC-47

Bowman Ashe Dunn
'Bo'

USAF KC-135 Pilot
Cell: 404-218-8834
BoDunn96@Gmail.com

My military story actually starts when I was a young boy growing up in Coral Gables, Florida. I enjoyed watching the airplanes fly over my house, in and out of Miami International Airport, and developed an interest in aviation. My mom noticed it also as she was a civilian pilot and Link Instructor during WWII. I was building model airplanes, while my friends were building model cars.

I got involved in sports growing up, mostly football, and got pretty good at it. I was fortunate enough to play on a State and National Championship football team at Coral Gables High School and was offered scholarships to play in college. I chose the University of Miami for several reasons. *One*, I really like the South Florida area, and *two*, my family was seriously engrained in the school; my grandfather was the first president of the school. My dad was an excellent Running Back in the 1930's, and he and my mom graduated from the 'U'. My sister and brother followed in the family footsteps after me and also graduated from Miami.

Now for the military part of my story. When I was a freshman in the late 1960's, the Viet Nam war was going strong and the military draft had been set up. To defer the football players from military service we were all assigned Army ROTC, in addition to our chosen major. My mom caught my dumb mistake of not telling the Academic Advisor that I wanted to be placed in Air Force ROTC. I had to participate in one semester of Army ROTC and then transfer to Air Force ROTC for the second semester, and the rest of my college experience. One interesting side note, the professor of Aerospace Studies *or* Commander of the ROTC unit was a graduate of the United States Military Academy at West Point. He also played football there and was the Quarterback for the famous duo of Doc Blanchard and Glenn Davis in the mid-40's. I had gotten married while in school just before I was supposed to go to ROTC summer camp at Charleston

AFB, so I had to delay our honeymoon until after that. Boy, was I ready to take a break. Anyway, it all worked out and I made it to graduation in January 1973.

Upon graduation I was issued my set of gold Second Lieutenant bars with an assignment to the Air Force Undergraduate Pilot Training (*UPT*) base in Valdosta, Georgia. Moody Air Force Base was to be our home for the next year. However, due to the winding down in military spending circa 1973, my report date was delayed several months, so I worked in my in-law's hardware store for a few months, and then reported to Moody AFB in May of 1973.

After a year of punching holes in southern Georgia skies, flying the Cessna T-37 and Northrop T-38, the Air Force assigned me to fly a KC-135 based at Robins Air Force Base in Warner Robins, Georgia. Prior to reporting there I had more training ahead of me. First, my wife and I packed one car. It was a new 1974 Buick Century for which I traded my 1968 Chevelle SS-396. I still miss that car to this day. Anyway, we packed the new car and headed west to Merced, California, home of Castle AFB, which was the training base for B-52's and KC-135's. After a few months of learning to be a good tanker Co-Pilot I was sent to Fairchild AFB to learn how to be a good POW. The lessons learned from some of the Viet Nam POW's were applied here and we were taught how to survive in the little boxes that those guys had to endure, and also how to E & E (*Escape and Evade*) the enemy in the woods of Washington state if we were ever shot down. After Land Survival School, I was sent to water survival school at Homestead AFB in Homestead, Florida. Homestead was about a 45-minute drive from where I grew up in Coral Gables, so it was like going home. I met my wife in San Francisco, where she stayed with a friend of hers while I was at Fairchild, and we packed the car again, and drove east to Homestead. In Water Survival School, we were taught how to use all the survival gear we might need if we were ever shot down over the water, and also did some parasailing into the water off of a specially equipped flat top barge/boat. While practicing floating in a survival raft, this one boat came by that looked fairly familiar, and it was my dad in our family boat, waving and watching all the training going on. I finally finished all the training, and it was time to get to work and get to my unit.

It was getting to the Fall of 1973 timeframe, and my wife and I packed the car once again, and headed north to Valdosta to pick up the car we had left with a friend after pilot training, and continued on to Robins AFB. We got into some temporary housing for a few days, and I finally reported to my unit -- the 912th AREFS (*Air Refueling Squadron*), which was part of the 19th Bomb Wing of the Strategic Air Command (*SAC*).

One thing I learned was that learning and practicing never ends in the military. I had to learn about all the nuclear security and procedures, and while we didn't carry any nuclear bombs, there was an active alert area where airplanes were loaded with nuclear bombs and the bombs were also stored on the base property. We carried some sensitive information in our airplanes, that concerned the EWO (*Emergency War Order*). It detailed our responsibilities if we ever had to launch from the alert facility to refuel the B-52's, in the event of an attack. Our navigator was responsible for checking out the weapon we carried on all our missions. Our normal schedule was to pull alert duty one week out of every month, where we would live in the alert facility for a week and be ready to launch within a few minutes in case the big balloon went up.

The rest of the month we would fly training flights to keep our proficiency up. We mostly refueled B-52's from our sister squadron, but we were also tasked with supporting the air refueling for the F-4 bases at Homestead AFB and McDill AFB in Tampa. We refueled not only the C-5's, but also the B-1's when they were in development, and the B-747 that was being tested as the Presidential aircraft.

I also had the opportunity to fly over in Europe for a short 35-day TDY, part of which we refueled some brand-new F-4's being delivered to Iran, when Iran was friendly. I flew another TDY to Hickam AFB in Hawaii to bring some F-111's from Southeast Asia back to the U.S. As a Co-Pilot, you are basically gaining experience for your turn to upgrade to the left seat as the Aircraft Commander. One of the best deals I experienced that I thought would never happen was that I was allowed to fly a T-38, in addition to flying as a tanker Co-Pilot.

The time period was in the 1970's and the fuel crunch had hit along with the winding down of military expenditures from Viet Nam. Training flights were cut back to save money so SAC and ATC (*Air Training Command*) got together and sent the spare T-37's and T-38's that weren't being used in ATC to the SAC bases, to let the B-52 and KC-135 Co-Pilots fly them to gain additional experience. It was dubbed the ACE program (*Accelerated Copilot Enrichment*). After all, it's much less expensive to fly a small twin-engine trainer for experience than an 8-engine B-52 or 4-engine KC-135. At Robins AFB, we were fortunate to get the supersonic T-38. It was *awesome*. While gaining my experience, I guess I did a good enough job to be assigned to a Stand-Eval crew (*Standardization Evaluation*). A part of my additional duties was to give simulator check rides. That assignment lasted about a year, before it was my time to upgrade to the left seat and become an Aircraft Commander. Again, in the interest of saving money, I was upgraded locally instead of having to go back to Castle AFB for the training. My Aircraft Commander was an Instructor, so he would put me in the left seat for our missions and we completed all the requirements to upgrade. One of the evaluators in our Squadron gave me my Check Ride and I was ready to go. I was assigned my own crew, and we flew together for about a year before I left the service after my 6-year hitch was up. One of the advantages of upgrading locally was that I didn't incur any additional commitments and could separate from the service on my original commitment of 6-years. Both my wife and I enjoyed our time in the Air Force and would do it again if we could. After my Air Force service, I was hired by Delta Air Lines and flew for them for 26-years in several different airplanes from Flight Engineer to Co-Pilot, and eventually promoted to Captain, and retired in 2005.

I am thankful for the **Veterans-For-Lunch-Bunch**. I enjoy the company of fellow Veterans, and hearing all the different experiences. Thank you T.D. for your leadership for our group.

My Vietnam Experiences

February 1968

I joined the Navy fully expecting to be stationed aboard a ship. Oops, I was wrong. I entered boot camp at San Diego. Graduated in April and Received orders to Boat Support Unit One at the Naval Amphibious Base Coronado, CA. When I asked my Company Commander what

Boat Support Unit One (BSU-1), he stated that he didn't know but maybe it had something to do with tugboats. After checking into my new command, I discovered that Boat Support Unit One had nothing to do with tugboats. BSU-1 was part of the Naval Special Warfare Group which included the SEAL Teams and other special boat units located at amphibious bases at Coronado, CA and Little Creek, VA.

Interestingly, BSU-1 had all the state-of-the-art boats in the Navy at the time which included the first hydrofoil boat the USS Tucumcari as well as the US Navy's PTF's. But I, (fortunately or unfortunately) was assigned to their SEAL Support boats and was destined for three tours with the SEALs in Vietnam.

I had extensive training during 1968 and 1969 including my basic electrician training, as well as specific training for small boats such as assault boat engineering, water survival, Survival, Evasion, Resistance & Escape Training (SERE) as well as training with the SEAL platoons that we would deploy with. Small arms training and field medical training at Camp Pendleton and operations with SEALs at Coronado and China Lake was on-going.

We utilized many types of boats in Vietnam but used three primary boats: Light SEAL Support Craft (LSSC), Medium SEAL Support Craft (MSSC) and Heavy SEAL Support Craft (HSSC). The LSSC and MSSC were state-of-the art aluminum, high speed, heavily armed, gasoline powered boats. Speeds were in excess of 40 knots, much faster than the many patrol boats (PBR's) used extensively in Vietnam. The HSSC was simply a diesel powered, slow, modified landing craft (think D-Day invasion boats with the drop ramp) modified with a helicopter landing pad on top to support extended operations away from a base.

LSSC's were 24' boats designed for SEAL Squad (7 SEALs) insertion & extraction MSSC's were 36' boats designed for SEAL Platoon (14 SEALS) insertion & extraction HSSC's were not used often for insertion or extraction but normally used as support boat for the smaller boats on extended operations. The ramp was welded shut and was not operable per the original design of the boat. Armament included an 81mm Naval Mortar, a 105 Recoilless mounted on a helo deck, a mini gun, several M-60 and 50 Caliber machine guns as well as 40mm grenade launching machine guns.

October 1969

First of three deployments to Vietnam. Unlike other Riverine Sailors going to Vietnam via commercial air, we flew over in old C-118 aircraft and carried our small arms with us to Vietnam and back. The rumor was that we were the only units using the VP Squadron out of Texas which justified their existence for keeping these old C-188 aircraft flying. They were 4-engine prop

planes which were very slow. Island hopping from North Island, CA to Tan Son Nhut airbase in Saigon with a 3-day stopover in Hawaii for booby trap school usually took us about a week to get there. We landed at Ton Son Nhut air base in the middle of the night and were loaded into a truck and rode to the Nha Be Naval Support Base about 10 miles South of Saigon. Our Team, Mobile Support Team -2 (MST-2) Detachment Alpha shared a two-story hootch with another MST-2 team and two SEAL Platoons. Our team worked specifically with one SEAL platoon but sometimes we would have joint operations with the other MST-2 and SEAL teams.

After about three months our team and one SEAL platoon moved to another Naval Riverine outpost in Sa Dec. Sa Dec was very small and since we had the only gasoline powered boats in Vietnam, they had to bring in a gasoline barge for us. It was a small barge, and the pumps were hand operated which were very exhausting (our boats held hundreds of gallons in multiple tanks). We operated out of this remote outpost for the remainder of this deployment.

During this deployment I experienced my first firefight on my very first operation (second day in-country). We had a rare day-time operation to intercept a sampan on a small river that our 24-foot LSSC could barely turn around in. We sat at ambush for about 6 hours with no activity. As we broke ambush and headed back the same way we came up the river, we came under heavy

machine gun fire. At the time I was standing aft and coming forward in the boat after turning on the battery-operated bulge pump at the back of the boat (we shut them off during ambush to reduce noise). A B-40 rocket was launched from the riverbank and missed me and a couple SEALs by less than a yard and exploded on the other bank. When the firefight broke out one of the SEALs in the boat grabbed my mounted M-60 machine gun to return fire. I proceeded to pick up that SEAL's AR-15 and returned fire myself. Since I was in an awkward position and trying to shoot left-handed, I put one bullet in the side of the boat. As you can imagine, I took a lot of flak for that.

June 1970

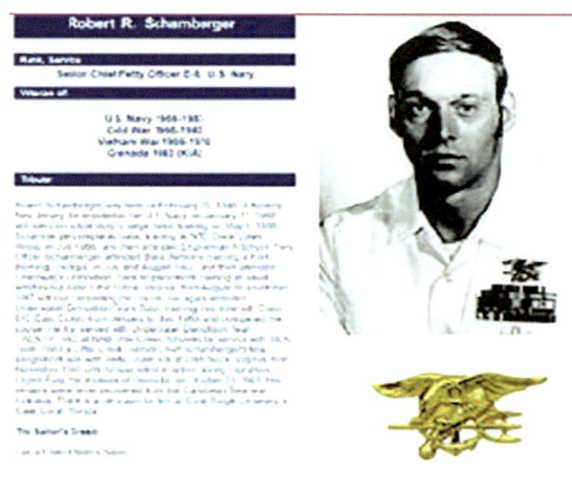

This was my second of three deployments. I was in MST-2 Detachment Delta this time and again, started out in Nha Be. After a few weeks we transferred to Dong Tam which was a joint Navy and Army Riverine Force Base near My Tho. Unfortunately, the base did not have room for us, so our MST-2 team, and the SEAL platoon shared a hootch on the South Vietnamese Army base adjacent to the U.S. base. Our hootch had no running water or sewer. We showered in the afternoon rain or from cisterns we installed to catch the rain. Our drinking water was from small "buffalo" tanks. Our nasty daily ritual was burning our waste daily in the half barrels that were used in our out-house to catch the waste. (It was a 3-holer).

One of the SEALs I worked with, Robert (Bob) Shamberger on this tour was later killed in action in 1983 at the invasion of Granada. His picture on the right with crutches with me (on right) and another MST-2 member "*Clutch*" in the center.

March 1971

This was my third tour of Vietnam. This time with MST-2 Detachment Charlie I was sent to Nam Can in the extreme southern tip of the Delta. The only way in and out was by boat or by air. The outpost had one of those small portable landing strips made with the metal plates (boy what a racket they made when landing!!). Prior to us arriving, it was called Sea Float since it consisted of barges and boats attached to the shoreline. By the time we got there, the name was changed to Solid Anchor due to all the hootches and buildings that were erected. Also, it was no longer a U.S. Naval outpost. The Vietnamese Navy ran it, and our three boats were the only U.S. boats on the base. All the other riverine boats were all under South Vietnamese flags.

One, interesting story from this deployment is that Admiral Zumwalt (The Chief of Naval Operations (CNO) at the time and originator of the Agent Orange operations)) came to visit. He had just previously authorized beards for the Navy and one of our teammates had a huge bushy beard. One of the U.S. commanders on the base told him he had to shave it (or trim it drastically). He refused and when Admiral Zumwalt saw the beard, he made the comment on how beautiful the beard was.

One other thing that was interesting is that we had to bring all our machine guns off the boats after every operation because they would be stolen by the South Vietnamese Navy. It was a long haul to the hootches, so we negotiated with an Army helo pilot to haul a jeep down from Saigon for us in exchange for some floor tile we had that he needed for his officer's club. Transporting the M-60's and 50 caliber guns from the boats to our hootch was a lot easier after that.

Here are some pictures from this deployment:

Boat Support Unit One evolved over the years and is now known as Special Boat Teams under Naval SpecialWarfare Group 4, Little Creek, VA. The Navy now has a special rating and qualification known as Special Warfare Combat-Craft Crewman (SWCC) and service members can now specialize and remain in the boat units for their entire career. History of the special boat units can be seen here: Navy SWCC – The Navy's Elite Boat Warriors |

Navy SEALs I initially left the Navy in December 1971 after my hitch was completed but I re-enlisted 65 days later and went on to finish a 20 year career in the U.S. Navy on various ships and duty stations and retired at Pearl Harbor in March 1988.

My Military Story

The following are my recollections of my return from Operations Desert Shield and Desert Storm:

Since I had only returned to the unit from qualification in the OV-1 Mohawk two days before our alert, there was no time to get my unit check-out in the Mohawk. Once we got the alert, we worked seven days each week, from about 5 AM until 10 or 11 PM. We did ranges and briefings, inoculations, painted vehicles, packed up and rail-loaded our equipment and convoyed to the port. Since there was no time for me to fly, I was chosen to take command of the company, deploy them to Saudi Arabia, and establish our base of operations. Consequently, at the close of hostilities, when we were preparing to redeploy, Captain Mike Drumm, the Company Commander, told me I could choose to fly a Mohawk back cross the Atlantic if I wanted to.

I was in fixed-wing and C-12 qualifications from August until December in 1988. I had spent all of 1989 in Honduras. I spent April and May of 1990 at Fort Rucker, and June and July in Fort Huachuca, Arizona. I just wanted to get back with my wife and return to a normal life. I remember telling Mike that I would rather exercise whatever option would put me back in the States one minute before the other. He said he would let me take command of the advanced party of A Company.

Colonel Clifton Aldridge (*AKA 'Simon Bar Sinister'*) had tried to come visit us in Theater before hostilities broke out, as we were detached from his Brigade (*504th M.I.*) and attached to another Brigade (*525th M.I.*). Cliff had been wisely denied country clearance and had made an impassioned plea to send his Command Sergeant Major to visit us, to check on the health, welfare and morale of the troops. When the CSM of the 504th came for a brief visit, Cliff had secretly sent the Brigade (504th) colors in his baggage.

As we prepared to return after the victory, the question arose among the troops: *Which brigade patch should we be wearing on our right shoulder as a combat patch?*

To the folks in the 525th, the answer was clear: *You wear the 525th patch, because that's the unit that owned the patch where you had been attached, since your permanent unit of assignment*

(504th) did not deploy. The answer was equally clear to the folks at the 504th: **You wear the 504th patch, because the Brigade colors DID deploy via a covert mission of the 504th's CSM.** Those of us not wearing any combat patch really didn't care. We just wanted to leave, and forget the whole unpleasant experience.

Our Battalion Commander, Psycho Joe Blanco, had selected Captain Mark Ohocki (*sp?*) to be the *"acting"* Battalion Commander. Mike Drumm was sending me back as the *"acting"* A Company Commander. The day finally arrived for us to leave, and I couldn't have been any happier. 50 soldiers of the 15th M.I. Battalion, plus myself, were bussed to the Airfield Departures and Arrivals Control Group (*ADACG*). At King Fahad Airport (*OEDF*). We were joined by an Infantry company of the 2nd Armored Division, 49 soldiers that included their Commander. In all, we were 100 soldiers. The ADACG folks quickly determined that I was the highest ranking passenger, and thus the plane load commander.

I learned from their Company Commander that this particular Infantry company was assigned to the 502nd Military Intelligence Battalion of the 2nd Armored Division. They were the Long-Range Surveillance Unit (*LRSU*) of the division, and they had been inserted 150 Kilometers behind Iraqi Lines before the Air War had ever started. In recognition of their heroic and selfless service they had been informed that they were not entitled to wear the Combat Infantryman's Badge (*CIB*) on their uniforms because they had not been part of an Infantry battalion, and thus had not earned it. I promise you, this really happened.

We were comfortably reclining against our baggage on the concrete pavement outside a hangar. Being the cool of the morning it was just shy of 100° Fahrenheit. I had been laden with my usual complement of a post-Civil War .38 caliber pistol, my aircrew chemical protective mask, my Kevlar helmet and my map case filled with papers and orders. Each of these treasures hung comfortably about my neck by a strap, and had been my constant companions to every meal, bowel movement, personal hygiene experience, flight, and crew rest session for the previous six months. Since I was leading the advanced party, I was given a spare M-16 and a set of night vision goggles, each conveniently equipped with its own strap for hanging around the neck. These additions would get sensitive items back to the States without hampering the main body of the battalion.

Suddenly, a truck pulled up and out jumped Major Thomas *"Bullet-Head"* Francis, the Battalion Executive Officer and Captain Steve Hirschkowitz, the Assistant S-3. *"The decision has been made!"* They announced. *"You are to wear the 525 patch. We didn't want you guys to return without your combat patch."* They produced a brown paper lunch bag and distributed 50, 525th patches and 50 corresponding Airborne tabs. I slipped mine into my pocket.

Soldiers immediately produced their field expedient sewing kits and proudly began to affix their newly earned combat patches to the right shoulders of their uniforms. I just pulled out my paperback copy of Stephen King's, **"IT,"** and tried to forget the previous six months.

"I'll tell you what," said Steve. *"As soon as you guys touch down in the States, people are going to be buying you beers and girls are gonna run up and hug and kiss you!"* That sounded nice, the beer part that is. I like girls and all, but I was really hoping to get home to my wife. I thought I had a pretty good chance of getting a little more than a congratulatory peck on the cheek. As for alcohol, I hadn't had a drop since we left Texas on 23 September 1990 (*unless you count the four ittle shootersof liquor my buddy accidentally dropped in a care package to me*).

We were finally told to amble aboard a luxurious C-141B Starlifter with its *"Comfort Pallet"*. The comfort pallet was a load of antiquated, worn out airline seats bolted to the floor of the aircraft in an aft facing configuration. There were precisely 100 seats. I was given a seat furthest forward, by the passenger door, which meant that all the other seats were in front of me as I looked aft. Now the C-141 was a pretty old aircraft. It, like my OV-1 Mohawk, had seen service in the Vietnam War. The four engines are what we call *"Straight Pipe"* jet engines. The thrust of the engines was produced, primarily, by the jet exhaust. I had learned from weeks of listening to C-141s idling on the apron near my tent, that whatever energy from the combustion of fuel was not translated into thrust was translated into noise. The result on the inside of the airplane was only marginally quieter than on the outside, by the engines. The pilots came to address us in the passenger compartment before we taxied out. They announced to us, in typical Air Force hubris, that we should feel honored to be the passengers of an Air Force Reserve crew, who were all Delta Airlines pilots in their civilian jobs. I attempted to lose myself in my paperback novel.

After what seemed like a month and a half of skull splitting noise and vibration, we touched down at some airport outside of London, England. Before we could pluck the ear plugs from our skulls, a crew van whisked away the benighted Delta pilots to a well-deserved steak dinner, an aroma therapy massage and night or two at a five star resort. An hour or so later a set of busses arrived to take me and my 99 fellow prisoners to the passenger terminal.

Not having any customs or immigration paperwork, we were imprisoned in a holding tank area that had about half as many seats as there were inhabitants. It being Easter Sunday morning in England, there was nothing but a couple of snack vending machines, at which we were all welcomed to shop with whatever British coinage we may have brought with us. There were two or three televisions mounted for us to view that played insipid British children's cartoon programs. Again, Stephen King was my hero, and I made significant progress in my book.

After a few hours of Anglo-bliss, the Air Force was able to produce a new crew for our aircraft, fresh from the resort. They loaded us into busses again, and I counted my 99 charges as we resumed our seats on the C-141 Luxury Liner.

After another eternity of noise and vibration, we touched down in the good, old United States of God-Bless-America. We had the good fortune of landing at McGuire AFB, NJ. It now being Easter Sunday in America, the terminal was completely abandoned. There was a long strip of tractor-fed paper hanging by one end, taped to the wall on which someone had generated a banner which read, **"Welcome Home 322nd TFG"**, or something like that. There were no pretty young girls anxious to hug and kiss us, and there were no good old boys lined up to buy us alcohol. In fact, there was only a small AAFES snack bar, and that was closed until about two hours before we had to board the plane again. When they did open, a few of the guys were able to buy themselves a couple of cans of Budweiser beer. One of my soldiers came up to me and said, *"Sir, you're not wearing your combat patch."* I told him that I didn't have a sewing kit, and he volunteered to sew my patches on for me; however, when I went into my pocket, I could only come up with the basic patch, and could not find the Airborne tab. I told the soldier to forget it, but thanked him for the sentiment.

I had the good fortune to have, as one of my soldiers on that journey, the Command Sergeant Major of our battalion, Ron Hintz. We had been sent another freshly massaged Air Force crew, and I instructed the soldiers to walk across the ramp and board the plane for our last leg of this painful journey to Robert Gray Army Airfield in Fort Hood, Texas. CSM Hintz and I stood at the passenger entrance of the plane and counted the troops as they boarded. As the last soldier entered, I asked CSM Hintz how many he had counted, including the two of us. His count was the same as mine: 99! We instructed the soldiers to get off the plane and try it again. They dutifully obeyed, and again the count was 99. CSM Hintz instructed all of the soldiers to remain seated as he counted them in their seats. Again, 99 soldiers. Just then, one of the infantrymen from the 2nd Armored Division said to CSM Hintz, "Well, Sergeant Schmo is not here."

CSM Hintz looked at him in disbelief and quipped, "*How long did you plan on sitting on that nugget of information!*" CSM Hintz came out of the plane and met me on the ramp. "*Stay right here, sir.*" He said, "*I'll be right back!*" He darted into the terminal, and came back dragging Sergeant Schmo who had been talking on the pay phone in the snack bar, oblivious to the fact that everyone had left. He had been excitedly telling his loved ones that he'd be home very soon! I settled in for the luxurious conclusion of my journey home to good, old Fort Hood and Robert Gray Army Airfield, contemplating my first day off in over seven months.

Now, at this point, allow me to describe the events leading up to our deployment. I had spent a year in Honduras flying missions against live targets for a year. When I told my colleagues that I had asked to go to Fort Hood on my return to the States, they all told me that the 15th M.I. Battalion was the lowest priority Special Electronic Mission Aircraft (*SEMA*) unit in the Army. I told them that this was precisely the reason I wanted to go there. When our alert came for Desert Shield, they said we would go to support XVIII Airborne Corps. I protested, saying that that Corps had its own SEMA unit, the 224th M.I. Battalion. I was told that the 224th couldn't be spared from their counter narcotics mission in the Caribbean. When I offered to relieve them in their counter narcotics mission, freeing them to go to the desert with their assigned corps, my selfless volunteerism was rebuffed.

III Corps Headquarters was at Fort Hood, along with the 1st Cavalry Division, and what was left of the 2nd Armored Division. George Patton's beloved '*Hell on Wheels*' division was being drawn down and all that remained was the Tiger Brigade. The 1st Cav and the Tiger Brigade of the 2nd Armored Division were both invited to '*the dance*'. Likewise, III Corps' Armored Cavalry Regiment, the 2nd ACR out of Fort Bliss, and III Corps Artillery from Fort Sill were selected. The Signal Brigade, the Military Police Brigade and the Corps Support Brigade were all included in the war plan.

Over at Hood Army Airfield, the vaunted 6th Cavalry Brigade (*Air Combat*) -- sometimes called, `6th CBAC` -- was readying to go. With their three squadrons of Apache attack helicopters, they were to be a very decisive factor in the war plan, until the true nature of their readiness (*heavily falsified in reporting*) became apparent. Civilian technical reps from McDonnell-Douglas, and other defense contractors, had been swarming around the 6th CBAC hangars until the word came down that they would not be going. Upon which, the contractors disappeared over to spin up 2nd Armored Division and 1st Cav aircraft. The 6th CBAC did give up their CH-47 Chinook unit, their aircraft maintenance companies and their air traffic control company, but the mighty Apaches of the 6th CBAC earned the moniker, "*6th Stay Back*".

Over on West Fort Hood was the venerable 504th Military Intelligence Brigade, consisting of an Operations Battalion (303rd M.I. – mostly hand wringers that populated the Corps' G-2 staff), a ground based Signals Intelligence Battalion (163rd M.I. - Tactical Exploitation sometimes called CEWI [Combat Electronic Warfare Intelligence – but we used to say "*Comes Equipped With*

Idiots"]) and the SEMA Battalion (15th M.I. – Aerial Exploitation). The green-eye-shade planners at the Pentagon use a tool called the *"Time Phased Force Deployment Data"*, or TPFDD. Your place on the TPFDD determined when your unit was to deploy, and consequently, its priority.

When word of Operation Desert Shield hit the streets, everyone on Fort Hood was very excited. Strange desert camouflage uniforms were being distributed, and some began to be worn around the Post. In the 15th M.I., we didn't get any of those uniforms, we were busy doing all the things that must be done when the Army suddenly makes its lowest priority SEMA Battalion their highest priority. I had a conversation with one of the officers in the 303rd M.I. Battalion. He was wearing the new uniforms we called, *"Chocolate Chips"*. I asked why he had that uniform, since we were leaving soon and they had not received their place on the TPFDD. *"Oh, your uniforms will be coming down shortly. We'll be deploying soon. Before Christmas, III Corps will relieve XVIII Corps. XVIII Corps doesn't have the combat power that III Corps has."*

Well, when word hit the logisticians and planners that the 15th didn't have their uniforms because the brigade had decided to give them to the Cone Heads first (*our name for ground based Military Intelligence types*), the fecal matter struck the blades of the rotary air circulation device. They were ordered to give them back, and distribute them to the 15th. This created a sense of envy in the already envious Cone Heads.

By the time Lieutenant General Luck, Commander XVIII Airborne Corps, was done picking through what he deemed necessary to prosecute the war, there was nothing left at Fort Hood but the III Corps Headquarters, the 504th M.I. Brigade Headquarters, two Cone Head Battalions, and three squadrons of broken down Apaches. XVIII Corps even took the 1st Infantry Division from Fort Riley, KS, away from III Corps. Luck convinced General Schwartzkopf that he didn't need to be relieved by III Corps, because all of their combat power had already been appropriated.

My wife wrote me a letter while I was there in the desert, saying that Killeen was so deserted that you could throw a rock at high noon down the middle of Rancier Boulevard, the main drag, and not hit anyone or anything. So, you can imagine that Colonel Clifton Aldridge, Commander 504th M.I. Brigade was a bit stung by not being invited to the biggest military dance in his lifetime; but, that was nothing compared to the indignation felt by Lieutenant General Richard Gordon Graves, Commanding General, (*what was left of*) III U.S. Corps. For the record, Lieutenant General Luck once punched me in the stomach following a Corps level Command & Staff meeting at his headquarters in Dragon City, an old cement plant outside of Damam, Saudi Arabia. He was just kind of *"feeling his oats"* as he came out of the meeting. I came to attention as he walked by, boxing the air with his fists. He saw me and asked, *"How's it going, Killer?"*... and landed one in my gut. He didn't stick around for my answer.

I only saw General Luck one other time during the conflict. I had just returned from another night mission. There was some need for me to ride an hour or so in the back of a pickup truck to the Corps G-2 during banker's hours, to be read onto some program (*just a bunch of lawyer documents, threatening to ruin your life if you ever told anyone the things you were going to hear or see, even though you never asked to hear or see them*). I was supposed to be sleeping. I needed a shower and a shave. My flight suit probably stunk and my buttocks were throbbing from five or six hours in an ejection seat. I wore an olive drab *'Boonie'* hat that I had modified by passing a semi-rigid wire through the bead of the brim so I could shape it somewhat. I must have looked like something that someone dumped out of a duffle bag. General Luck walked by and he stopped when he saw the threadbare Mohawk patch on my flight suit. *"Been flying much, son?"* he asked.

I looked up at him and said, *"Sir, I've been flying my ass off!"*

"Good!" he snapped, and was gone in a flash.

Well, to return to my last flight leg to Fort Hood and home on the C-141B Luxury Liner, I was filled with anticipation. My wife was preparing a crispy roast pork at my request, and she had six Corona beers on ice with fresh lime ready to slice. There were clean sheets on the bed, and I meant to mess them up something awful. No, it wouldn't be long now, and all the agony would be a distant memory. I feverishly devoured my paperback, hoping to finish it before we landed at Robert Gray Army Airfield.

The airplane arrived with a thump at about 2330 Hours local time on Easter Sunday, 1991. We taxied down the taxiway toward the ADACG. The airplane came to a stop, and the roar of the engines died down. The crew made an announcement that we were to remain on the aircraft. I began to gather my assigned and extra equipment and place each of the straps around my neck.. I slipped my unfinished paperback into the cargo pocket on my right thigh. From behind me, I heard someone yell, *"Where's the ranking officer on this plane!"*

I raised my hand and stood up, and answered, *"I am,"* as I turned around and came face to face with the spurned III Corps Commander. General Graves was a small man. I looked at him, and immediately came to attention and saluted. Without returning my salute, he turned and walked out the door and down the stairs to the ramp. *"What the Hell is his problem?"* I muttered to myself, as I picked up my night vision goggle case and struggled to the door under the weight of all my stuff.

"Well, at least I'm home," I thought to myself. I trundled out the passenger door and lumbered down to the bottom of the stairs. At the bottom of the stairs stood the strange little man who had declined my salute without comment. I suppose he was expecting a crisp salute, but I had completely lost all regard for him. I finally stood on the solid pavement of Robert Gray Army Airfield, a place I had dreamed of for six months. If he would simply get out of my way, I'd be home in my quarters at West Fort Hood in no time. My thirty-six hour journey seemed like it took at least a month. We stood and stared at each other for a few seconds. I suppose that somewhere in the recesses of the Pentagon, they had concocted the idea that each of us returning troops would be met with hero's ceremony and celebration, but nobody had briefed me. After a long pregnant pause, the Corps Commander thrust out his right hand to me, and said, *"**Welcome home**."*

I thanked the General and turned to walk over to the ADACG. Suddenly, some Captain from the Brigade staff was at my elbow. *"We're all really proud of the job you guys have done."* He said, as I angled toward the building. *"No. Let's go this way."* He corrected me so that our path went along the chain link fence that separated the ADACG from the parking apron. In the pitch black of the Texas night, I resolved to do whatever was necessary to get in to the building.

We turned at the break in the fence to go up the walkway to the ADACG. The moment my foot hit the walkway, the whole world exploded. Without warning, intense flood lights, aimed at my unsuspecting eyes, burst to life. Simultaneously the 2nd Armored Division Band began to play a rousing military march. A local television station camera was thrust in my face and some reporter began to interrogate me about my feelings of being home again. Not one thing felt like home, at all. The whole celebration was sprung on me like some sort of ambush. No one had briefed me as to how I was supposed to respond. I can assure you, they didn't want my visceral response to their celebration. I wasn't the one that disinvited them to the conflict. I didn't want to go, at all. I had just suffered one of the worst travel experiences that the U.S. Air Force could muster, and I had completely lost my sense of humor.

They ushered us into the seating area of the ADACG, and we were immediately beset by *Simon Bar Sinister* himself, Cliff Aldridge. Now, I had only spoken to Colonel Aldridge once before. It was during the early days of our deployment to Saudi Arabia. One of my Non-Commissioned Officers was experiencing some marital problems, exacerbated by the deployment. His wife was threatening to leave him for someone else, and take their children with her. I can't recall the exact purpose of my calling back to the rear at Fort Hood, but I was trying to reach the Brigade Command Sergeant Major, or a Chaplain, or someone to contact the disgruntled spouse. I was not, however, trying to contact the Brigade Commander. We had one telephone line for our Battalion that could be used for important calls to the rear, and I had been granted permission to use it for this purpose. I had to wait until late at night or early in the morning to make the call, due to the time difference. Unfortunately for me, Colonel Aldridge, anxious for news of his detached command, was waiting by the phone which would otherwise have been answered by a duty officer or staff NCO. He wanted to know why I was calling, and as I began to explain the assistance I needed, he angrily interrupted me and berated me for wasting his time. This phone was for official business, and not a morale line.

"*Who's the ranking officer here,*" he quipped? Although I had begun to become very weary of that question, I indicated that I was. "*You're the Battalion Commander.*" He informed me.

"No, sir. Captain Ohocki is the Acting Battalion Commander," I offered. "I'm the Acting A Company Commander."

"Who has date of rank?" he asked.

"Well, I do, but, ….."

"But nothing!" Colonel Aldridge interrupted. "*You're the battalion commander! And, I didn't say 'acting' commander, either. You brought the battalion colors with you; you are the battalion commander. And tomorrow morning you'll sign assumption of command orders in my office!*"

"Yes, sir."

"All of your soldiers are wearing the WRONG COMBAT PATCH," he corrected me! I turned my right shoulder toward him and pointed to the empty space there.

"I'm not wearing ANY combat patch." I protested.

"*You've got to get that fixed, first thing!*" he ordered me. "*I'm having a command and staff meeting in my office, tomorrow at 0800. I expect to see you there. You can sign the assumption of command orders then.*"

"Yes, sir." He then instructed me on the plan for dismissing the troops in a short ceremony.

The stay behind troops of the 504th M.I. Brigade collected all of our sensitive items; weapons, night vision goggles and chemical protective masks. They loaded all of our personal baggage into a '*duce-and-a-half*' truck and suddenly, I felt as light as a feather. Although I had eaten every meal I could, and an unending smörgåsbord of treats sent from home, I managed to return from the conflict twenty-five pounds lighter than when I had left Fort Hood six months earlier. I felt naked without the encumbrances around my neck. After six months of carrying those burdens, I was finally a free man (*except, of course, for my new command responsibilities*).

The hapless and undecorated Infantrymen of the 502nd M.I. Battalion, disappeared into busses and were dispatched to the Abrams Field House on main post, where nearly every other unit was welcomed home; all, but the soldiers of the 15th M.I. Battalion, whose hangar lie only a few hundred feet north of the ADACG along the main runway for Robert Gray Army Airfield. Fifty soldiers of the 15th lead by their new battalion commander, leisurely strode to and loaded onto two busses that had Military Police car escorts.

We all felt enormous relief. In a moment, we would pile off the bus and into a formation on the ramp in front of our hangar. I would stand at the head of the formation, and present a salute to Colonel Aldridge, telling him that we have returned from the battle. He would return my salute and dismiss the formation. It was all about to happen, *finally*.

As the busses began to roll down the taxiway toward our hangar, our Military Police escort turned on their flashing lights and suddenly switched on their sirens. This was the exact same siren that we had used for two months to alert our troops of imminent *SCUD Missile impact* in our general area. Doctor Pavlov would have nodded approvingly at the sight of 51 soldiers frantically trying to find their chemical protective masks after being separated from them only minute before, for the first time in months. I guess no one had briefed the stay behind troops of III Corps just what it was like. They were trying to honor us, but instead had panicked us.

We regained our composure and shortly reached the hangar ramp. We formed up, presented arms, and were dismissed according to plan. It was about midnight when the Hangar doors were slipped open, and the brightly illuminated hangar, filled with our loved ones and decorated with banners, seemed like a sort of paradise. I was overwhelmed with emotion.

It seems that the order from President Bush *(#41)* on down for all returning troops was that it would take no longer than thirty minutes from the time we left the aircraft until we were reunited with our families. Whatever else I may think of him, I will always be grateful for that order. If it were not for his insistence, I'm certain that my lecture as to the necessities of Command, shoulder patches, and heraldry, would have continued, ad nauseum, until morning's light.

As it was, I was whisked to my quarters by my loving young wife. She ran a hot bath for me and fetched me an ice cold Corona, complete with lime. I savored the beverage as she set my dinner of roast pork in order on our dining room table. I ate my feast, enjoyed the physical act of love, and then broke the news to my bride that I had to get up in a couple of hours to get to a meeting. She was somewhat incredulous, to say the least.

At 0800 Hours, Monday, 2 April 1991 (*the day before my wife's birthday*), I presented myself at the Brigade Headquarters for the meeting. I signed the Assumption of Command Order, as directed and took my seat. As a captain, I was the lowest ranking officer in the room, and one of only three Battalion Commanders. First on the list to speak was the brigade S-3. "*Sir, at 1400 today an aircraft with one hundred and fifty soldiers from the 15th M.I. will be landing here at Robert Gray.*" he said.

Colonel Aldridge immediately turned to me and demanded, "*What are the names, Social Security numbers and weapon serial numbers of those troops?*"

"*I don't know, sir,*" I offered. This response sent him into a tirade, lambasting me for my incompetence, my ignorance, my lack of concern for my troops, and my obvious unfitness for Command. Majors and Lieutenant Colonels watched calmly as the Brigade Commander dressed me down. When he had exhausted his rage on me, I simply said, "*Sir, this is the first I'm hearing of this. I was not informed of any such plan before I left Saudi Arabia; however, I will do everything I can to get that information for you.*"

Other business was shared and the Colonel gave his guidance. Last to speak at the meeting was the Brigade's Command Sergeant Major. He informed the group that tonight would be, **'*Right Arm Night*'** at the West Fort Hood Non-Commissioned Officer's Club; an occasion for Officers in leadership positions to socialize with their principal Non-Commissioned Officers. Colonel Aldridge issued his expectation that every Officer in Command or Leadership was expected to be present. He made special emphasis to me that I was to be there with Command Sergeant Major Hintz. I genuinely enjoyed the company of CSM Hintz, and was happy to have an occasion to share an adult beverage with him, as we often would sip a non-alcoholic beer together in Saudi Arabia. The troops were given an unlimited supply of **O'Doul's** alcohol-free beer that we affectionately referred to as "***Abdul's***". The only problem was that I now had to explain to my young wife that I would not be home for the evening, as we had planned.

I can't remember much about that first day of duty after returning from the war. I happily sent as many soldiers as I felt I could afford to go on *Ordinary Leave*. As I began to research the identities and vital information on that afternoon's returning troops, I got a call from the Brigade S-3. He explained that, *apparently*, he was mistaken about the returning troops, and none would be arriving today. One of the Captains from the 'REAL M.I." Battalions came over to have me sign for the Hangar. He told me that while we were goofing off in the desert, Vice President Dan Quayle had come to Fort Hood for a visit. He scolded me that the 15th M.I. Battalion had carelessly left the hangar in a horrible state of uncleanliness when we departed, and that the soldiers of the 163rd and 303rd Battalions had been forced to scour it and make it presentable for the Vice President's visit. I apologized for our thoughtlessness. I could just imagine Cliff Aldridge turning the VIP visit into something on the importance of *Operation Overlord*. I felt gratified that we had not had the benefit of his leadership in the desert.

That evening, I reported to the NCO Club, as ordered, for my Command Performance *at 'Right Arm Night'*. CSM Hintz and I spent some time together and toasted our successful return to Fort Hood. After some time, Colonel Aldridge approached me. "*I wanted you to know that I probably shouldn't have been so hard on you this morning*," he said.

As a new Lieutenant, I had been commissioned in the Infantry. At Fort Benning, I learned about what it takes to lead a group of men on very dangerous missions with limited resources, relying on each other, our courage and our physical strength. We were taught to build our Platoon into a team that could overcome the most difficult obstacles and face danger coolly, and with resolve.

In order to break into the field of Fixed-Wing flying, I had asked to attend the Military Intelligence Advanced Course in lieu of Infantry or Aviation. My experience at the U.S. Army Intelligence Center and School at Fort Huachuca, AZ, was demoralizing at best. Instead of learning to Command a Company, the course was designed to produce hand-wringing staff officers who knew how to produce graphics, prepare correspondence, and make coffee. The entire course had a single hour on the syllabus dedicated to instruction on *"Leadership."* That hour was taught (*no joke*) by the Chaplain. One Principle of Leadership I recalled from my days as an ROTC cadet was that you must correct and admonish your soldiers *privately*, but praise them in public. And, if you ever made a mistake yourself, you must frankly admit it publicly. Colonel Aldridge had actually found a way to diminish the low regard in which I held him. He had screamed at me and disparaged me publicly, and was now attempting to make his half-hearted apology in private.

"That's okay, sir." I quickly offered, *"I just came from a place where people were trying to kill me every day. If it makes you feel better, go ahead and yell at me. I can take it."*

"I wish all of my officers had an attitude like that," the Colonel replied! I wished that I had ever experienced leadership by an Officer above Company grade.

I remember thinking, *"Leadership is only practiced by Captains and Lieutenants toward enlisted soldiers."* Officers are expected to lead themselves. If they ever experienced difficulties, professional or personal, they had better suck it up and not let anyone know about it, or it would be seen as a sign of weakness. I was very sad.

So, I had spent all of 1989 in Honduras, returning only at Christmas to move my household to Fort Hood. I spent Christmas of 1990 in Saudi Arabia, driving around in a truck trying to visit my soldiers that had been farmed out to Division and Corps Headquarters. I was informed that, since the 163rd and 303rd Battalions had been compelled to do ALL of the holiday duties while the 15th M.I. Battalion was goofing off in the desert, the 15th would be required to provide an Officer to man the Brigade Headquarters for Christmas 1991. Since I ran the Duty Roster, and I had no children, I simply placed myself in that spot. All of the other captains had children with whom they needed to celebrate.

Late in the evening on Christmas Eve, 1991, I left my NCO in charge of the Headquarters, while I went with my driver over to the III Corps Message Center to pick up two bundles of message traffic: one *Classified*, and the other *Unclassified*. As I was being driven back to the Brigade Headquarters, I began to sift through the *Unclassified* messages. My eyes fixed on a very significant message from the Department of the Army. It read that my year group (1982) and one other year group (1978) were the targets of the coming Reduction in Force (*RIF*) that was to be the basis for the *"Peace Dividend"* that the weary American taxpayers were to receive, now that the Soviet Union had dissolved, and World Peace had broken out. This was my Christmas card from the Army. I had until 29 February 1992 to tender my resignation, or face the Boards that would give me a fraction of the money I would get for quitting.

Of all the slights, insults and indignities I had absorbed over the previous four years, this was the chief and came from the highest echelon. I still recall the disbelief of my superiors when I presented my resignation letter. Life got much better the moment I submitted my resignation, effective 1 June 1992. The other Battalions had been complaining that the 15th had not supplied any Officers to work on staff in the Corps G-2. "Psycho" Joe Blanco countered that his Officers were in Flying Billets, and that the Army expected them to maintain flight currency. The other Battalions declared that they would provide any Officer, that the 15th supplied, to fly two days each week. Blanco finally agreed to give up an Officer once my resignation came across his desk. I would spend the balance of my days detailed to the Corps G-2 staff.

I reported to my new assignment at the G-2, where I met Major Harold Waybright, an M.I. Officer, who had spent years in the XVIII Airborne Corps, and had hundreds of parachute jumps.

Although he was nearly unable to walk, due to his numerous hard landings, he regarded anyone who was not on jump status as a lesser soldier. Major Waybright was to be my supervisor in the G-2 Collection Management Section. I soon learned that the only thing lower, in his opinion, than a non-Airborne soldier was an Aviator pretending to know anything about Military Intelligence. This arrangement suited me just fine.

Two days each week, I reported to the Flight Line, and if no other aircraft were available, I was given one. This was part of the deal made for my services at the G-2. The other days I sat and typed my applications for airline pilot jobs, and worked on my log books, and civilian ratings. Major Waybright was loathe to give me any real G-2 work to do, for fear that I might succeed. He was particularly irritated whenever the Colonel, who was the principle G-2 officer, came by. I can't recall his name, but he had Commanded the School Brigade when I was at Fort Huachuca in the M.I. Advanced Course. He remembered me well and would often stop by to ask about my experiences in Desert Storm. This infuriated Waybright, as not only was he among those disinvited to the fight, but I had served as an augmentee to XVIII Airborne Corps. Around the time I finished my time in the G-2, I heard that Major Waybright was being medically retired as a major (*AIRBORNE!*).

These are the events as I recall them. I hold no animus toward any of the leadership failures I witnessed, during my time in the Army. They paid me $54K to quit in 1992. I got my first DD Form 214 on 1 June 1992, when I resigned my Regular Army commission. I was told, as a Cadet, that if you ever resigned a Regular Army commission, you could never have another. I received my fourth DD Form 214 when I retired from the Regular Army on 30 June 2011. I finished paying back the Army for the $54K separation bonus 1 July 2020. I get my Direct Deposit from the U.S. government the first of each month. I retired from flying two years ago, after more than 12,000 flight hours and more than 200 flights around the world.

Thanks for reading.
Respectfully,
Philip D. Forsberg, LTC
U.S. Army - *Retired*

TOM FOSTER
US Army
25th Infantry Div Tet '68
Cell: 404-906-5266
Foster_Tom@Bellsouth.net

My Vietnam Story

SPECIALIST– 4 TOM FOSTER WAS JUST A CITIZEN-SOLDIER

Tom was not a military-oriented young man, but was drafted into the U. S. Army (*a citizen-soldier*) in 1966, 2-months after his 19th birthday. But an indicator of Tom's worth to the Army was immediately recognized, as he was awarded the *American Spirit Honor Medal* when graduating from Boot Camp. He then went to Ft Carson, Colorado, as a member of the 5th Infantry Division (*Mechanized*). He didn't think he would be sent to Vietnam, so he got involved playing football, and was getting ready to start training for boxing, but fate had a different course for him.

Tom found himself recognized for his bravery under fire, and part of his **Silver Star Citation** reads:

"For gallantry in action … Specialist Four Foster distinguished himself by heroic action on 28 April 1968, while serving with Company A, 4th Battalion, 23rd Infantry on a combat operation in the Republic of Vietnam. When his unit came under intense enemy fire, Specialist Four Foster took command of his platoon after all of its leaders had been wounded. He fearlessly rallied his men and organized them to continue the attack against the enemy. Exposing himself many times to this intense enemy fire, Specialist Foster directed the fire of his men, then climbed on the platoon's Command Personnel Carrier to give a situation report to the Company Commander. He supplied his men with ammunition, directed the evacuation of the wounded, and finally directed the platoon in a withdrawal at the order of the Company Commander. Specialist Foster's personal bravery, aggressiveness, and devotion to duty are in keeping with the highest traditions of the military service and direct great credit upon himself, his unit, the 25th Infantry Division, and the United States Army."

On the Dedication page of the book, "**Rolling Coffins**", authored by **Brain Esher**, Tom is mentioned, and further on pages 122, 123 and 124, Tom's actions, while a member of the 25th Infantry Division in 1968, is *immortalized*.

It is remarkable that in one fire fight Tom took a glazing round that hit a hand grenade attached to his flak jacket and did not detonate. Tom was wounded **twice** while in Vietnam, once before the action cited in this *Silver Star Citation*, and once afterwards. He was sent to the 7th Field Hospital in Tokyo, Japan, and later evacuated to the 377th Medical Evacuation Hospital in South Korea, before returning home to the U.S.A.

After returning stateside, Tom was an ardent activist regarding the treatment of returning Veterans and wrote several newspaper articles, and was the subject of a personal letter from General Norman Schwarzkopf for voicing his opinion in Atlanta regarding the liberation of Kuwait in 1991.

Several of Tom's articles appeared in the *Peoria Journal Star* and later in the *Marietta Daily Journal*. He was also the subject of articles in the *Soldier of Fortune* magazine.

Tom became an international businessman as the President/Chief Executive Officer of his company – *ConCure, Inc*. Concure, Inc. is a Coldwater Mist Curing System company, a system that was introduced in the domestic and international marketplace to include the likes of Australia, and many other countries to include the Soviet Union. Tom was even debriefed by the CIA upon his departure from an international tradeshow and concrete convention.

After leaving the service, Tom has shown his continued patriotism for this country. Just one of many examples is … for the past 15-years Tom has been actively involved with the History and Social Studies Department at the Newnan High School, Newnan, Georgia, in the Student-Vet Connect program. According to **Steve Quesinberry**, *Department Chair*, Tom is the most heavily involved Veteran in the history of the Veteran programs, and he plays an integral part of the student's knowledge of history regarding the Vietnam War era. He involves himself with the Vietnam Class Email Project and has helped shape the future of hundreds of students.

This program was made especially for Georgia's Heroes, of whom **Tom Foster** certainly fits the bill!

DEPARTMENT OF THE ARMY

HEADQUARTERS, 25TH INFANTRY DIVISION

APO SAN FRANCISCO 96225

25 June 1968

GENERAL ORDERS

NUMBER 4583

AWARD OF THE SILVER STAR

SP4 E4 THOMAS L. FOSTER

Co A, 4th Bn, 23rd Inf, 25th Infantry Division

Award: Silver Star, Date Action: 28 April 1968, Theatre: Republic of Vietnam

For gallantry in action: Specialist Four Foster distinguished himself by heroic action on 28 April 1968, while serving with Company A, 4th Battalion, 23d Infantry on a combat operation in the Republic of Vietnam. When his unit came under intense enemy fire Specialist Four Foster took command of his platoon after all of its leaders had been wounded. He fearlessly rallied his men and organized them to continue the attack against the enemy. Exposing himself many times to this intense enemy fire Specialist Foster directed the fire of his men, then climbed on the platoon's command personnel carrier to give a situation report to the company commander. He supplied his men with ammunition, directed the evacuation of the wounded, and finally directed the platoon in a withdrawal at the order of the Company Commander. Specialist Foster's personal bravery, aggressiveness, and devotion to duty are in keeping with the highest traditions of the military service and direct great credit upon himself, his unit, the 25th Infantry Division, and the United States Army.

Chief of Staff

By direction of the President under the provisions of Executive Order 11046, dated 24 August 1962, and USARV message 16695, dated 1 July 1966.

B. F. Hood

Colonel, GS

Chief of Staff

Above: Our own **Tom Foster,** being honorably inducted into the Georgia Military Veterans Hall of Fame.

My Military Experiences

I was a Marine Corps H-34 helicopter pilot with a Vietnam tour from late 1965 to 1966 and was essentially stationed in four different places: Danang, Danang East, helicopter carriers and Chu-Lai. Here are several memories that stand out.

When we first arrived in Vietnam, we lived in the old French BOQ on Da Nang Air Base and there was a flight scheduled at dawn. I was up earlier than most and when I attempted to wake up another pilot, his instinctive reaction was to grab his .38 revolver, immediately jump from his bed, cock it, and point it directly between my eyes. Needless to say, I never attempted that wake-up maneuver on another person.

The next incident happened at the end of a Training Mission, in which I was instructing a Vietnamese student at Da Nang.

Pilots are normally very smooth at the controls, but he was the exact opposite, when moving side-to-side, or back-and-forth, he'd move the "stick" sharply in all directions, despite being consistently instructed in the proper method. I took the controls for the mission's final approach, but when adding power to land I had an emergency, which petrifies all helicopter pilots -- a 100% tail rotor failure. One of Newton's Laws of Physics, "For every action there is an equal and opposite reaction" was proven – the helicopter blades were moving in one direction, and we went into an uncontrollable circle in the opposite direction. With an emergency like this, there is no time to think. There must be an immediate reaction, and mine was simply to totally reduce the power ASAP, which resulted in the tail wheel being ripped off, but miraculously the aircraft remained in an upright position. When the Master Sergeant-in-charge of Maintenance looked at the helicopter, he said, *"Congratulations Lieutenant, you're the first person to ever survive a complete tail rotor failure."*

HMM-261 was the first Squadron, which moved from Da Nang Air Base to the newly constructed Da Nang East. When we arrived on the new base, the Seabees who were making tent frames large enough for 12 of us, looked down and said something like, *"Hey JarHeads, if you want air-conditioning roll the canvas up, when you don't, roll it down."* They enjoyed a great laugh.

My Squadron flew combat and supply missions from aircraft carriers as a group called the **BLT** (*Battalion Landing Team*). The combat missions generally involved the insertion, resupply, and removal of Marine Corps ground troops, and my Operations Officer created an original approach, which required an *autorotation*. An autorotation is reducing your engine power to idle, causing a rapid rate of descent, and in the H-34's case, it would be a maximum rate of 3,000 feet per minute. When the helicopter came close to the point of landing, the pilot pulled back on the stick, transferring the airspeed to lift, and allowing a landing at its desired point (*see photo on Page-1, as an example*). This approach was in direct contrast with those utilized by Army helicopters in the original phase of the war, when they all were lined up together at a very low altitude and airspeed, making them ideal targets for the Viet Cong.

We pilots would quietly talk about how grateful we were *not* to be "*Grunts,*" but one time in the Carrier Wardroom we happened to mention it to them. Those Lieutenants and Captains immediately looked at each other, smiled and then began laughing. When asked what was so funny, we were told how the combat situation totally changed when we were resupplying them. Almost no shots were fired at the Battalion when they were on the ground by themselves, but when we landed … the amount of rounds aimed increased *dramatically*. Then they told us they were much happier being Grunts then Pilots.

As our length of time in Vietnam increased, most combat missions required us to fly in flights of four. There were several times when we were on the ground in a **LZ** (*Landing Zone*) waiting for the Grunts to return, and scores of rounds were shot at us. On three of these missions, all three of the other helicopters in my flight were hit by several bullets; one with 25. And when we returned to our base of operations, every one of them was grounded. On all three of these missions, the total number of hits my helicopter sustained was ***zero. Nada***. Needless to say, this was noticed by all the other Squadron Pilots.

When based at Chu-Lai nearing the end of our tour of duty, we inserted troops in an area around a rice paddy, but when taking off my engine lost power, and we were forced to land. Anyone who has seen a rice paddy knows in the initial phase of growth it's completely under water, and that's what all four of our crew members jumped into. In high school I had been the Quarter Mile Champion of our 8-school League, and while running to the other helicopter it must have looked as though I'd break my quarter mile record. During that run, one of the Pilots still flying above quietly made the remark that because of me, he felt like he had to go back to church.😊 When asked why his comical response was, "Frankle's helicopters not ***only didn't take any hits, but now I'm watching him run on water.***"

Amen brothers and sisters. Thanks be to God!

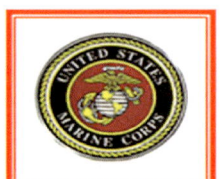 

My Military Experience(s)

I started my Army time in Basic Training at Fort Benning, Georgia, on Sandhill side. After that, I was assigned to Fort Gordon, Georgia, for Advanced Infantry Training. I was chosen for Radio Relay & Carrier Systems.

They sent me to Germany when I finished. It was a 4-month school. When I got to Germany, they didn't need carrier personnel, so I was reassigned to another school -- *Radio Repair*, for almost four more months. ☹It was rough duty being assigned right next to a ski resort adjacent to Garmisch, Germany. I finished that school and was put into an Armor unit, working on intercoms in tanks and fixing radios.

Next, we went onto Maneuvers, played War Games in tanks with the German Federal Army, rail-headed tanks on trains, rode across country, and slept on the trains. It was all fun, except for the snow and cold temperatures. I stayed there for over a year.

I had it made. I had just made Sergeant and it suddenly became *easy duty* for a change. At least I wasn't, *You Know Where* [**Nam**], BUT … one evening, the Company Clerk came down our hall grinning, and waving a sheet of paper with ***RVN*** on top of that page. The next day, I was called into the Orderly Room. The C.O. told me to go to Mannheim, Germany, pick-up a prisoner at the Stockade, and take him to Würzburg to see his lawyer, and then take the prisoner back to Mannheim. I was 20-years old kid, who only weighed 120#, soaking wet. I told the C.O. that I wasn't an M.P., but he just said this was not an M.P.'s job, and that I was *next* on Duty Roster.

So, I checked out my .45-Pistol and ammo, got a truck and driver, and off we went across Germany in the snow. When we got to Würzburg, he saw his lawyer, and I went to check on my

Orders. I **knew** they had me pegged for Nam. The guy just looked at me and asked what I was doing there. He said I was on **my** time, and I was *supposed* to be in Acworth, Georgia. It had taken several days to get to Mannheim & Würzburg, and our truck would not run in the cold, and was vapor-locking, so we put some pure alcohol into the gas tank to help get it started. I called my company clerk, and he got the Executive Officer (X.O.) to come and get me. The X.O. came in his red Mustang with his wife and baby.

 I turned the prisoner over to a U.S. Air Force Officer. I got our 1st-Sergeant's jeep the next day and cleared in one day. I made it home *BUT*, had a rather short stay. Next, it was onto a plane to Washington State for Jungle Training.

 Once there, we jumped off of our truck, and ran into woods. I tripped a booby trap, and an Officer came running over and yelled, **"DEAD*!*"**

 I thought that was a bad omen. Anyway, next was a plane to Viet Nam. We landed at Cam Ranh Bay. I saw a pretty beach, and wooden sidewalks. I thought, *I can make it here a year easy.* I got to stay there for 2-days. Next, I got onto a C-123 plane to Ban Mê Thuột. After landing there I observed a dirt runway, a small building with 4' x 8' plywood sign that said, **"Home Of The Dirty Dozen."**

 I was by myself, a 21-year-old NCO, who had no clue where to go. About that time, a native *Montagnard* came up to me trying to sell me a crossbow. Finally, I hitched a ride in a jeep to a Firebase about 10-miles out to *NoWhereLand*. When I got to the Firebase, there was nothing there but six small guns and sandbags; NO tanks or radios to work on … just red dirt dust and sandbags.

 I found the C.O., and he told me, *"I want commo, here."* We ran commo wire to the guns, listening posts, and FDC. We built bunkers, we got hit with rockets and mortars, and we built a Hootch to sleep in; LOTS of sandbags. We tried to get comfortable before the monsoons were scheduled to arrive. Guess what**?** We moved to start another one of the same.

 I met a lot of interesting people there. We had an OLD E-7 (*probably 40-years old?*). He was a *Lifer* and *loved* it all. Made me think of General George S. Patton. When we took mortars, he would punch me and say, did you hear it? Here comes three**!** He *loved* it. We called him, '**Chief Of Smoke**.'

 One evening, we got hit. We all took off to our place, or ran for cover. Don't know where she came from, but there was a young girl, who had fallen to her knees crying, **"Buddha, Buddha*!*"** I slung my M-16 to my other arm, ran out there, scooped her up, and ran with her to a bunker. She probably thought I was *Buddha*. I guess she is a true *Buddhist* now. Never heard any more about her, or why she was there.

 Another funny thing we did was when one of our Officers flagged a convey down. We

5-Finger-Discounted a deuce and half full (**2.5-Ton Army Truck**) of popcorn, oil, and big popper. The First Sergeant turned it over to me. I had popcorn coming out of my ears. I traded popcorn for everything. Some Special Forces guys were living in a little compound outside Ban Mê Thuột. I would go there and trade popcorn for flashlight batteries for our *Field Phones*. We set up the Popper so we had popcorn with our warm beer, *when* we were able to get beer.

We got hit real hard the night before I was to get out of there. All I could think of was the stories of guys getting hurt the last day. I don't think anyone got hurt bad and guess what? I got to Ban Mê Thuột Air Base, and got on that C-123 to Saigon, and then onto a *real* Plane to *The World* – to **MY Home Sweet Home!**

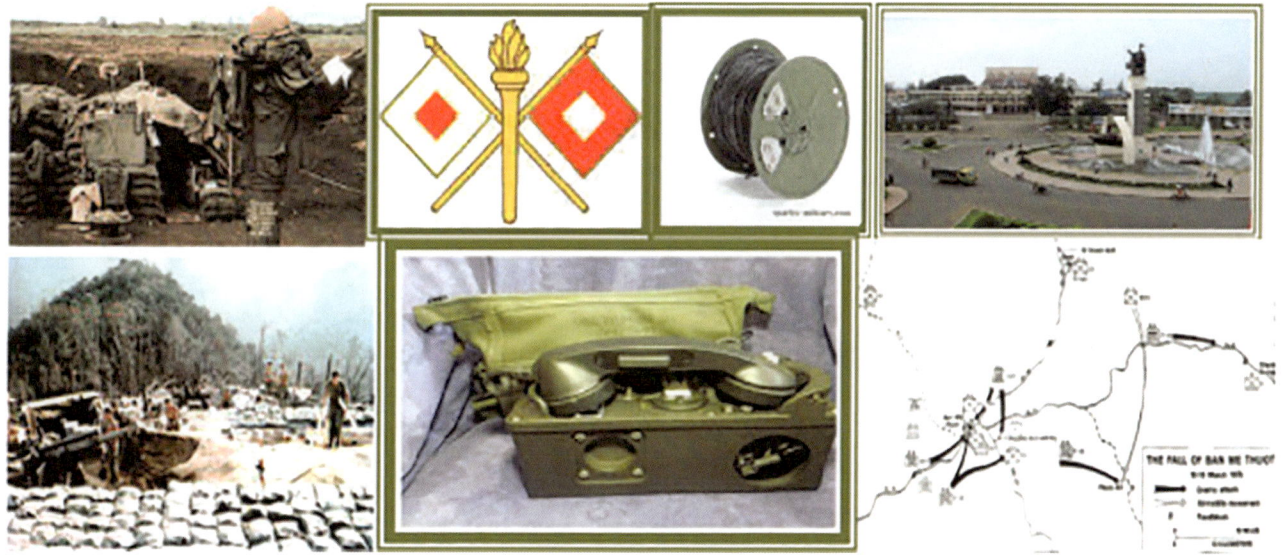

BRUCE GODDARD

U.S. Navy
Submarines
Cell: 678-523-3384
BruceGoddard@yahoo.com

MY MILITARY EXPERIENCES

Because my parents could not afford to send me to college, I joined the United States Navy. I served 3-years and 3-months on active duty in the U.S. Navy, from 1959-1962. The odd time was because of the "*Kiddy Cruise*" (*if you went in before your 18th birthday, you got out the day before your 21st birthday*). I was released from the Navy in September 1962, and the **Cuban Missile Crises** started in October 1962. I served on three submarines out of Key West, Florida -- the USS Balao SS285, the USS Chopper SS342, and the USS Sea Cat SS399. The Balao was used in the filming of the movie `**Operation Petticoat.**`

While in Boot Camp in San Diego in 1959, I took the Fleet-Wide Exam to the Naval Academy and passed, and was sent to Bainbridge, Maryland, to attend the Naval Academy Prep School for one year to prepare to take the College Boards for entrance into the U.S. Naval Academy (*U.S.N.S.*). The Prep School had military men from the U.S. Navy, U.S. Marines Corps, and U.S. Air Force, and we attended daily classes studying math, science, and English, similar to a freshman in college, preparing to take the College Boards exam. I failed on *English Comprehension*, and since I had been in the Navy for one year, they told me I could go into any area in the Navy, so I chose submarines.

After Submarine School (`**Subs**`), I was assigned to the Submarine Base in Key West, Florida. I had no specific rating or technical schooling in the Navy, so I was assigned to a Chief Petty Officer, who was a Quartermaster, and therefore, I became a Quartermaster, as well. A Quartermaster in the Navy is responsible for *visual communications and navigation*. Most of my time in subs was aboard the USS Chopper, and all three boats were diesel boats. During one deployment, we spent three months in the North Atlantic off the coast of Murmansk, Russia, recording the *Sonar*

Screw Signature of all the Russian ships going in and out of Murmansk, so that Sonar Operators would recognize the sound of a specific type of ship. We were within the 3-mile coast of Russia so it was a very tense time. Other deployments included Bermuda, New Orleans during **Mardi Gras**, Guantanamo Bay, Cuba, and Montego Bay, Jamaica.

I obtained the rank of QM3(SS), a Quartermaster Third Class Petty Officer. The SS-designation at the end of my rating indicates I was qualified on Submarines. This qualification requires that an individual to be able to take over any position on a sub, if someone is injured, or dies. This requires you to know what each and every valve and button on the sub is for, and how to operate each of them.

I left the Navy in 1962, and attended college on *The G.I. Bill*, graduating from the University of Florida in 1969 with a degree in Civil Engineering. My freshman year at Florida in 1964, when I was 23, *Steve Spurrier* was the Sophomore Quarterback for our football team. I was very popular with the men in my dorm, as I was the only one *over* 21, and could buy beer for my good friends. Because of my military experience, I was mature enough to study, and graduated *cum laude*. Before graduation, I got married, and had a daughter, and lived in *Married Student Housing* during my Junior and Senior years at Florida.

I became a *Professional Engineer* and was registered in more than 10-States throughout my professional career. I have been around the world doing engineering projects in China, Chile, Alaska, Hawaii, Saudi Arabia, Germany and Turkey. I finally decided to retire from engineering at the tender age of 79, after a *long* and *fulfilling* career.

In 1998, I started going to Haiti as part of a *Medical Mission Group* from our Parish Church -- **Transfiguration Catholic Church** in Marietta, Georgia, supporting the Medical Team with engineering needs. When the Medial Doctor (**Dr. Gerry Lluberas**) contracted Cancer in 2003 and died, **Ted Waldbart** and I started a non-profit organization called, `**Health and Education Relief Organization, Inc.**` (**HERO**), in memory of Dr. Gerry. Since then, as President of HERO, I made more the **50**-trips to Haiti, and built an orphanage, two medical clinics, four schools, five water systems, and numerous education libraries in remote villages throughout the country. HERO is a registered-nonprofit organization with the Federal Government, and the Secretary of State of the State of Georgia, and information on HERO can be obtained through our web site . . . www.herononprofit.org

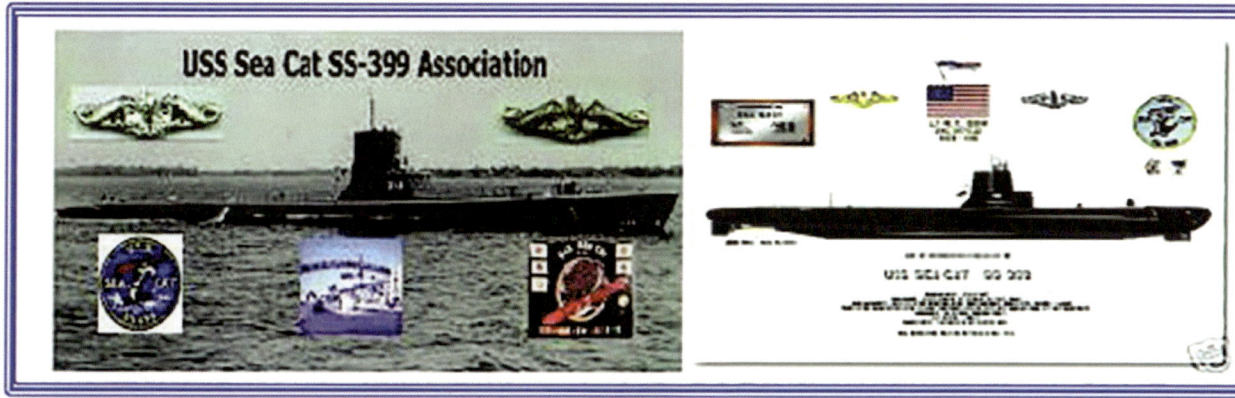

DICK GODDARD
U.S. Army
770-973-6687
IPSD378269@Yahoo.com

My Military Experiences

It was a dark and stormy day on 9 Sep 1941 . . . when I was born in Chicago, and grew up in the inner city, attending high school when not sitting in the Wrigley Field bleachers, or playing sports with friends in local parks, *[or streets]*. **Next stop:** 6-years at the University of Illinois, where I earned Management and Law degrees on 15 Jun 62, and an ROTC Commission in the U.S. Army. After a lovely year in Oregon, teaching law and clerking for a Supreme Court Justice, the Army said, *"Son, Fort Lee, Virginia, has missed you, but wonderful experiences are awaiting you; "Y'all come now, ya`hear?!"*

So, I came. Having transferred from Quartermaster to the ***Army's Judge Advocate General's Corps*** [*a.k.a., JAG*] to avoid the musty smells of Army supply rooms, I was soon immersed into the musty smells of law books at the University of Virginia Law School, where the Army JAG School was then located. After JAG School, I volunteered for a couple of those wonderful experiences. I attended *Armor Officer Basic* at Fort Knox [*Winter Armor lesson:* ***Nothing*** *is as cold as a Tank!!*], and I arrived at Fort Benning, Georgia, just in time to enjoy the change of seasons at Airborne School, where the Black Hats enjoyed giving all the s**t duties to me and the 3 other JAG's in our class.

After 10-months on active duty, I finally was forced to go to work. My two years at the 82d Airborne Division passed quickly, defending, and prosecuting, felony court-martial cases, and the next promised experience loomed large . . .

Our flight landed at Bien Hoa, Vietnam, and after 2-days of drinking lots of beer, my law clerk from the 3d Brigade, 82d arrived to drive me to our base, ***Camp Red Ball***, just north of Tan Son Nhut Air Base. After the usual introductions and minimal orientation, I had arrived. Being a quick study, I immediately learned the location of my hooch, the legal shack, the mess hall, and the latrines. Then work commenced. I was the only JAG in the Command, but I was blessed with two fine legal clerks, one a lawyer SP4, to whom I could delegate many of *my* legal chores, which gave me time to expand my horizons -- drinking beer at our miniscule "Officers' Club," which became a priority, but lacked excitement. I had acquired some civil affairs and *Psy Ops* Training while at Bragg, and thought I might put it to some good use, so I sought out our S-5 Section. Learning that the S-5 Chief, a *Major,* was the only one in the office with relevant training and experience, I volunteered my services on a part-time basis, and was immediately welcomed into the section. Let the games begin!

Most of my time with 3d Brigade was spent as a *de facto* S-5, working *civic action projects* with nearby villages, coordination with ARVN host units in the area, scoping out Saigon's bars and restaurants, and the serious duties -- endless leaflet drops, *a.k.a.,* litter-bugging western III Corps and War Zone-D, and **MedCAP**, **DentCAP**, and **VetCAP** Missions to win the hearts and minds of the locals [*It was partially successful, because they only went to war at night.*]. In December 1969, 3d Brigade redeployed to CONUS, leaving me behind as a Trial Lawyer with the **Big Red One**, until the *Freedom Birds* rescued the entire *BRO*, four months later.

As I had deployed without complaining, never contracted an **STD** *["shrinking bird" disease]*, and never reported my superior officers who did, I was rewarded with the assignment of my choice: Fort Ord, California, on the shores of Monterey Bay, in a time before California turned left, and went *woke*, and it was still a beautiful state.

Fort Ord was a pleasure, but there was lots of work for all. There were many personnel problems and personnel shuffles. When the smoke cleared, I was a CPT(*P*), a captain selected for eventual promotion, serving in a Colonel (*O-6*) slot, as the Staff Judge Advocate of a major installation and Infantry Training Center, working for **Major General Hal Moore**. He was an outstanding Commander, and a wonderful boss, who remains one of my heroes to this day. While I was at Ord, a multiple murder [*fragging*] case was transferred to us from US Army Vietnam, giving me a short TDY back to Nam and to Camp Zama, Japan, as an Investigating Officer.

All good things come to an end, and after 33-months, I returned to Fort Bragg, NC, as a Military Judge. This was not an Airborne assignment, and Ft. Bragg is no place to go if you aren't Airborne; like they say about a Harley-Davidson, *"If you ain't Airborne, you ain't s**t!"* My soon-to-be boss and dear friend was **Colonel Reid Kennedy**, the *Lt. Calley Court-Martial Trial Judge*, who was wrapping up a 36-year career as the Senior Circuit Judge in the Southeast, trying the cases of his choice, and golfing with fellow Judges at several posts, before retiring to Marietta, Georgia. Colonel Kennedy had been the Army's first JAG to become a *Master Parachutist*. Understanding that I wanted an Airborne slot, he allowed me to negotiate an Attachment to the 82d, and I became the only [*ever!*] Military Judge on active Airborne status. I left this post to briefly fill a vacancy at the **XVIII Airborne Corps** office. And then, the music died . . .

I was selected to fill a somewhat prestigious post with the **U.S. Army Legal Services Agency** in Falls Church, Virginia. It SUCKED! I was now a suburbanite in Fairfax Virginia.   *It was 1974.* An unpopular war had ended, my subordinates had disgustingly long hair, and we were encouraged to wear our uniforms only one day a week - Wednesdays. I did this job for two years, was denied transfer to any hardship area [*which I considered the D.C. area to be*] and resigned my *Regular Army* Commission. If I was going to serve like a civilian, and live like a civilian, I might as well be one!

Fast forward to the finale; **it's Happy Hour!!**

I went to work as an overpaid, over-grade litigation attorney for a federal agency. Three years after resigning from the Army, and bored to tears with my job, I received a call from my Falls Church boss, who had been promoted from Colonel to Major General, *The Judge Advocate General of the Army*, and he advised me to re-Commission in the Reserves, and I could immediately expect an excellent assignment. So, I did, and received Command of a

Legal Detachment in Harrisburg, Pennsylvania, just as Fort Indiantown Gap was filling up with Cuban refugees from the Mariel Boat Lift, and my Unit went on an extended active-duty assignment. It was three years of a great assignment, some active-duty time in Grenada, and legal support to the *Army War College*. Three years followed as a second detachment Command in Norfolk, Virginia, and more time in Grenada. Then, my tenure expired . . .

So, I was again seeking an assignment, not easy at the Lieutenant Colonel level, as the pyramid gets narrow at the top, and the Reserves have far more LTC JAG's than available jobs. I found one!! Commuting from Fairfax to Atlanta was a snap, to a sleepy little post **(Fort McPherson)**, which harbored a sleepy little Command – **Third United States Army**, which became **ARCENT**, the Army Element, U.S. Central Command, upon a future deployment to Southwest Asia. The assignment featured many training opportunities and TDY's to Egypt and Somalia, until 5 August 1990.

The balloon went up! Saddam Hussein had invaded the Kuwaiti oil fields, and CENTCOM issued its deployment order. 9 August saw me on a C-141B at Dobbins ARB, heading for the sandbox. As the first ARCENT JAG in country, I became the Legal Adviser to our 3-star Commanding General and his Staff, the Legal Adviser to ARCENT's Operations and Intelligence Center, and the Legal Liaison to SJA CENTCOM. As our JAG Office closed in theater, I retained the latter two jobs for the duration of the war. After serving as a member of the Joint Service Targeting Board and spending a week closing down the small legal section we had maintained in Manama, Bahrain, I returned to Riyadh, Saudi Arabia. Two days later, my war was over. The Command Section, my deputy and I returned to CONUS on a chartered L-1011 on 12 May 1991, with refueling stops at Shannon, Ireland, [*lots of beer and stout consumed in 90-minutes*] and Bangor, Maine, the site of my last meaningful memory. Wait for it . . .

The last dark and stormy night. It was a dreary, foggy morning in Bangor, but it was AMERICA! As we entered the terminal during the refueling, there were 150+ civilians there to welcome us home! My deputy's comment was that it was a hell of a way for all of these folks to perform their community service. Shortly thereafter, an American Legionnaire asked all Vietnam Veterans in our group to take a left turn at an intersection in the terminal concourse. We did, and about 50-yards ahead was a huge sign that read, *"Welcome Home, Vietnam Veterans!"* . . . For many of us, including myself, it was the first time we heard these healing words.

I returned to Fort MacPherson, helped to out-process our Reserve personnel, and remained on active-duty until my 364-day hitch expired. Although I was getting long in the tooth, I still had one more assignment remaining. Pending promotion to Colonel, I was assigned as the Staff Judge Advocate of the 377th Theater Army Area Command, headquartered in New Orleans, Louisiana, literally on the shores of Lake *Pontchartrain*. In my two years there, I enjoyed one return trip to Saudi Arabia and Kuwait, and one CAT-4 Hurricane. Retirement was beckoning . . . and so, on Nov 2002, I finally began my *Golden Years*.

In the 30-years of my checkered career, I have made and lost friends, and garnered memories, almost all of them wonderful memories, that I will take to my grave. I have had the honor and the pleasure of serving my country, the greatest country in the world.

God *Bless* America *and* her troops. Fade to *Black*

FRED HALE

U.S. Army Reserve

770-422-4914

Email: 04206ce@comcast.net

Martin Frederick Hale
BSME, MS, Juris Doctorate

A REALISTIC NON-COMBAT

When I was 12, my first cousin (who retired as an Army LTC, and served three tours in Vietnam) and I played army with canteens, pistol belts, etc. I always knew I would be in the Army, not Navy, because I couldn't swim; not Air Force, because I couldn't fly, but Army, because I could walk a long way. The Marine Corps wasn't even considered as I wasn't tough enough, or mean enough.

When I went to Georgia Tech, in 1958, ROTC was mandatory for two years, I signed up for an additional two years at $90 a month for one day a week drill and the military classes also counted toward graduation. After I graduated in 1963 (yes, it took me 5 years, as I was a co-op student with Georgia Power/Southern Company at their steam electric generation plants, worked 3 months, and went to school 3 months), with a Bachelor of Mechanical Engineering degree. Summer camp was mandatory, and I went to Fort Benning for 6-weeks of Basic Training with a Cadre of commissioned Officers, Captains and above. They were relatively easy on us as one day we may out rank them.

We all had to take turns in the mess hall, so I chose DRO (dairy room orderly), as we got there first and got to leave first. The absolute worse was kitchen pots and pans, but we all got our turn. One thing about the mess hall was the sign, "Take all you want, but eat all you take." I chose what I thought was steak, but it was really tough. I turned it over and it was green, when I went to discard my tray, the captain was guarding the garbage can. He said, "Cadet why didn't you eat what you took?" I responded with, "Sir, I didn't know it was liver and I don't eat liver. He said, "Carry on, then." We had some really good chow for the most part. Some have said that the Army purchases the best, but the cooks screw it up.

At the end of basic training (9-week wonders?), I was commissioned as a 2nd Lieutenant in the Corps of Engineers, and awaited assignment for active duty, which came in November 1963 to Fort Belvoir, VA. This Engineer Officer Basic Course was pretty tough, as Virginia was really cold from November to January. Having completed the course, I was designated as a Distinguished Military Graduate, #5 in a class of 60. I said, "Then, I would like to choose my assignment, I wanted Hawaii". But they said, "No engineers in Hawaii, but we will give you Germany, Korea, Fort Leonard Wood, MO or Fort Jackson, SC". I asked about Fort Benning since it was 90 miles from Marietta. Me and four others from my EOBC class were assigned to the 72nd Engineer Company, attached to the 197th Infantry Brigade, which supported the Infantry School with various tasks, as well as Engineer tasks.

After being there for 2-months, I was chosen to apply for Instructors Training Course (ITC), which was one of the toughest courses I had thus far taken. As a 2nd Lieutenant, I was in a class with 3-Captains, 2-Majors, and 1-Lieutenant Colonel. One can criticize the other Officers, as long as one prefixed the comment with, "Sir, that was terrible." We had to make 1-60 minute presentations. I taught field fortifications (based on previous wars), but the instruction changed with information coming from Vietnam. I also taught the use of the demolition kit assigned to Infantry companies. Composition C-4, Detonating Cord, TNT, Blasting Caps, both electric and non-electric. I was paid $105 a month, because I was responsible for clearing mis-fires caused by others (Thank goodness for my brave NCOs, who helped in this endeavor. I respected each of them).

I was assigned to instruct Officer Candidate School candidates, Infantry Basic Officers and Rangers in the use of expedient explosives. We had a static display showing the use of Bailey bridge-building, potable water units and other engineering equipment. I was explaining the use of the potable unit to a group of CARR Captains (I had to fill-in because the other Captains on the Engineer Committee were unavailable that day). One of the smart-ass Captains asked me when was the last time I had used the equipment, knowing as a 2nd Lieutenant that I didn't have that experience. The Major on our committee overheard that comment and chewed the Captain's ass out, stating a new Major out ranked the most senior Captain. The Captain was totally embarrassed.

My term of service (being USAR) was about to expire when the Tonka Bay incident in Vietnam occurred. I was sweating bullets that the Reserves would be activated. Fortunately, that didn't happen as I was discharged in November 1965 and went to work at Lockheed-Martin of Georgia in Marietta as a mass properties engineer on the C-5A Galaxy. Because the program required critical skills, I was given a deferment for the remainder of my 8-years of service. I had been there about a year when one of my co-workers was drafted and went to OCS. He was commissioned in the Corps of Engineers and wanted to buy my uniforms (Engineers have different button on their uniforms). He was sent to Vietnam, assigned to LT. Col David Hackworth's unit and was killed by, "Friendly Fire". He was buried in what used to be my Dress Blues.

Lockheed offered me the opportunity to go to graduate school to get a master's degree in Aeronautical Engineering. School would be held during company time, they would pay for books, tuition and the Georgia Tech professors would come to Lockheed to teach the classes. I was getting the G.I.-Bill education benefits (Don't throw me in the briar patch, Brer Rabbit). In 2-years and 3-months, I got my M.S. degree in Aeronautic Engineering.

I became involved in local politics and zoning issues, I called a politician a liar, and he said, "I will sue you for slander". As I didn't know my rights or obligations, I decided to use the rest of my G.I.-Bill for education benefits by going to John Marshall Law school at night. After 2-years and 3-months, I took the State Bar Exam and passed it the first time. Now to decide whether to be an engineer or a lawyer. I decided to do both. Engineer during the day and have a Law Office at night. I retired after 38 years at Lockheed, and I am still a paid active member of the State Bar of Georgia in good standing.

Now this is NOT a story about narrow escapes in the jungle of Vietnam, and the number of Viet Cong that I killed, but I am proud to have served and to be called a Vietnam Era Veteran. By the way, my wife considers herself a half veteran, as she served with me. She was a Civil Service Federal Government employee and worked for a full Colonel in the Artillery Committee of the Brigade and Battalion Operations Department at Fort Benning. She worked for my bosses' boss, who was a Lt. Colonel, I got the scoop on everybody before my boss even knew.

**DAVID W. HAMBRICK
CAPTAIN, U.S.M.C.**
(Retired)
Cell: 770-315-3942
Email: DHambric@BellSouth.net

It has been 57 years now, and who would have thought it. And, I rarely think of my tours in Vietnam unless there is a sound, a smell, a flash of light, a glimmer of movement in the trees behind our back yard. Instead, I see small vignettes, some are vivid but most are mundane. Asked, what are some of my first, or most vivid, memories that affected my senses – some are:

The smell of Nuc Mam.

The heat, dust, and humidity.

The blue exhaust of cycles clogging the streets.

Local villagers, including women, relieving themselves along the dusty roads and trails

Curious eyes behind the questionable smiles of the villagers.

Naked children running in the villages

The sight of young women with their flowing Ao Dais

Water buffalos moving gracefully, for their enormous size, down a rice paddy dike with a small boy in charge

The smells of rotten vegetation

Monsoon rains that seemingly would never end

The smell of your feet that never seemed to get dry

From the cotton and soybean fields of northeast Arkansas and southeast Missouri, who would have known that the young 17-year old high school drop-out would be in a war, so far from home in a matter of just a short year. Dave Hambrick joined the Marine Corps in September 1964 and by the spring of '65 he had joined Company "A", 7th Engineer Battalion at Camp Pendleton, California. It was the lead company, of the engineer battalion of Regimental Landing Team-7 of the 1st Marine Division. Along with his unit, he boarded the USNS General Blatchford transport ship in San Diego harbor and headed for, *"Destination to be determined"*. Twenty-two (22) days later we arrived on Okinawa and completed some training and then boarded the LST-1166 Washtenaw County and headed for Vietnam [*even though we did not know that then*], arriving there after 7 more days at sea on August 16th.

Through the next year many large and small events occurred. Teams sweeping several road ways and trails for mines and booby traps.

Heavy-duty equipment building roadways. Construction workers building hard back tents. Building sandbagged surrounded bunkers. Pulling guard duty. Sitting on a listening post in a garbage dump invaded by rats. Movement to the left or movement to the right, report it up the chain. 122mm rockets and B-40 rockets launched down the hill headed for the Da Nang airstrip. Death along the roadway. Tracers bouncing through-out the compound. A little shrapnel in left kneecap and right ankle. Spider bite on the thigh that had to be drained by the Corpsman several times within a couple of weeks. Pain in the right ankle; it was broken. Hill 41 and Hill 55. Seeing Ann Margaret and Joey Heatherton over at Freedom Hill. Next to the Da Nang Air Base in October 1966 to catch the Freedom Bird, but mine went to Iwakuni, Japan, instead of stateside. After Japan, I was sent to a reserve communications unit in Cincinnati, Ohio, to teach the Reserves what to expect if they were called to in-country [RVN].

Next tour was in 1968 through 1969. I flew this time and once I reported in to Division Headquarters I told them that I was already a one tour vet and I wanted to go as far north as I could. I was assigned to "A" Company, 1st Tank Battalion and they were located on the Gia Le Combat Base southwest of Hue City and Phu Bai. Got there in time for the back side of the **Tet Offensive** and the company I was with had multiple Bronze Star and Silver Star recipients and I was happy to be in a unit that was very involved with the support, not only of many Marine Infantry units, but supported the 101st Airborne that was stationed at Camp Eagle at the time. By this time, I became the Unit Administrator and supported all of the many operations; some casualties, both KIA and WIA's.One Tank Commander got a back shot – through and through by an outlying sniper. Received H&I [*Harassment and Interdiction*] mortar fire within the compound. Major wire breach had gunships overhead – hot brass falling down our flak jackets. VA and NVA bodies in the morning at first light, they were already bloating. Time to leave this country, this war, as it was taking its toll on me and I didn't know at the time it would be called PTSD later.

Several years later I would be serving my third overseas tour, this time back in Okinawa. I was assigned as the Squadron Administrative Chief. Seemingly just getting there, the squadron was chosen, along with many others to go afloat on the USS Hancock and/or the USS Blue Ridge with the challenge, and opportunity, to help perform the extraction and evacuation of Americans, South Vietnamese and some Cambodians in Operations Frequent Wind and Eagle Pull from their Embassies. That was done.

The photo below best depicts my tours in South Vietnam over 10 years. Between 1965-66 Combat Engineer [*see bottom left*], second tour 1968-69 with the 1st Tank Battalion, and at the end, in a helicopter squadron as depicted in the top right.

So here I am. Fifty-seven years ago, a young 17-year-old, left the cotton and soy beans fields as a high school drop-out. Joined the Marine Corps. Went to sea. Went to war. Got experience and got hurt. That was over 50 years ago. And forty-seven (47) years ago this month, was involved with the extraction of our soldiers from that war and the relocation of the Vietnamese boat people back in California. In between that, I served another tour in that war zone.

I got educated thanks to Marine Corps mentors along the way – high school completed, Bachelor of Public Administration (BPA) degree achieved, got a Master's of Business Administration (MBA) degree and pursued another Master of Science Degree until I began instructing at an Aeronautical University as an adjunct professor/instructor of Management. Rose in the enlisted ranks from private to Gunnery Sergeant, served in the Warrant Officers through Chief Warrant Officer-3, and later became a Captain, and served both as a Squadron Executive Officer and a Company Commanding Officer.

That's my military, and now veteran, saga.

BILL HARPER
MCPO — Retired
U. S. Navy
Cell: 770-359-9207
inov8r@windstream.net

My Navy Story

Beginnings - Born in 1951, and if I was going to be a part of the Vietnam experience, it was going to have to wait while I finished college. Starting in the Fall of 1969, I enrolled into the **University of Kansas** – the Navy was paying for my education under the **Navy ROTC program**. I would have graduated and commissioned as an Ensign in 1973. It was voluntary – I wasn't dodging the draft.

When that didn't work out, I enlisted in December 1970, with a plan that would take me to **Navy Nuclear Power School**, **Boot Camp in Orlando**, and **Machinist Mate "A" School in Great Lakes**.

And then I met my future wife, and realized I wouldn't be the ideal "nuke," so I gave the NPS Prep School in Mare Island/Vallejo, California, a convincing enough story that they canceled me out of training, and sent me to Treasure Island, California, to await re-assignment in October 1971.

I was assigned to **USS Roark (DE-1053)**, homeported in San Diego – a Knox-class escort ship that was multi-purpose when it came to the ways it was used in the Vietnam era, in plane guard, escort, and NGFS (*Naval Gunfire Support*) roles; the latter, when the gun at least worked!

I reported to Roark in November 71 – the ship had finished its first deployment earlier in the year, including an engine room fire that had delayed redeployment, after being towed back to Pearl Harbor from somewhere west of Midway Island. Today, that crew remains very close, and meets annually for a *"Buddy Check"* – sadly, quite a few have been lost to effects of the fire and Agent Orange.

WestPac 1972 was my first deployment, and first experience with "*exotic*" Asia and the tropics – an eye-opener it was, though not my first time in Pearl Harbor, but from there we went on to Midway Island, a famous place in WWII history for the U.S. Navy.

There wasn't a lot of evidence of *war's wounds* remaining, and the clear, pristine lagoon, where the ship was moored to refuel, gave no evidence of the violence that had taken place there only 30-years prior.

I also experienced my first Navy *"Beer Call"* at Midway, while we were refueling, and we were given time off of the ship to play softball, have a cookout, and explore a bit of the famous island.

First deployment for me also brought an introduction to Singapore, including the Raffles Hotel (*very British given the Colonial aspect of Singapore*), the Philippine Islands, Subic Bay, Olongapo, a solo trip to Manila over a weekend, Cebu & Cebu City, Hong Kong, China Fleet Club, and, of course, Vietnam … from a distance. More about Subic Bay in a minute…

As I said in the 4th paragraph on page-1 above … the Roark was the type of ship that was used for carrier escort/plane guard duty, and Naval Gunfire Support – at least when the gun worked**!** We endured many challenges that the *"lowest government bid"* approach to ship acquisition put before us with the Knox-Class ship design … vertical-mount fire pumps that were constantly failing … and a real *PITA*-to-align comes to mind, as one of the worst *FUBAR*'s of the ship design, for an essential system supporting many shipboard functions.

Subic Bay was a maintenance and "***R&R***" port, and learning how *"the system"* worked to get things done on the maintenance side, was quite an experience in and of itself – and then putting things back together correctly, as the ship was often on short-notice to return to the *"hot"* war area, and trying to get underway on short notice, due to some emergent event or weather, and/or with earlier consumption of too much San Miguel that would still be sweated out of our bodies, all made for some rough times.

Phoning home from Naval Station Subic Bay in 1972 was an adventure as well, and relatively *expensive* back then. *Mail Call* was a *REALLY* big deal, and whether we got mail (*and/or movies*) while at sea, or once in port, where mail that had been chasing us all around the South China Sea, finally caught up with us, the tension relief was worth the wait. Sometimes, it hurt to see some mates not receive mail, or to receive that *"Dear John"* letter. I'm so lucky that I didn't.

As to liberty, once we caught up with the mail, it was time to give my Sea Legs a rest, as I was wary of crossing that bridge over *"Shit River"*, but eventually I did … another story for another time, mostly forgotten, *on purpose*, I think it's safe to say.

I found the safety and relative comfort of what was available on base to be more than enough to keep me happy. Trouble was still waiting at the on-base Enlisted Club, but many more sailors headed out the Main Gate and into Olongapo on a nightly basis, where the music from home, *especially Country & Western*, was amazingly reproduced faithfully by a bunch of provincial Filipino bands. The talent was quite a thing to experience. Much more happened in Olongapo, but that's part of that *"another time"* that I've largely forgotten.

Some of the fun things to recall about the time spent in Subic Bay – the Go-Kart track, the base theater, many restaurants, including the Sky Club over on NAS Cubi Point. I went there one night and **Mel Torme** was entertaining – quite a surprise, courtesy of the **USO** tour program.

I wanted to mention this - upon return from that first deployment, I weighed in at 172# - well under my ideal weight, and over 100# less than I weigh today**!**😳 It was discovered, much later, that Roark was in the **Agent Orange Exposure Zone** over **30** times during our 1972 deployment – something we knew next to nothing about, being on a small ship out in the ocean, even though we were operating in the coastal waters of Vietnam. 50- years later, many have been impacted by the effects of exposure to this chemical, including myself.

WestPac – again - 1973 brought another deployment – back-to-back-to-back for the ship, so it was beginning to need some restoration and renovation. But this time, I had gotten married before heading west. I was an E-4 (*Machinist Mate 3rd class*) or E-5 – promoted in 1973.

During the 73 WestPac, we were supposed to rotate movies with other ships, but the crew was *SO* hooked on the original **Walking Tall** with Joe Don Baker, we hung on to it for *weeks*. I also watched `American Graffiti` at the Subic Base theater in 1973 – a fun movie even today.

The highlight of the 1973 deployment for me was actually at the end, when we arranged for my two step-sons, Ed & Don, nine & eight years old, to travel to Hawaii and return on the ship from Pearl Harbor to San Diego – a 7 - 8 day trip, known as a *Tiger Cruise.*

My time on USS Roark ended in 1974, when I re-enlisted and took orders for **USS Tarawa LHA-1**, a pre-commissioning assignment. I did not deploy again until 1982, and that was after advancing to MMC (E-7) in 1979, changing rate to GSMC - *Gas Turbine Technician, Mechanical* - and returning to sea duty on **USS John Young DD-973**. By then, Vietnam was just a memory.

There's much more, given my 30-years served in the U.S. Navy – it will have to wait for another day to tell more of my story. I retired on **January 1st, 2001**, as a *Master Chief Marine Gas Turbine Inspector*.

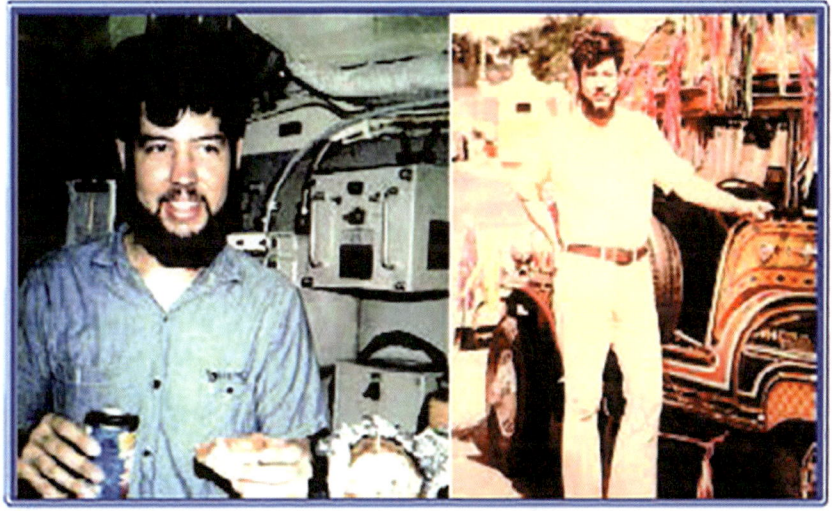

Chowin` down on Mama's C.A.R.E. Package of Banana Bread.

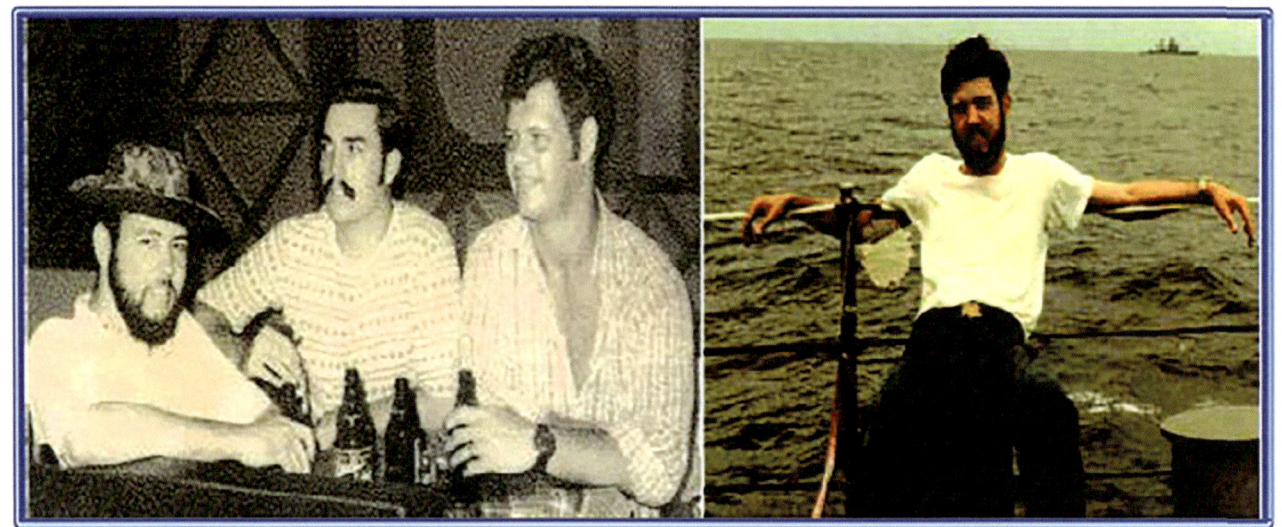

Shipboard leisure time, and Port Call Beer Time!

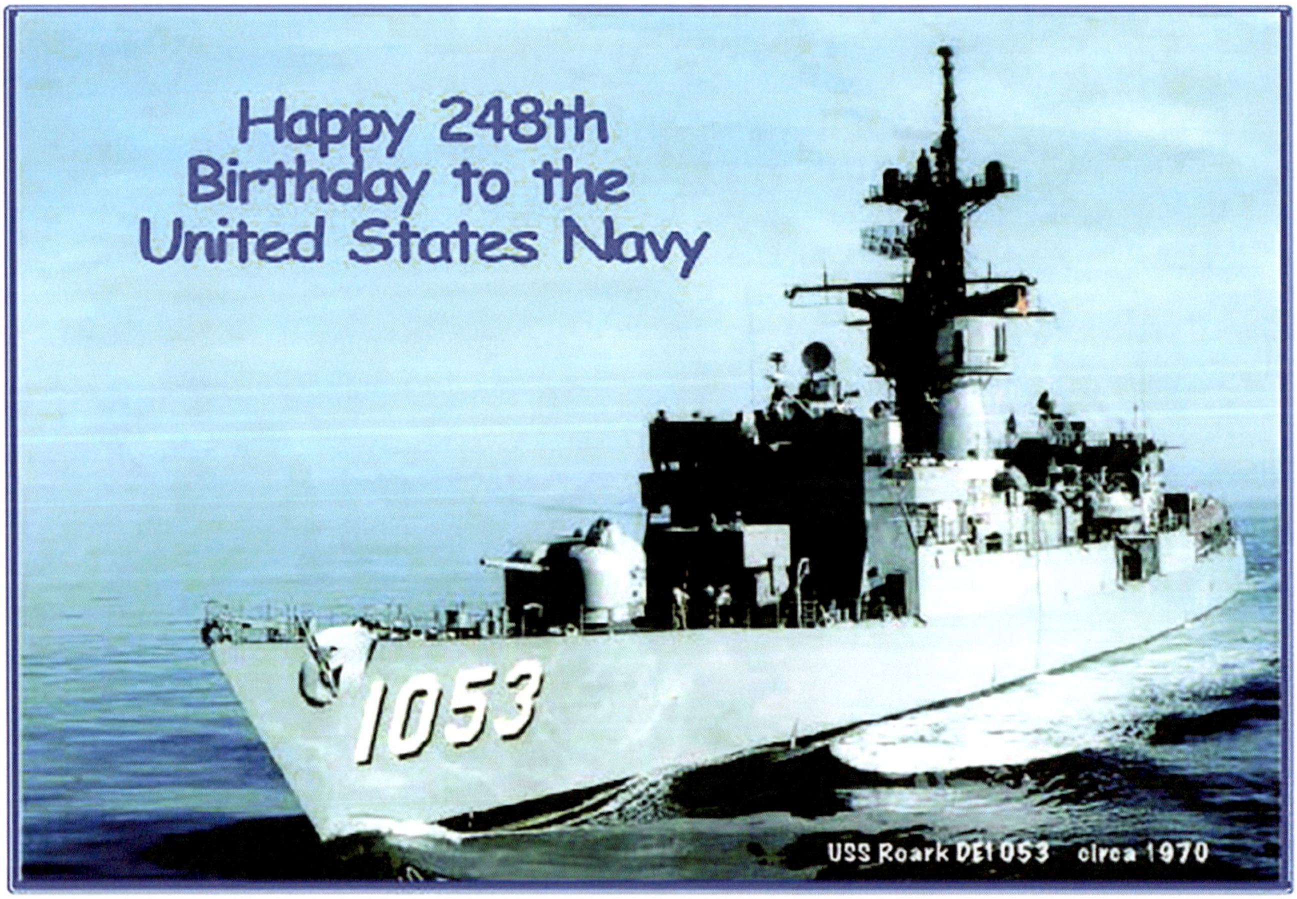
Happy 248th
Birthday to the
United States Navy
1053
USS Roark DE1053 circa 1970

AL HEFLIN
US Army
Cell: 404-317-5201
RAH791@Gmail.com

Entered the Army July 25, 1967 Arrived in the Republic of Vietnam in December 1967, and was assigned to the 18th Engineer Brigade. Returned to the U.S.A. in December 1968, and was assigned to III-Corps Headquarters in January 1969. I separated from active-duty on July 24, 1969.

It was early in February 1968. The infamous TET Offensive had been underway for a week or so. I was approached by a Lieutenant looking for volunteers. The story goes that there were some villagers a few miles outside of our compound that wanted to get to the base, but were unable to travel, because of heightened Viet Cong activity. The Lieutenant asked if I would come with him and a few others, and bring along my M-60. I had always heard the adage that when in the service you should never volunteer. I'm a slow learner. I agreed to go and loaded up for this excursion. I believe our *"Patrol"* consisted of four of America's fine young men. I was the oldest at 22-years.

It was dark that night. For some reason during TET the nights seemed even darker. In prepping for this exercise, and remembering my Boy Scout years, I grabbed every piece of armament I could find. I was wearing my flack jacket. I had several grenades, and belts of ammo for the 60, and I could barely stand up. My weapons included the aforementioned M-60, an M-14 over my left shoulder and an ammo belt fully loaded.

Our vehicle was a 3/4 ton Army truck with wooden slats fencing in the bed. We left the base unknowing what was lying in wait for us. We proceeded down the unpaved road. It was checkered with ruts and at times made for a rough ride.

As we were moving through the first village, we began to slow down to about 5-10 mph. The truck had hit one of the ruts and threw me to the left. The magazine in my M-14 dislodged and flew out of the truck into the road. To my surprise, the Lieutenant said to me, "*Go get it. They'll use it against us.*"

In what seemed like an eternity, I processed this order with some measure of disbelief. The Lieutenant looked at me and repeated his "*request.*" Some impolite words came to mind. With my pucker factor at an all-time high, I jumped off the back of the truck and ran back toward the location of the magazine. As I moved away from the truck (*which continued to move at a slow pace*), I pictured dozens of eyes staring at me from the buildings along the so-called *road*.

I picked up the magazine and turned toward the truck. I ran back as fast as I could. Now remember, I had many pounds of gear on my body. I caught up to the truck and with all the strength I could muster, leaped into the bed of the truck. It was a feat worthy of an Olympic athlete. If you offered me a million dollars to replicate this feat, that *ain't* happening.

I learned the awesome power of adrenaline, remembering the adage: **NEVER VOLENTEER**! We were able to complete our mission, and gather the indigenous personnel, and return safely to our base.

Just another 1968 February night in the Republic of Vietnam

Al Heflin

18th Engineer Brigade Republic of Vietnam, 1968

~ The End ~

THE TRUCK

THE PIG

HAROLD HOLLINGSHED

USAF

Security Service
Cell: 678-576-6883
HaroldShed@att.net

"Music gives a soul to the universe, wings to the mind, flight to the imagination, and life to everything."
~ Plato ~

Plato, the 428 BC philosopher, must have been envisioning my life's journey, because music has been my inner guiding light for almost 60-years.

I was born on 2 November 1949, and raised on a small farm east of Kennesaw, Georgia. I was the only child and responsible for all of the chores to maintain the family farm. I still reside on the family farm with Linda, my wife of 49- years, and describe my childhood as being, "*very busy*," as I reflect back over my past.

When I was 14-years old my father bought me an old Silvertone electric guitar and amp, which inspired my musical journey. My cousin taught me how to play the cords, and how to sing, and promised to put me on the stage, when I perfected my performance.

During my time at North Cobb High School in Acworth, I joined a group of fellow musicians and formed **"The Kennesaw Strays."** I worked at McLaurin Company for six months after graduating from high school in 1968.

The Vietnam War activated *The Draft*, which found me and my close friend Larry Lewis contemplating our future and waiting for our draft notices. So, we decided to visit the U.S. Air Force Recruiter. The next thing we realized was that we enlisted in the Air Force, and on 16 January 1969, we were on our way to Lackland A.F.B., Texas, for Basic Training. Upon completion of Basic Training on 3 March 1969, I was selected for Advance Training at Sheppard A.F.B., in Wichita Falls, TX, for a 34-week Tech School in Communication & Relay Center as an Equipment Repairman in Electro/Mechanical.

During my training at Shepard A.F.B. I lived in old WWII open bay barracks. I received Orders to Misawa, Japan, upon finishing Tech School, but they were canceled, and I was assigned to Advanced Tech Training, because of my high scores. In fact, I was selected to attend the prestigious **U.S.A.F. Security Service School** (*Freedom Through Vigilance*).

On 5 January 1970, I entered an 8-week Security Tech School at Goodfellow A.F.B., San Angelo, TX. The school was for training Special Teleprinter Maintenance Technicians. My orders for Misawa, Japan, were canceled again, because I was selected to go TDY to Keesler A.F.B., Biloxi, Mississippi, to attend classes for High-Speed Paper Tape Equipment. I was in for another surprise upon returning to Keesler.

Goodfellow A.F.B. from Keesler A.F.B. I was informed that my pending trip to Misawa, Japan, in three days was once again *postponed*, because my 1st Sergeant informed me that I wasn't going *anywhere* until I went home first, for a 30-day Leave. The 1st Sergeant pulled some strings, and I was on my way home for a 30-day Leave.

On 28 June 1970, I was finally headed to Misawa, Japan, for my first duty assignment after attending several training schools for maintaining equipment over the past 18-months and completing my 30-days Leave. I started my six-month O.J.T. training upon arriving in Misawa, Japan, to achieve my 5-level, so I could be promoted to E-4/Buck Sergeant. I was an E-3 / A1C for 26-months and promoted to E-4 in October 1971.

During my tour in Misawa, Japan, I serviced the equipment the operators used to maintain the freedom and safety of the United States. My supervisor and mentor was an E-8 named Walter McKee, and in December 1971 I was told that I wouldn't be leaving Misawa, because I was the only technician in the compound that maintained the high-speed paper tape equipment, and my replacement had not arrived. In fact, my tour was extended for another six months (**Hurray!**).

During my two years in Misawa I was involved in several activities such as bowling in two leagues (*Japanese/American Goodwill Bowling Tournaments*), attended Cherry Blossom Festivities twice in Hirosaki, Japan, and played my guitar in bands.

During my two years there, I owned three cars, and travelled all over Northern Japan to visit farming and fishing villages and enjoyed meeting many Japanese locals during my journeys. On 16 July 1971, 25 Airman travelled 400-miles by train from Misawa to the Waco train station outside Tokyo and boarded a bus for the ride to visit Mt. Fuji.

Upon arriving at Mt. Fuji (*elevation 12,389 ft.*), the group rode horses up to the first two levels, and then started to climb by foot. We spent the night at the 8th Station, and arose at 0200 to climb to Mt. Fuji's summit to behold the spectacular sunrise at 0410-hrs. I still cherish my memories of that breathtaking view, after hiking up Mt. Fuji, and that 9- hour train ride!

During my two-year tour in Japan, I played my guitar and entertained for several events and parties. And, with only five months remaining in my enlistment, I was transferred from Misawa to Goodfellow A.F.B., San Angelo, TX, and assigned to the 6948 Mobile Squadron. After a 30-day Leave, I was Honorably Discharged on 15 January 1973. Shortly after returning home, I married my childhood friend, **Linda McPherson**, on 1 June 1973. Interestingly, we first met when we were only 6-years old at the Shady Grove Baptist Church in Acworth, GA.

Harold & Linda's wedding, 1973.

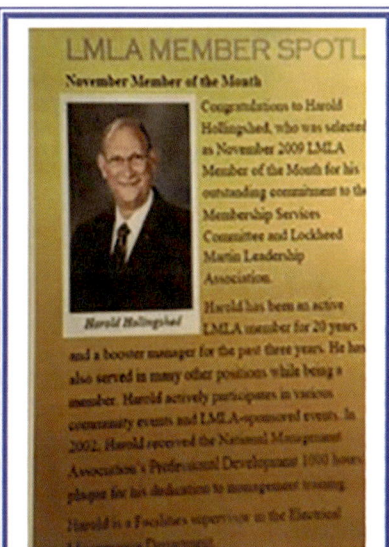

Harold retired after 32-years with Lockheed-Martin Aerospace.

Harold, USAF Airman 1st Class.

ABOVE: **Various jamming sessions with bands I played with during my USAF days.**

Harold Hollingshed   Air Force

One of my favorite country singers was Johnny Cash, who also served honorably in the USAF Security Service Command in Germany (1950-1954).

Today, I continue to enjoy playing my guitar, singing, and performing with "The Tunnel Rats" band. In November 2018, it was my honor to be inducted into the Atlanta Country Music Hall of Fame.

Linda & Harold, above in more modern times, than back in their Shady Grove Baptist days in 1st Grade.

The End

JAKE JACOBS

USAF Fighter Pilot
CallSign: Jake-The-Snake
Retired Delta Air Lines Pilot
Cell: 850-830-4744
RJacobsSr@aol.com

My Military Experience

MY LOVE OF AIRPLANES & FLYING, BEGAN WHEN I WAS A YOUNG BOY

I vaguely recall watching airplanes take-off and land into, and out of, the local Airport when I was a young lad growing up, and thinking . . . I'm gonna fly one of those fast birds someday.

And, when I became of age to go to college, I enrolled into Georgia Institute of Technology right here in Atlanta, Georgia. And, because I still loved aviation and day-dreamed of the time I might become a pilot, and actually fly those fast airplanes . . . I took up the major of Aerospace Engineering and tried to keep focused while I also found new friendships that have lasted to this very day, in the Alpha Tau Omega Fraternity (ATO's). Some in our Fraternity also chose the Aviation field after graduation, and one Fraternity Brother (Orson Swindle) was shot down over north Vietnam and spent six-and-a-half years in the Hanoi Hilton, but I wouldn't learn of his imprisonment, and relentless torturing, until years after graduation.

When I graduated from Georgia Tech, I entered the U.S.A.F., and went into the Flight School program. Those were some of the most interesting years of my young career, and I found my Aeronautical Engineering degree to be of great value to me in my understanding of the laws of flight, lift, thrust, aircraft attitude, etc.

Following graduation, I found my niche and was living my dream of flying, as I also enjoyed my time being assigned to Laredo AFB, Texas, training new, wanna-be Pilots.

But I soon yearned for "The Bigger Birds," to fly, and found myself applying for a job to fly for Delta Air Lines and was subsequently hired not long after my military assignments at Laredo & Randolph AFBs in Texas.

Most pilots starting out with Delta had to take on a 2nd-job to help get them through their first 3- years, financially, until Delta began paying pilots the "real money," we had heard about, and dreamed about, in our early years with the company.

Well, my particular 2nd-job was flying with the Texas Air National Guard out of Ellington AFB, in Houston, Texas. And one of my acquaintances I met while flying out of that unit, was a young Junior Officer named, **2LT George W. Bush**. George and I were once roommates for a couple of nights there during one of those summers, while we both trained at Ellington and Tyndall AFB's.

What's interesting, as this story continues . . . is that "**W**," as he was called later in his life of politics, following life as an owner/operator of the **Texas Rangers MLB** team in the Dallas metroplex would take a trip to Upper Michigan (*a.k.a., The* **U.P.**), specifically **Marquette**, Michigan, and become the **1**st**-EVER** U.S. President to visit that part of the State of Michigan, as a sitting President. "**W**" was seeking re-election, and this was his visit to rally his supporters in the U.P. (*where inhabitants there are referred to as,* "**Yoopers**" *– they get their moniker from the use of the letters,* "**U**. *&* **P**." *as in* **UP***'ers*).

Well, as luck would have it, my wife Susie and I had *JUST* arrived in Marquette after a very long 2-day drive from Sandestin, in the Panhandle of Florida, to begin our usual-and-customary summer sabbatical of 6+ months, and we had heard of "**W**'s" pending visit to Marquette and decided to attend. We were standing along the cord-on that kept fans out of the way, so "**W**" and his entourage could pass by and get to the stage & podium.

THAT's, when I blurted out, "**102's!**" . . . to which "**W**" replied, "*Are you still flying those things?*" ☺

An *Afterthought* from back in my days of flying in Europe with the U.S.A.F. -- After spending **2-1/2** years at Zaragoza AB, Spain, my Squadron was transferred to Ramstein AB, Germany.

We would be spending time there pulling alert in the Squadron. One day, we had the alarm sound to scramble our flight, as there was a sighting of possible Russian MiG's that crossed the Iron Curtain border. I was lucky enough to be *Second Lead* in the Scramble, and shortly after launching our Fighter Jets, we were then advised that we had *authorization* to shoot down what was supposed to be a Russian MiG. My heart was beating harder than normal, thinking that I might have a *Red Star* on the side of my plane the next day, for shooting down a MiG. We were told by the *higher-ups* that we *could* shoot, but **first** we had to *authenticate*. The *Authentication Codes* that were given to us each day would cover a 6-hour period, and they changed each day. We also had to have memorized the *silhouettes* of all the airplanes that were being flown in the area, by each country's forces, friend-and-foe. We got the *Approval* that it was ok to shoot down the thought-to-be MiG. **But** I still didn't feel comfortable doing that, because it was twilight and I didn't really have a good sighting of this supposed MiG aircraft.

Again, I was given the clearance to fire, but then I let the *higher ups* know that I **could** finally confirm that the plane was *NOT* a Russian MiG, but a **French Mirage**. They were doing the same thing as my Squadron, but they were on a different radio frequency.

In the end, the day was *saved*, and the **Brigadier General** that was waiting for me at the Flight Ops Tarmac, told me . . . *"Captain, you probably SAVED me getting my 2nd-Star today. Well done!"*

Jake-the-Snake (*sitting atop his F-102 on left*) with his Crew & friends at the Wheelus AB in Libya. Is that Bikini-clad lady a member of the Crew, Jake? Nice German Lady!

Jake-the-Snake enjoying a cold adult beverage on the beach at Wheelus AB, Libya.

The Superior Dome is the largest wooden-structured Sports Arena in the world.

This is also where the U.S.A.'s Winter Olympic Team's Sports athletes practice many of their events' crafts, in preparation for the next Olympic Games. Northern Michigan University's Wildcats play their football, ice hockey, and basketball games there, as well.

Former Detroit Lions Head Football Coach, and lifetime friend of MSU's Head Basketball Coach Tom Izzo (*both natives of Iron Mountain, MI*) Steve Mariucci introduces George W. Bush inside the Superior Dome in Marquette, MI, on July 13, 2004, on the occasion of "*W*'s" Re-Election Rally there.

T.D. JORGENSEN

CAPTAIN, U.S. Army, May 1967 – July 1973
Commissioned at Engineer O.C.S., into the Transportation Corps
U.S. ARMY DUAL-RATED AVIATOR & Instrument Flight Examiner
Bronze Star Medal, 7-Air Medals, 2-Army Commendation Medals,
National Defense Service Medal,
Vietnam Service Medal, Vietnam Campaign Medal.

Cell: 404-680-0735 | Email: Nurnberg62@aol.com

MY VIETNAM EXPERIENCE

It all started with my being required to register for **The Draft** on my **18**th birthday, and my U.S. Marine Corps father reminded me to register, about 5-seconds AFTER he wished me a, "**Happy Birthday**," over in Fürth / Bavaria, Germany, a suburb of Nürnberg, where I had graduated from **Nürnberg American High School** that same day.

Fast-Forward … to about 4-years later, and I'm in my **1**st-Senior Year at **Michigan State University**, and I thought, *"My Marine Corps father always preached to me that it was important that I always try to be **#1** at something in my life!"* Well, he got his wish – when the U.S. Postal Service mailman dropped off our mail that day in my off-campus apartment, I opened a letter from the U.S. Government, and I couldn't understand why they'd be writing me? Nonetheless, my curiosity prevailed, and I opened the letter, and read . . . and became aware that my father's dream had come true!!! **I *WAS* #1 at something** . . . I was **#1** *at my Selective Service Draft Board* in Marquette, Michigan, which was where I had put down as my "**hometown**" in the U.S.A., while registering in Fürth, Germany (*which, by the way, was the birthplace of our former Secretary of State* **Henry Kissinger**).

It was pretty much an uphill climb thereafter for me, starting out in May 1967 at Ft. Dix, New Jersey for both Basic Training as well as Advanced Infantry Training, before entering Engineer Officer Candidate School at Fort Belvoir, VA. After I was commissioned a 2nd-Lieutenant in the *Transportation Corps*, and left immediately thereafter in my brand-new Chevrolet Camaro Super Sport, for Fort Eustis, VA, for the U.S. Army's Transportation Corps Basic Course, which involved much weekend training at Virginia Beach, where we were forced to utilize our Greasy EyeBallz to gaze upon members of the opposite sex for hours at a time, while they were scantily-attired in nature's most precious Bikinis, and giggled like little school girls attempting to troll for young junior officers at this particular "*Officers Beach*" at **67**th-**Street** in Virginia Beach. Life was tough, but someone had to do it, I was reminded of, every single weekend day by my former O.C.S. classmate **Roger William Gardner**, who I continue to correspond with via emails and texts almost daily, despite the fact that we're at polar ends of the political spectrum. I guess this is proof positive, that opposites **CAN**, in fact, get along, and we don't need to hate one another like Democraps and Conservatives seem to believe is the only way these days? Nonetheless, life is good, as we approach our octogenarian days, which will begin on June 2nd, 2024 – The Year We Re-Elect **Donald J. Trump**, or one just as good, in case The Trumpster decides *NOT* to run?

Then, following Officers Basic Course, I was off to Fixed-Wing Flight School at Fort Stewart Georgia's Wright Army Airfield, followed by Multi-Engine transition, and O-1/Bird Dog Tactical phase of aviation training at Fort Rucker, Alabama.

The Army needed more aviation maintenance officers, so I was transferred back to Fort Eustis, VA, for A.M.O.C. (*Aviation Maintenance Officers Course*), which trained me for test pilot training, which was followed by Helicopter Transition course back at Fort Rucker, Alabama, in the OH-13 Sioux, as

well as weeks flying the UH-1B, UH-1C gunship, UH-1D, and eventually the UH-1H Huey. I was now ready for mortal combat in the semi-Republic of (*South*) Vietnam.

I arrived in Saigon, Vietnam, on **April Fools' Day** 1970, and would fly home to the Land of Round Door Knobs ALSO ON **April Fools' Day** 1971. So, **April Fools' Day** has MUCH more appreciative meaning for this former Army Aviator, than most. I CELEBRATED that Special Day each year after arriving Home, *Safely* . . . but, I also contemplate those we lost over there during that time in that high temperature / HIGH Humidity / Hell-Hole, and pray for their Souls, that they might Rest In Peace. We lost my roommate in Flight School (**Franklin Lee Weisner**), whose father was a 4-Star Admiral. Lee's name appears on '*The Wall*" in Washington, D.C., which I visit when I go there.

There were DAILY skirts with death & destruction, which brought you down to earth, mentally, *BUT* . . . there were also moments of great joy & appreciation for being alive, and avoiding prematurely, your early demise, EACH DAY.

Like a lot of American Servicemen in that overseas conflict, there were days where you could enjoy a good smile or laugh; especially when **Bob Hope** and his **USO Show** came during Thanksgiving thru the Christmas Holiday Season. Somebody had to transport those beautiful ladies in the Bands that accompanied several of those USO Acts, and I was fortunate enough to be one of them, *once*. I'll never forget `*Drooling*` all over myself, as I google-eyed over the most beautiful of the female members of the band that my 2-day Huey Taxi Service could render. (*See Photos*, ***below***).

After dropping off the band at their next performance site, I was ordered by Flight Ops, to drop off 4-Nurses who attended the USO Show, back to their ship – the U.S.S. Sanctuary off Da Nang's coast. After I dropped them off, my 5th-stage disc turbine in my engine blew up, and I autorotated safely to the ground, to fly another day. The Good Training we had in Transition School, was good enough to walk away, alive!

I can remember Test Flying UH-1H Hueys each night, in the pitch-black dark, with only your red nav-lights on **in** the cockpit, so you can realize you were at level attitude and not flying up-side-down. The maneuvers we Test Pilots had to perform with each test flight, were scary enough. *BUT*, to test fly the 30–40-minute test flight required that you **NOT** fly ANY exterior Navigation Lights "**ON**," at any time while airborne. Think about it! YOU are up there performing those almost acrobatic maneuvers to test the Huey, to insure it will be ready for flight missions in the morning when they launch at Early-Thirty. **BUT SO ARE ALL THE OTHER Aviation Maintenance Officers, who are Test Flying THEIR aircrafts** (other Hueys, CH-47 /Chinooks, AH-1G's, and even a Flying Crane / CH-54 unit around the revetment from "**The Castle**," which is where "**The Kingsmen**," parked their aircraft in our home base of **Bravo Company** / 101st Aviation Battalion / 101st Airborne Division (AirMobile).

It was a VERY BUSY place, and your only thought was to *PRAY* that no other aircraft was flying *where* **YOU WERE**, at the **SAME TIME**, as we all knew that 2-aircraft **CANNOT** occupy the same space at the same time. **DEATH** was imminent, and we knew it, **EVERY DAY !** **CRAZY. ABSOLUTELY DEATH-DEFYING CRAZY ORDERS** to get the aircraft ready for flight in the morning, and the Higher-Ups wanted **"85% Availability."** I do NOT know HOW in the world we did it, but we did; except for "**Operation Lam Sohn-719**," where **several HUNDRED** helicopters were blown-away by the V.C. and North Vietnamese Army forces (**NVA**) in Laos, as if they had expected us when we arrived. **CRAZY !**

We did **NOT** have **85%** the next morning for the 101st Airborne Division Commanding General. It was believed that he gave us time to get our shit together in one suitcase, collect our thoughts, thank our lucky stars we were above ground level, and vertical, and gave us time to bury our dead, or DEROS them back to The World, to be buried by their families. That was a bad day for America.

Somehow, *luckily*, I was spared by The Good Lord Above, and remained alive, and DEROS'd back to The World, out of Cam Rahn Bay on an American Airlines 707 Silver Bird, and the story was interesting on how I got on that flight home. When I arrived at Cam Rahn Bay, and checked in, I was told that it might be **3-4 DAYS** before I would get on a bird home. I was not happy about it, and so I did the most prudent thing to kill time – I went to the Officers' Club, and began to consume cold adult beverages, starting around 1600-hrs. on March 31st. I decided I'd better go find my quarters, and bunk bed, before I forgot where I was, because whatever I was consuming, was affecting my better judgement, *AND* directional-finding apparatus in my brain. I found my bunk, and crashed, around midnight. **WHEW!**

At approximately **0330-hrs**., some Private tapped on my bunk bed frame and asked, *"Are you Captain Jorgensen, Sir?"* I did not answer him right away. But, after 3-persistent taps on my bunk bed frame, he awakened me, got my undivided attention, and after admitting I, *indeed*, was Captain Jorgensen, he gave me an ultimatum. I could either sleep in, and wait 3-4 more days to leave Vietnam, **OR** . . . I could accompany a convicted soldier, who was on his way back to Fort Leavenworth for his new *LIFETIME* residence . . . and, I'd be flying out at 0830-hrs., that very day.

H*mmmm* … difficult decision … *Sleep-In*, and give your HangOver a slight chance of suppressing, **OR**, improving your attitude within a few hours, **but** launching homeward bound <u>**THAT**</u> MORNING!

DIFFICULT choice, but I was NO FOOL, despite what I must have looked like that morning, once dressed in my TW's, and reporting for HANDCUFFS to be place around my one wrist, while the other was around the wrist of the soldier-prisoner, where he'd remain until we made refueling stops at Midway Island, and Honolulu, Hawaii, before heading for SEA-TAC (Seattle-Tacoma) International Airport, to turn over the prisoner to the M.P.'s.

The M.P.'s took the prisoner, marched him off the plane, and the rest of us began deplaning. I can vividly remember that day when we entered the terminal, through the gate, and were greeted by a large band of enthusiastic Hare Krishna-ANTI-WAR Protestors that I'm sure Jane Fonda organized, and as I passed them by, a couple of them began to hack some large luggies my way, as they screamed those usual and customary expletives for Armed Forces members serving & defending their country. I went to the restroom to wash-and-wipe off the luggies. Ready for homeward bound.

I must say that I am **DELIGHTED** to see the nation's total reversal in attitudes towards the American Servicemembers, to one of support, and affection, so I feel a lot of pride for our current Servicemembers, and affection towards fellow Americans, who show their support towards Servicemembers. We'll be **GREAT** again, and sooner than later. Our best days ARE ahead of us. KEEP the **Faith**. Here's our `Calling Card,` (*below*) from back then, in case you care to send *The Very Best* . . .

T.D. Jorgensen Nurnberg62@aol.com Cell: 404-680-0735
Marietta, GA 30066

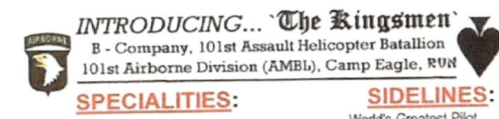

Below-Left: T.D. Jorgensen w/ UH-1H.
Center: Major John Coleman, Capt. Tony Santella, Capt. T.D. Jorgensen, and Capt. Chuck Shedd (*Staff Officers of the 5th Trans Battalion at Camp Eagle – my 2nd RVN assignment*).

Far Right, below: Military Wedding, June 14, 1969. Still going strong, **55+** years later.

We enjoyed the camaraderie and relationships we developed over there, which have prevailed to the present day.

Franklin Lee Weisner

K.I.A./RVN

At Camp Eagle, we <u>NEVER</u> had Flush Toilets. We became accustomed to the Pissoir outside, and Papasan's 55-Gallon Drum Outhouses. We had a 2-Seater, lined in Shag Carpet. **Gross**, eh?!

Five Pennies For Your Thoughts?!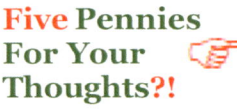

To the left some of Jack Driscoll's & Johnny Brown's B-52 Craters left after one of their runs, near Phu Bai, north of DaNang, in I-Corps.

Above, the various planes I flew in my Army career: U-21 KingAir, O-1 Bird Dog, T-42, and the UH-1 Huey.

CLIFF JUDKINS

Source : Chapter 7 in author Ron Knott's new book : ' *SUPERSONIC COWBOYS* ' (sharing forty-five Crusader stories)" *I Fell 15,000 Feet And Lived*" by Cliff Judkins {abridged}

CHAPTER SEVEN
I FELL 15,000 FEET AND LIVED CLIFF JUDKINS

"Jud, you're on fire, get out of there!"

Needless to say that startling command got my attention. As you will read in this report, this was just the beginning of my problems!

It had all started in the brilliant sunlight 20,000 feet above the Pacific Ocean as I nudged my F-8 Crusader jet into position behind the lumbering, deep-bellied refueling plane. After a moment of jockeying for position, I made the connection and matched my speed to that of the slowpoke tanker. I made the graceful task of plugging into the trailing fuel conduit so they could pump fuel into my tanks.

This in-flight refueling process was necessary, and routine, because the F-8 could not hold enough fuel to fly from California to Hawaii. This routine mission was labeled *"Trans-Pac,"* meaning Flying Airplanes across the Pacific. This had been going on for years.

Soon, after plugging into the tanker, my fuel gauges stirred, showing that all was well. In my cockpit, I was relaxed and confident. As I was looking around, I was struck for an instant by the eeriness of the scene: here I was, attached, like an unwanted child, by an umbilicus to a gargantuan mother, who was fleeing across the sky at 200 knots as though from some unnamed danger. Far below us was a broken layer of clouds that filtered the sun's glare over the Pacific.

In my earphones, I heard Major Van Campen, our Fight Leader, chatting with Major D.K. Tooker, who was on a Navy destroyer down below. Major Tooker had ejected from his aircraft, the day before, in this same area, when his Crusader flamed out mysteriously during the same type of refueling exercise.

Crusaders in-flight refueling from a KC-130 Tanker

At that time no one knew why his aircraft had flamed out. We all supposed it had been some freak accident that sometimes happens with no explanation. One thing we knew for sure, it was not pilot error. This accident had to be some kind of mechanical malfunction, but what? Our Squadron had a perfect safety record and was very disturbed, because of the loss of an airplane the day before.

"Eleven minutes to mandatory disconnect point," the Tanker Commander said. I checked my fuel gauges again. Everything appeared normal.

My thoughts were, *"In a few hours I knew we'd all be having dinner at the Kaneohe Officers Club on Oahu, Hawaii. Then after a short rest, we'd continue our 6,000-mile trek to Atsugi, Japan, via Midway and Wake Island."* Our whole outfit - Marine All Weather Fighter Squadron 323 - was being transferred to the Far East for a one-year period of operations.

"Nine minutes to mandatory disconnect."

My fuel gauges indicated that the tanks were almost full. I noticed that my throttle lever was sticking a little. That was unusual because the friction lock was holding it in place and was loose enough. It grew tighter as I tried to manipulate it, gently.

Then - **thud!** I heard the crack of an explosion.

I could see the RPM gauge unwinding and the tailpipe temperature dropping. The aircraft had lost power – the engine had quit running – this is a flame-out!

I punched the mic button, and said, *"This is Jud. I've got a flame-out!"*

My thoughts were, *"In a few hours I knew we'd all be having dinner at the Kaneohe Officers Club on Oahu, Hawaii. Then after a short rest, we'd continue our 6,000-mile trek to Atsugi, Japan, via Midway and Wake Island."* Our whole outfit - Marine All Weather Fighter Squadron 323 - was being transferred to the Far East for a one-year period of operations.

"Nine minutes to mandatory disconnect."

My fuel gauges indicated that the tanks were almost full. I noticed that my throttle lever was sticking a little. That was unusual, because the friction lock was holding it in place and was loose enough. It grew tighter as I tried to manipulate it, gently.

My thoughts were, *"In a few hours I knew we'd all be having dinner at the Kaneohe Officers Club on Oahu, Hawaii. Then after a short rest, we'd continue our 6,000-mile trek to Atsugi, Japan, via Midway and Wake Island."* Our whole outfit - Marine All Weather Fighter Squadron 323 - was being transferred to the Far East for a one-year period of operations.

"Nine minutes to mandatory disconnect."

My fuel gauges indicated that the tanks were almost full. I noticed that my throttle lever was sticking a little. That was unusual, because the friction lock was holding it in place and was loose enough. It grew tighter as I tried to manipulate it, gently.

Then - **thud!** I heard the crack of an explosion.

I could see the RPM gauge unwinding and the tailpipe temperature dropping. The aircraft had lost power - the engine had quit running - this is a flame-out!

I punched the mic button, and said, *"This is Jud. I've got a flame-out!"*

Unfortunately, my radio was already dead; I was neither sending, nor receiving, anything via my radio.

I quickly disconnected from the tanker and nosed the aircraft over, into a shallow dive, to pick up some flying speed to help re-start the engine. I needed a few seconds to think.

I yanked the handle that extended the air-driven emergency generator, called the Ram Air Turbine (*RAT*), into the slipstream, hoping to get ignition for an air-start. The Igniters clicked gamely, and the RPM indicator started to climb slowly, as did the tailpipe temperature. This was a positive indication that a re-start was beginning. For one tantalizing moment, I thought everything would be all right. But the RPM indicator hung uncertainly at 30% of capacity and refused to go any faster. This is not nearly enough power to maintain flight.

The fire warning light (*pilots call it the panic light*) blinked on. This is not a good sign. And to make matters worse, jet fuel poured over the canopy like water from a bucket. At the same instant, my radio came back on, powered by the emergency generator, and a great babble of voices burst through my earphones.

"Jud, you're on fire, get out of there!"

Fuel was pouring out of my aircraft; from the tailpipe; from the intake duct; from under the wings and igniting behind me in a great awesome trail of fire.

The suddenness of the disaster overwhelmed me, and I thought: *"This can't be happening to me!"* The voices in my ears kept urging me to fire the ejection seat and abandon my aircraft.

I pressed my mic button and told the flight leader, *"I'm getting out!"*

I took my hands off the flight controls and reached above my head for the canvas curtain that would start the ejection sequence. I pulled it down hard over my face and waited for the tremendous kick in the pants, which would send me rocketing upward, free of the aircraft.

Nothing happened! The canopy, which was designed to jettison in the first part of the ejection sequence did not move. It was still in place, and so was I.

My surprise lasted only a second. Then, I reached down between my knees for the alternate Ejection Firing handle and gave it a vigorous pull. Again, nothing happened. This was very surprising. Both the primary, and the secondary ejection procedures had failed, and I was trapped in the cockpit of the burning aircraft.

The plane was now in a steep 60° dive. For the first time, I felt panic softening the edges of my determination. I knew that I had to do something, or I was going to die in this sick airplane. There was no way out of it. With great effort, I pulled my thoughts together and tried to imagine some solution.

A voice in my earphones was shouting: *"Ditch the plane! Ditch it in the ocean!"*

It must have come from the Tanker Skipper, or one of the Destroyer Commanders down below, because every jet pilot knows you can't ditch a jet and survive. The plane would hit the water at a very high rate of speed, flip over, and sink like a stone, and they usually explode on impact.

I grabbed the control stick and leveled the aircraft. Then, I yanked the alternate handle again in an attempt to fire the canopy and start the ejection sequence, but *still* nothing happened. That left me with only one imaginable way out, which was to jettison the canopy manually and try to jump from the aircraft without aid of the ejection seat.

Was such a thing possible? I was not aware of any Crusader pilot who had ever used this World War II tactic to get out of a fast-flying jet. I had been told that this procedure of bailing out of a jet, was almost impossible. Yes, the pilot may get out of the airplane, but the massive 20-foot high tail section is almost certain to strike the pilot's body and kill him before he falls free of the aircraft. My desperation was growing, and any scheme that offered a shred of success seemed better than riding that aircraft into the sea, which would surely be fatal. I disconnected the canopy by hand, and with a great *whoosh*, it disappeared from over my head, never to be seen again. Before trying to get out of my confined quarters, I trimmed the aircraft to fly in a kind of sidelong skid: *nose high and with the tail swung around slightly to the right.*

Then I stood up in the seat, and put both arms in front of my face. I was sucked out harshly from the airplane. I cringed as I tumbled outside the bird, expecting the tail to cut me in half, but thank goodness, that never happened!   In an instant, I knew I was out of there, and uninjured.

I waited ...*and waited* ...until my body, hurtling through space, with the 225-knots of momentum started to decelerate. I pulled the D-ring on my parachute, which is the manual way to open the chute *if* the ejection seat does not work automatically. I braced myself for the opening shock. I heard a loud pop above me, but I was still falling very fast. As I looked up, I saw that the small *pilot chute* had deployed.(*This small chute is designed to keep the pilot from tumbling until the main chute opens.*) But, I also noticed a sight that made me shiver with disbelief and horror! The main, 24-foot parachute was just *flapping in the breeze,* and was tangled in its own shroud lines. It hadn't opened! I could see the white folds neatly arranged, fluttering feebly in the air.

"**This is very serious**," I thought.

Frantically, I shook the risers in an attempt to balloon the chute and help it open. It didn't work. I pulled the bundle down toward me, and wrestled with the shroud lines, trying my best to get the chute to open. The parachute remained closed. All the while, I am falling like a rock toward the ocean.

I looked down hurriedly. There was still plenty of altitude remaining. I quickly developed a frustrating and sickening feeling. I wanted everything to halt while I collected my thoughts, but my fall seemed to *accelerate*. I noticed a ring of turbulence in the ocean. It looked like a big stone had been thrown in the water. It had white froth at its center; I finally realized this is where my plane had crashed in the ocean.

"*Would I be next to crash?"* were my thoughts!

Again, I shook the parachute risers and shroud lines, but the rushing air was holding my chute tightly in a bundle. I began to realize that I had done all I could reasonably do to open the chute and it was not going to open. I was just along for a brutal ride that may kill, or severely injure me.

I descended rapidly through the low clouds. Now, there was only clear sky between me and the ocean. This may be my last view of the living. I have no recollection of positioning myself properly, or even bracing for the impact. In fact, I don't remember hitting the water at all. *At* one instant, I was falling very fast toward the ocean. The next thing I remember is, hearing a shrill, high-pitched whistle that hurt my ears.

Suddenly, I was *very cold*. In that eerie, half-world of consciousness, I thought, "*Am I alive?"* I finally decided, and not all at once, "*Yes, I think I am ...I am alive!"*

The water helped clear my senses. But, as I bounced around in the water I began coughing and retching. The *Mae West* vest around my waist had inflated. I concluded that the shrill whistling sound that I had heard was the gas leaving the CO_2 cylinders, as it was filling-up the life vest.

A sense of urgency gripped me, as though there were some task I ought to be performing. Then, it dawned on me what it was. The parachute was tugging at me from under the water. It had finally billowed out (*much too late*), like some Brobdingnagian Portuguese Man-of-War. I tried reaching down for my hunting knife located in the knee pocket of my flight suit. I had to cut the shroud lines of the chute before it pulled me under for good.

This is when I first discovered that I was injured severely. The pain was *excruciating*. Was my back broken? I tried to arch it slightly and felt the pain again. I tried moving my feet, but that too was impossible. They were *immobile*, and I could feel the bones in them grating against each other.

There was no chance of getting that hunting knife, but I had another, smaller one in the upper torso of my Flight Suit. With difficulty, I extracted it and began slashing feebly at the spaghetti-like shroud line mess surrounding me.

Once free of the parachute, I began a tentative search for the Survival Pack. It contained a one-man Life Raft, some canned water, food, fishing gear, and dye markers. The dye markers colored the water around the pilot to aid the rescue team in finding a down airman. All of this survival equipment should have been strapped to my hips. It was not there. It had been ripped away from my body upon impact with the water.

"How long would the Mae West sustain me?" I wondered.

I wasn't sure, but I knew I needed help fast. The salt water that I had swallowed felt like an enormous rock in the pit of my gut. But worst of all, here I was, completely alone, 600 miles from shore, lolling in the deep troughs and crests of the Pacific Ocean. And my Crusader aircraft, upon which had been lavished such affectionate attention, was sinking thousands of feet to the bottom of the ocean.

At that moment, I was struck by the incredible series of coincidences that had just befallen me. I knew that my misfortune had been a *one-in-a-million* occurrence. In review, I noted that the explosion aloft should not have happened. The ejection mechanism should have worked. The parachute should have opened. None of these incidents should have happened. I had just experienced three major catastrophes in one flight. My squadron had a perfect safety record. *"Why was all of this happening,"* was my thinking?

In about ten minutes, I heard the drone of a propeller-driven plane. The pot-bellied, four-engine tanker came into view, flying very low. They dropped several green dye markers near me, and some smoke flares a short distance from my position. They circled overhead and dropped an inflated life raft about 50-yards from me.

I was so pleased, and tried to swim toward the raft. After attempting to swim two strokes, I almost blacked-out, due to the intense pain in my body. The tanker circled again and dropped another raft closer to me, but there was no way for me to get to it, or in it, in my condition.

The water seemed to be getting colder, and a chill gripped me. I looked at my watch, but the so called *unbreakable crystal* was shattered, and the hands torn away. I tried to relax and surrender to the Pacific Ocean swells. I could almost have enjoyed being buoyed up to the crest of one swell and gently sliding into the trough of the next, but I was in such *excruciating* pain. I remembered the words that **W.C. Fields** had chosen for his epitaph: *"On the whole, I'd rather be in Philadelphia."*

In about an hour, a Coast Guard Amphibian Plane flew over and circled me as though deciding whether or not to land. But, the seas were high and I knew he couldn't make it. He came in very low and dropped another raft; this one had a 200-foot lanyard attached to it. The end of the lanyard landed barely ten feet from me. I paddled gently backward using only my arms. I caught hold of it and pulled the raft to me. Even before trying, I knew I couldn't crawl into the raft due to my physical condition. I was able to get a good grip on its side and hold on. This gave me a little security.

The Coast Guard Amphibian gained altitude and flew off.

(*I learned later that he headed for a squadron of minesweepers that was returning to the United States from a tour of the Western Pacific. He was unable to tune to their radio frequency for communications. But this ingenious pilot lowered a wire from his aircraft and dragged it across the bow of the minesweeper, the U.S.S. Embattle. The Minesweeper Captain understood the plea, and veered off at top speed in my direction.) I was fully-conscious during the two and a half hours it took the shop to reach me. Soon, its great bow was pushing in towards me, and I could see sailors in orange life-jackets crowding it lifelines. A bearded man in black rubber suit jumped into the water and swam towards me).*

"*Are you hurt?*" he asked.

"*Yes,*" I said. "*My legs and back.*"

I was now very cold and worried about the growing numbness in my legs. Perhaps the imminence of rescue made me light-headed, for I only vaguely remember being hoisted aboard the ship. I was laid out on the ship's deck as they cut away my flight suit.

"**Don't touch my legs! Don't touch my legs!**" I screamed.

I don't remember it. Somebody gave me a shot of Morphine, and this erased part of my extreme pain. An hour or so later, a man was bending over me and asking questions. (*It was a Doctor, who had been high-lined over from the* **USS Los Angeles,** *a cruiser that had been operating in the area.*)

He said, "*You have a long scar on your abdomen. How did it get there?*"

I told him about a serious auto accident I'd had four years earlier in Texas, and that my spleen had been removed at that time.

He grunted, and asked more questions while he continued examining me. Then he said, "*You and I are going to take a little trip over to the USS Los Angeles; it's steaming alongside.*"

Somehow, they got me into a wire stretcher, and hauled me, dangling and dipping, across the watery interval between the **Embattle** and the cruiser.

In the **Los Angeles**' Sick Bay, they gave me another shot of Morphine, *thank God*, and started thrusting all sorts of hoses into my body. I could tell from all the activity, and from the intense, hushed voices, that they were very worried about my condition.

My body temperature was down to 94°; my intestines and kidneys were in shock. The doctors never left my side during the night. They took my blood pressure every 15-minutes. I was unable to sleep.

Finally, I threw-up about a quart or more of seawater. After this, my nausea was relieved a bit.

By listening to the Medical Team, that was working on me, I was able to piece together the nature of my injuries. This is what I heard them saying. '*My left ankle was broken in five places. My right ankle was broken in three places. A tendon in my left foot was cut. My right pelvis was fractured. My number 7 vertebra was fractured. My left lung had partially collapsed. There were many cuts and bruises all over my face and body, and, my intestines and kidneys had been shaken into complete inactivity.*'

The next morning, Dr. Valentine Rhodes told me that the **Los Angeles** was steaming at flank speed to a rendezvous with a helicopter 100-miles from Long Beach, California.

At 3:30 that afternoon, I was hoisted into the belly of a Marine helicopter from the **USS Los Angeles'** FanTail, and we whirred off to a Hospital Ship, the **USS Haven**, docked in Long Beach, CA.

Once aboard the **Haven**, Doctors came at me from all sides with more needles, tubes, and X-ray machines. Their reaction to my condition was so much more optimistic than I had expected. I finally broke down and let go a few tears of relief, exhaustion, and *thanks* to all hands *and God*.

Within a few months, I was all systems go again. My ankles were put back in place with the help of steel pins. The partially-collapsed left lung re-inflated and my kidneys and intestines were working again without the need of prodding.

The Marine Corps discovered the cause of my flame-out, (*and that of Major Tooker, the day before*), was the failure of an automatic cut-off switch in the refueling system. The aircraft's main fuel tank was made of heavy reinforced rubber. When the cut-off switch failed, this allowed the tank to overfill and it burst like a balloon. This then caused the fire and flameout.

We will never know why the Martin-Baker Ejection Seat failed to work, since it is at the bottom of the Pacific Ocean. The parachute failure is a mystery also. Like they say, **"Some days you are the dog, and others you are the fire-plug."**

Do I feel lucky? That word doesn't even begin to describe my feelings. To survive a **15,000-foot fall** with an unopened chute is a fair enough feat. My mind keeps running back to something Dr. Rhodes told me in the Sick Bay of the **Los Angeles** during those grim and desperate hours.

He said that if I had had a spleen, it almost certainly would have *ruptured* when I hit the water, and I would have *bled to death*. Of the 25-pilots in our Squadron, I am the only one without a spleen. It gives me something to think about. Maybe it does you as well.

Cliff Judkins

Semper Fi - 23 May 2009

[Author's Note: Amazingly, Cliff Judkins not only survived this ordeal, but he also returned to flight status. He was flying the F-8 Crusader again within six months after the accident. After leaving the Marine Corps, he was hired as a pilot with Delta Air Lines and retired as a Captain from that position.]

Thanks to Ron Knott for permission to use the story from his book, and thanks again to Cliff Judkins for sharing his amazing experience with us. Finally, thanks and God Bless both men for their service to our country.

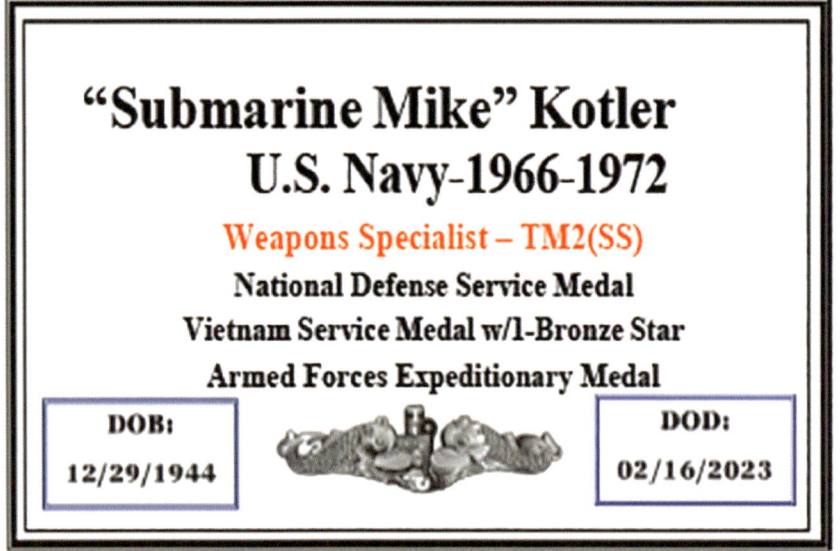

Admittedly, I am a Procrastinator !!!

Sub-Title: **Water can be Dangerous to Contend With- Take it from a US Navy Submariner**

Like most of the Veterans in our Monday for Lunch Bunch Group, I did not heed the urging of our fearless leader, T.D. Jorgensen, to sit down and write our brief memoir for this journal. It was not until I was viewing the devastation in Florida, with the damage that Hurricane Ian wrought on September 28-29, 2022, that I felt compelled to recall an incident during my service in Vietnam that brought back memories and nearly cost the loss of 120 of my fellow shipmates….. but more on that, later. First, let's travel back to how I wound up entering that deep, dark, undersea world.

When I was 12, a TV series in black & white entitled "*The Silent Service*" aired for 2-years in 1957-58.

The reenactments depicted the true exploits of men in submarines during WWII. It was both captivating and molded my future choice for military service. Eight years later in 1966, about to graduate from college, my dad called to tell me I had a letter from the Yonkers, NY, Draft Board. Following graduation, with a new A-1 status, I drove to the New London Submarine Base in Groton, CT, and inquired if they were accepting enlistees. After the recruiter learned that I had recently graduated college, I was signed up.

The typical 6-year reserve enlistment would include 2-years Active Duty, followed by 4-years Active Reserve. However, for Submarine Candidates, it was 1-year meetings, plus a 2-week summer cruise, followed by 2-years Active Duty and then 3-years Active Reserve. It was done this way to weed-out any enlistees, if the Navy felt they would not be able to qualify for Submarine duty. This way, rather than release them from their military obligation, they could be transferred to the Surface Fleet.

With the 1955 launching of the USS Nautilus SSN-571, the first Nuclear Powered Submarine, the 60-day Submarine School that had been conducted prior, was changed to a 6-month Nuclear

Power Program and the normal 4-year (*regular Navy enlistee active duty*) was extended to 6-years active duty.

Nuclear power was in its infancy and the Pentagon only budgeted for 1-1½ Nuclear Submarines each year. By the mid-1960's, only 15-18 "nukes" had been commissioned since the Nautilus, yet 250-300 WWII-type diesel-electric submarines were still in operation. The senior enlisted personnel serving on those boats were the same 18-19 year olds that enlisted in 1942, after Pearl Harbor. Having completed 20+ years they were due to retire. The Navy had two choices; create another 60-day Submarine School Program to teach the diesel-electric, or mothball the entire fleet. The Vietnam conflict left only one choice -- A 2nd Submarine School was established at Hunter's Point / San Francisco (*nearer to San Diego, serving the Pacific Fleet and, naturally Vietnam*). That's where I went, graduating 2nd in my Class of 81.

I reported aboard the USS Pomodon SS-486 following SP/SG Sub-School. Pomodon had recently returned from her 1967 Vietnam trip and was in Mare Island for upkeep. She transited to San Diego and I boarded her, expecting that I would join the ranks of the new-enlistees and the mess-cook brigade. I caught *"lucky break #1"*. The new Mess Cooks, 5-in-all, were picked from the new enlistees that had joined the boat in dry-dock at Mare Island, while I was in Sub-School. So, I became part of the deck-crew, chipping rust and repainting in typical flat-black paint.

Lucky-break #2 came only two weeks later when the COB (*Chief-of-the-Boat*), heard that there was an opening in San Diego's Weapons School for a Torpedoman. He asked, I said, "Yes," and I was gone for 3-weeks. I returned to the boat in time to take the 3rd-Class Advancement Exam for TM (*Torpedoman*).

Fresh in my head from A-School, I made 3rd Class. This was lucky break #3. The pathway to mess cooking was traditionally, non-rated, then non-qualified. Since the 5-Mess Cooks had 60-days till release, all had about 3-weeks left when I made 3rd Class TM. There were still about 8-10 new recruits that would serve before me. My next goal was to earn my Dolphins.

Earning your Dolphins means becoming a Qualified member of the crew. What does that mean? A simplified explanation is if you are part of a 5-man tank crew, you would cross-train so that all 5 men could do the other crewmembers' job. In a Submarine, it is different. There are over 100-systems, including high-pressure air, low-pressure air, the trim & drain system, hydraulics, and the equipment that makes that happen; ***e.g.***-IMO Pumps (*which we called-I Move Oil*) … how they work, and how to fix them if they don't, *etc.* The reality is that you must know every handle and every valve in all 10-compartments; what they turn on or off … what they open or shut … and how you can save the boat if called upon. The normal qualification time for enlisted men to get *"signed-off"*, plus the rigorous Officer Review that follows is 6-months to a year. I qualified in 42-days, ending my Mess Cook days. At my Dolphins presentation, my Captain said, "You may not be the best man in case of an emergency; ***you may be the only man!***"

Now for the promised water incident that almost lost the Pomodon and her entire crew

Shortly after the Pueblo was taken by North Korea in January 1968, we headed to Yokosuka, Japan, the Navy Base for Vietnam jumping-off point. We headed toward Vietnam, en route from waters close to Red China. At about 2 AM, most of the crew was asleep, except for submerged watch-standers. We had been Snorkeling (*a submerged operation that allows a submarine to run her engines to recharge her batteries at the same time*), when the Collision Alarm rang throughout the boat.

I leaped out of my bunk (3rd level up), and hit the deck in the After Torpedo Room (*my berthing compartment*). The sonar sounding from the Control Room stated 110 feet to the bottom on the 1MC. At 110-feet, you are pretty close to the China mainland. I ran over to the depth gauge near the After Room Torpedo tubes and it read 120-feet. That meant our "*attitude*" was already bow-up, stern-down. Our screws had to be in the mud at 130-feet. I heard the call for "*Blow Bow Buoyancy and Blow Negative*". These are two ballast tanks that would normally provide the negative buoyancy to stay submerged. But, we had taken on 10,000 gallons of sea water into our Forward Engine Room in 30-seconds….with no explanation.

We were able to stabilize the boat through a series of controlled shifting of water in the trim & drain system, and able to prevent from "*broaching*" the surface that would have exposed our submarine to any observers on the Chinese coast. We stayed submerged and left the area for the safety of international waters; then surfaced about 5 AM to find what caused the malfunction.

The Pomodon was commissioned in 1945. Too late for WWII, and it never suffered any enemy attack or depth-charges, making it perfect to become the 1st Diesel Boat to get converted with a revised German Snorkel System. The U.S. version employed two-masts, elevated by hydraulics from the Control Room to recharge the boat's Twin-256 Battery Cell Compartments. The intake mast has 3-electrodes that close the head-valve when a wave goes over, minimizing the water that would drain into the main-induction line. When we surfaced, we could see why we took in so much water and nearly lost our boat.

Travelling so close to shore, the recent event of Hurricane Ian showed this as well. Oil slicks and debris usually occur near land. When we made it to the bridge in the early morning hours, we saw that a truck tire floated over the snorkel-head-valve, jamming it open, not enabling the electronic closing or manual shut-down, allowing the 10,000 gallons to enter.

Take it from an undersea dweller, <u>NOTHING is scarier than Water</u>. Beside flooding, it can cause electrical failures and fires. If these happen in a submerged Submarine, it is all-hands-on-deck

JACK KOWALL
U.S. ARMY
Scout Dog Handler
Cell: 770-560-5564
JackKowall@Bellsouth.net

My Military Experiences

In the summer of 1969, I received my grades for the Spring Trimester at California State College and was notified that I was **NPR** (*Not Permitted to Register*) for the next trimester of school. Knowing that my overall GPA was high enough, all I had to do was ask, and I would be readmitted in the fall. Not to worry right? **Wrong**! I lost my deferment, and the Draft Board was notified. So, I got drafted, and was inducted into the U.S. Army on September 9, 1969. I became **Privat** Kowall. If anybody remembers, I went on the last call-up before the Lottery took effect. When they began drawing numbers … mine was **289**. I would never have been *Drafted*. Too late. I was already in the Army.

At Fort Jackson in Columbia, SC, I arrived at the Reception Center, where you are tested, and told how great thou art. I was offered all the different kinds of training. I remember being told that I could go to any school the Army had; it was just a matter of how much time I wanted to extend my Draft status. Being the agreeable person I am, I declined all of it and said, "*I just want to get out as quickly as I can*." Next, I went on to **Basic Training**. When that was completed, I was sent to **LPC** (*Leadership Preparation Course*). It was only three weeks, so I didn't have to extend, and they made me a Squad Leader in **Advance Infantry Training** (*AIT*). I got a *private* room. All I did was stand at the end of the line in formation. Graduation followed, and a lot of troops were sent to Vietnam and other places, while a lot went on to other jobs. Me? I was lucky; I was put on a bus with about 15 other troops and sent to Fort Benning, Georgia, for **Non-Commissioned Officers** (*NCO*) **School**.

Got there about 0300-hrs. and sent to bed. When we got up in the morning, I was told the class I was in started on Monday *but* was full. Not to worry… I was to be a Company Clerk, and wait for the next class to start. *Great*, right? The catch was, when you complete NCO school, you must have at least one year left to go in your Army service contract. Being one month short of the time necessary, I was told I could extend for the time I needed. I thought about it, and decided **not** spend more time than I was already committed to. So, I was sent to a casual company to await new Orders.

I was again interviewed, and offered training, and as usual, more time in the Army was required; for everything! So, I asked the interviewer if there was a school that I could get into that didn't require any more time for me? He answered, "Sit tight," and walked away. When he returned, he said, "**There was a Scout Dog School starting on Monday, and I could get in**." I became a **Scout Dog Handler** at that time, and later found out what I had done. I had signed up to be a *Point Man* in Vietnam.

In Vietnam, I was part of a 30-man Platoon. We were usually led by a Lieutenant and/or a Platoon Sergeant. Our Sergeant was an E-7, and we would rarely see each other. Our job was to go out with a Line Company in the field, and as they moved, we would walk point and lead the way. We would usually go out on a supply chopper and return 3-5 days later on the next supply run. I have many stories to tell on those missions.

My dog's name was **Eric**. Eric was an all-black Shepherd and Lab mix. He was a wonderful dog, whom I'm sorry to say, I've not been able to find out his fate. When I left Vietnam, Eric was assigned to another Handler, and continued his job as a true hero. We spent almost an entire year walking the trails of Vietnam, and I returned home with *not a scratch*. At night we would camp on a hill and put claymore mines on the trails leading to our site. One night I was awakened by the sound of one of the claymores going off. Scared the shit out of me. Next thing I know, everyone is firing rounds into the dark and then. a few grenades were thrown. No one thought they might bounce off a tree and come back. In the morning nothing was found at the site; no remains, no blood, nothing. Guess we got lucky.

I always had someone walk my *slack*, (*watch my Six/Back*), as I was watching my dog. One day, as I was walking, the guy behind me was carrying a LAW (**Grenade Launcher**), with a grenade in it. Luckily, because if he would have had a shot gun shell instead, I would not be writing this today. I heard a thump as the launcher went off and then felt a swish by my ear. I still think it nicked me. He said a twig had hit his trigger and it went off. The shell hit a tree about 10 yards up and fell to the ground. I asked for a different slack man.

I guess you can say I achieved my goal. In July 1971, my tour was up and I returned to the States. I only had 2-months left to fulfill my 2-year obligation, so I was Honorably discharged. I only spent 22-months in the Army.

As I look back, if I knew then what I know now, I may have done things a little differently.

BELOW, OUR PLATOON OF DOG HANDLERS

BELOW, JACK WITH ERIC

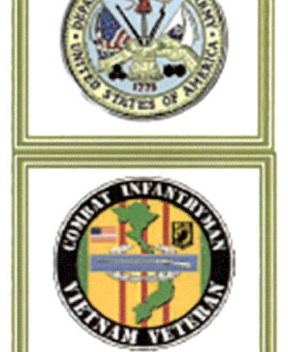

BOB LANDIN, VIETNAM, ONE ADVISOR'S EXPERIENCES

In 1965, I was the Commandant of the Anti-Tank Missile (ENTAC) Gunners School at Ft. Gordon, GA. While on leave, I stopped at the Pentagon to visit Infantry Branch to check my official records. My Branch Assignment Officer was a friend from the 1/7 Cavalry in Korea. Earlier in the year, I applied for a Regular Army commission and was selected. He informed me that all R.A. Officers fight in a war and there was a small one going on. I volunteered and was told that Orders would be sent. I received them in September for direct assignment to MACV, but without attending Advisor or Language School enroute. My report date was in November. My flight from Travis AFB, CA, was direct with a fuel stop in Manilla. In-processing and shots took 3-days, and I was assigned to the 10th ARVN Division Advisory Detachment in III Corps.

I flew to Bien Hoa, Vietnam, the next day to sign in at Corps Headquarters (*HQ*), then on to Xuan Loc and Division HQ. When I got off the Huey, the Captain that met me asked for my Branch. I told him Infantry. His response was "No, your *real* branch, not your detail." I replied that I wear the EIB, so Infantry is my *real* branch. Apparently, they had not received an Infantry Officer for about 8-months. I stayed there for three more days, and received my assignment as the Senior Advisor for the 4th Battalion, 48th Regiment, which was a new Battalion, still in training at the Training Center in Phouc Le.

The rest of my advisory team (*1 officer, 2 NCO's and 1 RTO*) joined me two weeks later. The Battalion completed training for four more weeks, and we moved to the regimental Area of Operations (A/O) northwest of Bien Hoa Air Base along the Dong Nai river. We located to the west of the Regimental Compound and began patrolling and performed road security for the MSR in our area. In early April, we were awakened by automatic weapons fire. The First

Company on our western flank, was under attack. I got on the radio and notified the Regimental Advisor of the situation. Within 15-minutes, I had a FAC overhead and described the situation. He flew to the engagement area and began dropping flares to mark the engagement area for the fighters. First on station were the Vietnamese Air Force (**VNAF**) A6's, dropping cluster bombs and strafing. They were on station for about 40-minutes. The next were U.S. Fighter Jets from Bien Hoa, and they continued to bomb and strafe. In total, we had 4 - 5 sorties as I guided the FAC to where we needed them the most. After 2-1/2 hours the Viet Cong withdrew, taking their dead with them.

At first light, we checked First Company. It had lost about **35 %** of their troops. Worst were the dependents of the soldiers that were killed in the attack. (*It was common for lower ranking soldiers to have their families accompany them to the base camp*). Later that afternoon, personnel from III Corps came for a briefing, and to observe where the action took place. Patrols for the next few days were finding unexploded cluster bomb ordnance, which they were happy to show us.

The remainder of the month was without activity. Our main event was when a convoy of Armored Personnel Carriers (**APC's**) from the 1st Division came through the area, and we levied a toll for the use of the highway. The Commander of the lead track didn't believe me when we told him it would cost a case of `Charlies,` before he could proceed. He gave us 3-cases, and we appreciated the American food.

In May, the Regiment conducted a Battalion swap and the 4th changed location with the 2nd Battalion. Our new area was south of the Headquarters with the main mission of protecting the MSR. Battalion HQ was located next to a small hamlet of a few houses and a National Police (***a.k.a.,*** *White Mice*) checkpoint. The rifle companies were located west and north of our location. The 1st Infantry Division was southeast of us. Directly to our west was a Vietnamese Leprosarium that the Viet Cong would raid for medical supplies. The Battalion and the 1st Division would alternate running patrols into the area to provide protection.

In July, the Viet Cong (**VC**) blew up the police check point at night, killing two of the cops, but they did not come near our compound. Our primary mission was to protect the MSR from Regiment's location to the north, and then south from our location for about 10-miles.

Housing for a Vietnamese unit in the field was rudimentary. Regimental HQ had buildings, but the Battalions and Companies had to rough it. Initially, we were able to set up in a Pagoda that was only used once each year. That enabled the team to sleep in an open, but covered, building and have a place to eat and relax out of the sun. A two-burner kerosene stove enabled us make coffee and do some basic cooking for breakfast, and an occasional dinner. Lunch and dinner were eaten with the Battalion Commander and his staff.

After we moved to the new location, our housing was a large hole-in-the-ground, where our cots were three feet *below* the surface. We improved the overhead protection by getting 2 x 12's, that were used as dunnage by the ships, from the port outside Saigon, and we were able to swap our M2 *Grease Gun* for enough Perforated Steel Plating (*a.k.a., PSP*) to also cover the roof. With a tarp to keep out the rain and 3-layers of sandbags, we were fairly well protected overhead. The team Hut was set up at the entrance to the hole with a covered roof, and with sandbags from the ground up to 4-feet, and screen wire from above the bags to the roof to keep out the bugs. Further improvements were made by obtaining a propane powered refrigerator that had been turned in for repair and never reclaimed.

My assistant was able to obtain new metal bunks and double wall lockers from the Air Force (*a story for a different time*). The separators for the conversion to bunk beds enabled us to be able to raise the bunks to just below ground level and provide some cooling. The addition of the fridge meant cold beer and soft drinks, without worrying about a supply of ice. It also improved our meals.

A captured weapon could be traded for a case of meat, the field bakery gave us free bread. A friend of mine at Long Binh arranged for the Mess Halls to give me the excess canned vegetables they received in the small grocery store sized cans. With the new availability of American food, we were able to cook and serve all our meals, ourselves.

In August, I was notified that I would be reassigned to a new posting. After my replacement arrived and we reviewed everything that Battalion had done and was doing, we met the Battalion Commander, and I departed for my new position as the Senior RF/PF Advisor of Binh Tuy Province, with location in the town of Ham Tan on the southeast coast.

My new team was 2-Officers and 2-NCOs. We were the Advisors for the military staff and the Provincial Training Center. My counterpart had 1-Battalion, 7-Independent Companies, 10-Independent Platoons, and 12-Independent Squads at various locations within the Province.

I was able to participate in a patrol to a local village, where we were to set up a Medical Clinic for the day. I was amazed to see a village of pregnant women and children, but no young men. I was also the back-up for the PsyOps War Officer, so I spent time doing leaflet drops, and playing propaganda tapes from USAF aircraft. The FACs would let me fly with them on missions. Since I had a civilian license, they were kind enough to let me fly the aircraft. The only action we had in the area was when the U.S. Marines did an operation into the Viet Cong area south of the Province. I was allowed to send my Deputy as a Liaison. In October, I received *Authorized Leave* (**R&R**) to go to Bangkok, Thailand, for family shopping. My number for R & R came up in November, two weeks before my DEROS, so I went to Hong Kong, China, to buy clothes and a Rolex. My last week in-country went fast as I turned everything over to my Deputy, and then I was off to Saigon, to clear for departure and leave for CONUS.

A U.S.M.C. Experience

"Nothing in life is so exhilarating as to be shot at without result."
~ Sir Winston Churchill ~

Here's a story about a Vietnam experience I had. It's excerpted and up-dated from my 2005 book, *"Never Beat the Boss at Horseshoes."*

was a Radio Operator in the **1st Bn., 7th Marines**, stationed on **Hill 10**, southwest of Da Nang, near "**Happy Valley**."

"Expect to be back tomorrow afternoon and be prepared to get hit!"

Those were the last words my squadmates and I heard from the Marine Guard at the gate as we marched off towards "**Happy Valley**" -- if ever a place on earth was misnamed, that was it – from our home on Hill 10.

A squad that went out earlier had been hit hard, sustaining many casualties, and our job was to help. As firm as our resolve was to help, there were equally resolute bands of Viet Cong determined that we wouldn't be given the opportunity. Something rang in our ears a time or two during that mission, and it wasn't Churchill's words, quoted above. However, when we regrouped back on Hill 10 the next day, we did talk about what happened, and especially of the brief *farewell advice* from the Marine at the Gate. To a man, we agreed that *somehow* the expectation of a safe return had a positive impact on our behavior. A little more confidence, a little less apprehension, and a definite feeling of being ready, all came with our positive expectation. Those words remembered from over 54-years ago that our unknown Gate Guard

Marine uttered, which have continued to resonate with me to today, and have been a beacon - expect the best from every situation, while being prepared for whatever the situation may bring.

Oh, and the words of Sir Winston Churchill at the beginning of this story? I would agree with them, as well ... though *perhaps* worded just a tad differently! So, that's my story, T.D., and I'm stickin' to it.

I made sure I found time to enjoy some Leisure Time while in Vietnam, but also posed for a couple of John Wayne-type Photos whenever the opportunity posed itself.

A Radio Operator's typical equipment pack that he carries on his back to keep in communication with his T.O.C. (*Tactical Operation's Center*).

One might say my 1st *Official* 'Quarters' in Vietnam was a bit under-rated? But, at least I had nice Palm Trees in the distance for my viewing pleasure.

U.S. Marines' H-34's insert Infantrymen into an LZ in early years of Vietnam's war.

P. DICKSON LESTER
U.S. Navy
Cell: 678-836-4391
PDL721@BellSouth.net

My Military Experience

1972 INFO HISTORY OF THE

USS Waddell DDG-24

On May 5th, 1972, **Painter Dickson Lester** was called by Captain Herberger, to the Crip Room, where the two of them reviewed a *TOP SECRET ORDER /TELETYPE* from President Nixon, Washington, D.C., and *the teletype read as follows:*

STOP* PROCEED TO HAIPHONG HARBOR STOP*

STOP* IF CAUGHT STOP*

STOP* YOU ARE ON YOUR OWN STOP*

I was told by the Captain to memorize this message, read it back to him 5-times, and he read it to me 5-times, and then, we practiced without the message. When we knew we had it committed to memory, we burned it.

We prepared to travel to North Vietnam's Haiphong Harbor along with several other ships. We had Intelligence that said that 17 Russian ships, then loaded with weapons, ammunitions, and fighting equipment, were going to Haiphong Harbor at midnight, and we were to cloak ourselves and follow them in as close as we could get. Then, we were to help mine the harbor entrance, to prevent them from escaping, and so that President Nixon could fly in a spy plane, and capture aerial photos of the Russian cargo ships in daylight, to prove to the world that they were aiding and abetting the Vietcong Communist regime, even though the Russians had been denying it for years.

We proceeded northbound, and as we traveled, we made all preparations to eliminate any lights outside the ship that could be seen. The night was going to be cloudy and very dark. We were also given orders by our Captain Herberger that once we entered a certain area of the South China Sea, we would receive a signal and no one would be allowed to speak. Instead, we would use note pads to write notes to one another.

As part of my duties in the Engineering Department Engine Room we were given Orders to reduce all motors and equipment noise to the *bare minimum*. We shut down power to everything, except enough equipment to run one generator, 1200-lb. Steam Engine, and one screw of our power plant.

We were told that there was a Russian Submarine escorting the flotilla of Russian Freighters, and they would be listening, and if they heard English speaking voices, they would know something wasn't right.

We finally found the flotilla of Russian ships and fell in at a distance behind them, and following them right up to the point when they began to enter Haiphong Harbor. When the last Russian ship was approaching the entrance, we called in the Air Drops of the Mines, and all chaos broke loose … the clouds broke open … and the moonlight was bright enough for the last of the 17-Rusian ships to see us behind them, and they tried to back out, but damaged their rudder and prop causing them to actually help in the blocking of the Harbor.

We were already at General Quarters, so the Captain told us to `Light Off` the entire ship's power, and weapons. In the process, one of our Electricians broke a handle on the power grid board, and that caused a cascade of shutting down all power, leaving us *Dead-at-Sea* with **no** weapons to protect ourselves and **no** engines to pull us away.

As part of the duties of our Electrical Team, we began the Emergency processes with portable diesel generators to bring the ship back up with power, which took some 15 - 20 scary minutes as the Vietcong started realizing what was happening and started firing at us and the aircraft flying in to drop more mines. We finally got power up for everything (*in a record time I might add*), and Captain Herberger gave the orders to fire for affect against the weapons shooting at us, as well as at the warehouses around the Russian ships causing huge fire storms of ammo explosions going off, and fires engulfing the warehouses. It was one of the most incredible fireworks shows we had ever seen.

Meanwhile, we were soon getting up to speed to vacate the area and missiles were being fired at us. One, went in-between our smoke stacks and one across our Fantail (*rear of the ship for civilians*) exploding in the ocean several hundred yards past us, but the concussion beneath the water did cause buckling of some of the plates of steel below our decks, but no *serious* damages.

A MiG aircraft was trying to find us and shoot at us, as well as drop a bomb on us, but some Navy Fighters removed him from our A/O (*I think they shot him down, but I was not a witness to that reality*).

We finally made it back out to sea to regroup with the rest of our ships. Then, we proceeded back to duty near the De-Militarized Zone at the Quantri Province area in Northern I-Corps.

In June, we were defending U.S. Marines and U.S. Army soldiers in the Battle of Quantri, where hundreds of Marines and Army personnel were pinned down in a major thrust by the Vietcong. We spent 49 days and nights on the gun-line, and burned up a set of Belgium 5' 54-Caliper Cannons firing nonstop, 13 miles inland with the aid of a spotter plane.

THE USS WADDELL DDG 24 (*Guided Missile Destroyer*) and all its crewmembers (*including yours truly*) received the Navy Unit Commendation (NUC) MEDAL for outstanding *heroism-in-action* against the Vietcong enemy in support of military operations for the month of June 1972, supporting and saving hundreds of U.S. MARINES and U.S. ARMY lives in the Battle of Quantri. (*non-stop 49-days and nights in the Quantri Province gun-line, just below the Demilitarized Zone*). The **Navy Unit Commendation** (**NUC**) is a United States Navy unit award that was established by order of the Secretary of the Navy James Forrestal on 18 December 1944.

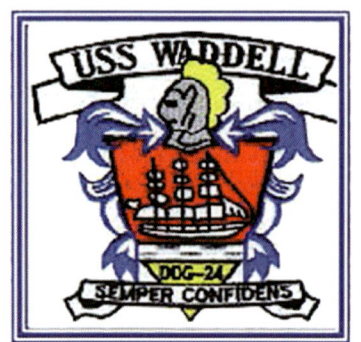

MY USAF EXPERIENCE

Richard `DOC` Liposky

U.S.A.F.

Cell: 724-333-5123

DrLiposky@DSA-LLC.net

A YEAR AND A DAY IN VIET NAM

The Mission: Treat Dental/Facial injuries in Viet Nam war zone.

Training: Twelve months of specialty training in primary management of dental/facial Injuries. The USAF selected 27 for this special training out of the 4,000 new graduates. It was an *Honor* to be selected but, little did we know what they had in mind for us.

Deployment: Sent to Tan Son Nhut A.B. dispensary TDY to Binh Thuy A.B. in Mekong Delta.

Duty: From dental surgery to being part of USAF surgical team, which morphed to working at the *Cần Thơ* Regional Hospital treating facial wounds on civilians. This was expanded to working in the villages and hamlets treating patients who needed immediate surgery in the field ... *literally*. Working in the field also help provide needed military intelligence. I assumed that we were being watched... and we were. Two important missions were accomplished: help the people and help our own soldiers with information.

    Binh Thuy Air Base was a refueling base in the delta. When the pilot and I landed at the base, the pilot feathered one engine so I could climb out with my bag. By the time, I walked to the side of the runway, he was rolling. What was up with that? I was a pilot, so I knew a little about the process. I had commented in the air that I didn't know that they had irrigation farming in Viet Nam. The pilot corrected me. "Captain, those are B-52 bomb craters, **not** irrigation patterns like state side." Interesting observation.

    My first instructions from the medical commander was to, "*Always know where the nearest bunker is and how to get there with your eyes closed.*" Proved to be great advice. Mortar attacks were common. Usually at night and hopefully early enough that we could get to sleep. After each attack, our Army would go after the enemy. We were hit three to four times a week. Charlie was mainly trying to take out our fuel depot and power supply. They also would hit our dispensary when we had wounded waiting for evacuation. We had to "*dispose*" of our civilian janitor for the dispensary when we found that he was letting Charlie know when and how many wounded were waiting for evacuation. Our dispensary would get hit and he would conveniently not show up the next morning for cleanup. After that revelation, we had to evacuate all wounded by dark.

Surgery at the *Cần Thơ* Regional Hospital was an educational experience which became the foundation of my professional career. Security was issue so I had to be off the roads and back to the base by 1800 hr. We had four operating rooms in a separate building. The family wheeled the patient across the dirt courtyard among the animal and people, and up to the door. They knocked. We took in the patient, and they waited on the ground outside. When we finished surgery, they took the patient back to the ward. Three patients would use each bed, with the family sitting on the floor around the bed. One patient laid down, and two sat-up at the foot of the same bed. They would switch-off, so that each had a chance to lay down.

There were so many wounded, (*all civilians*), that Triage was critical. Operations that would take four to six hours were post-posed to treat patients with surgery that would take one to two hours. Less time, more patients could be treated. Some who waited, died. Scary. Sad, but true.

The facial wounds were extensive and equipment and supplies limited. The windows were blown out and it was not unusual for a bird to fly in or have a chicken sitting on the windowsill watching the surgery. Sterility was an issue, but the chickens seemed to enjoy it.

The TDY of only 6 weeks lasted 6 months, while I helped develop the medical civic action program (MEDCAP). I got called back to Saigon to setup the MEDCAP program for the capital military district.

The MEDCAP missions grew from 4 missions to over 80 per month with priority helicopter support, second only to combat. My teams included volunteer physicians, dentists, nurses, and medics. State department or Command identified the need, location and provided interpreters.

Security was provided by ARVN and US Army troops. The 82nd and 101st provided most of my security. They secured a location. We dropped in to treat patients and then were pulled out.

Helicopters watched from above and pulled us out when necessary. Most visits lasted no more than a couple hours.

Since my medical teams were made up of volunteers, their safety and security were a high priority. Picking the right people was also important. Most team members were very sincere and wanted to help. I was so proud them, and humbled by their compassion and dedication. Those who just wanted to go along for the ride didn't volunteer for another mission.

In my spare time, I went to the Don Bosco Franciscan orphanage and attended to the boys who had dental infections or needed extractions. I enjoyed just visiting with them, listening to their stories and trying to offer hope in a very difficult time in their lives. They were being taught trade skills. They were very talented young men.

I had 3-months left on my service commitment and they was wanted me to go to the Pentagon to write MEDCAP protocols. But, there was no slot for a Captain. OK. I'll head home.

During all this, Irene and I had our second little girl whom I wouldn't get to see until she was 10 months old. That's right. I was deployed in the seventh month of her pregnancy. It was a war, you know!

I came home and started my 5-year residency in facial and reconstructive surgery at the University of Pittsburgh. Would I do it all over again? I did. I provided surgery for the Contra's in Central America in their fight for freedom as part of International Medical Corp.

More stories can be found in my book: *"It's Not What I Know…It's how I learned it."* . . .

This was the surprise `*Vietnam Honor Medal,*` presented to seven men in front of 1,000+ troops in formation. Humbling, but proud honor, that I received the day before I left Saigon. It is also in my book, entitled, *"It's not what I know…"*

My book #2, *"Grandpa and Andy"* is **sold out** right now, but more are on the way from my publisher.

JOHN LULA

My Military Experience

I joined the U.S. Air Force on July 1st, 1963 and discharged honorably on August 30th, 1967.

After Basic Training at Lackland AFB, Texas and Advanced Jet-Aircraft Maintenance Training at Amarillo AFB, Texas, I was sent to MacDill AFB in Tampa, Florida, following my course completions. I was assigned as part of the 12th TFW (Tactical Fighter Wing) and were the first to get the brand-new F-4C Phantom Jets.

My Squadron was the 555th (The Triple Nickel). We were a unique group, because we stayed as a continuous unit from November 1963 to November 1966.

In December 1964, our unit was sent to Naha (Okinawa Island), Japan, for a 90-day rotation. The following November, we went back to Naha to relieve one of the other Squadrons, so they could go home, and we were supposed to go to Cam Rahn Bay, Vietnam, but ended up going to Udorn (Royal Thai Air Base), and then on to Ubon (Royal Thai Air Base). My enlistment was extended by 2-months to get a Stateside Assignment to Shaw AFB, SC.

I came back, and got married, and we decided I should leave the Air Force. For the past 20-years we of the Triple Nickel have been getting together for our Air Force Reunions, but COVID-19 and its variants gave cause for us to cancel, or postpone, this year.

I wish everyone of this formerAir Force group the very best of health, and hope everyone enjoyed their time in service to our country as much as I did.

The F-4C Phantom Fighter Jet

Going to Vietnam changed my life.

I joined the Army when I was 19 because I was bored, not because I was going to be drafted. I had a student deferment, and I still had braces on my teeth which, believe it or not, gave me a medical deferment. I signed up hoping to get into the *Bird-Dog Program* because it looked like a cool job. That's how big of an idiot I was. It reminded me of WWI. The program closed and so I signed up for the *Army Diver Program*, another stupid idea, and then that program closed while I was in Basic Training at Fort Knox, KY. I remember the day the Company Commander called me to the office to tell me that the school was closed, and I had other options. I could go home because my contract was broken, I could go to Ft. Monmouth to go to the USMA prep school program, I could go to the defense language Institute in Monterey, or because I was already a Registered *OR* Tech from a summer job, I could get immediately promoted and go to Ft. Sam Houston, Tx. Or, I could even pick something new. He gave me an hour to think it over. Generous of him, I thought at the time. I picked photography, another dumb idea. And that's how I got to Vietnam.

It is not an exaggeration to say that I was a smart-ass child of the 60s and had very little respect for institutions, or anybody over the age of 30. Quite frankly, after the events from 1963 to 1969, I wasn't sure any of us were going to live past thirty. And so, after learning how to shoot and develop pictures, and becoming even more of a smart ass, I got orders for Vietnam, and off I went. Before I went, I married my fianceè Sharon, and that was the only smart thing I did that year. We are still together, and we now have three sons, three daughters-in-law, and one granddaughter.

The closest comparison I can make to my little Band of Brothers in Nha Trang (*no disrespect to the actual Band of Brothers*), is to compare us to the crew in Catch-22 by Joseph Heller. We were misfits, but interesting. Our little group was like the comic strip Beetle Bailey. We had PhD's, two high school dropouts, and our future ambitions ranged from being a truck driver to going back to surfing on the North Shore in Hawaii. Honestly, our group was not the most ambitious of future citizens. Our average age was twenty, or twenty-one.

The first thing that happened when I got to my unit was, they gave me a set of Orders for travel anywhere within the Republic of Vietnam on any transportation, and the armorer gave me a M-1911 sidearm. Secondly, I was advised never to wear any rank, so that no one would know if we were military, or CIA, or just passing through. Somewhere in Nha Trang was a First Lieutenant, who was supposed to be our OIC (Officer-in-Charge). I may have seen him twice in a year. We literally did whatever we wanted to do if it involved cranking out pictures. Our hooch was behind the Grand Hotel (*First Field Force HQ*) and across the street from the beach on Nha Trang Bay. Every three or four weeks we would bundle up our work, make sure it all had captions, and fly down to Saigon to personally deliver it to the Department of the Army record office. That was fun.

Everywhere I went, I took pictures… firebases, villages, orphanages, leper colonies, feasts when a VC would repatriate, most everywhere up to the DMZ. In our group were combat artists, remarkably talented guys, and I often wonder what happened to their work.

I turned twenty-one over there and celebrated by going to Saigon to deliver some pictures. I told my buddies I wanted a lobster dinner, a gin and tonic, and I wanted to go to an opium den just like in *The Heart of Darkness* by Joseph Conrad. That is the book that **"Apocalypse Now"** was based upon. The opium den was down a very long, very dark alley by the Saigon River. My first thought during the experience was… **"never do this again!"** But, I checked the block. I have spent a lot of my adult life in the medical and mental health business and to say that I understand the power of addiction is an understatement. I'm 100% convinced that if I had ever taken a second puff, I would've been an addict. It was not the smartest move of my year, but it was educational.

We often made up our own missions and a lot of them did not involve patrols or firebases. I did a story on orphanages run by French nuns, a leper colony in Cambodia, and one on the Vietnamese Naval Academy in Nha Trang. It is still there. Look it up.

My experience in Vietnam changed me. I saw people do things for each other that still bring me to my knees in awe. It gave me an appreciation of how wonderful *normal* is compared to *misery & despair*, and how everyday Joe's can become heroes when you least expect it.

I was lucky and the only hospital I saw was the one I woke up in after passing out from amoebic dysentery. Don't ask. Dumb way to lose weight, trust me.

When I was leaving Vietnam at the end of my tour, I was '*detained*' by the Military Police in Saigon. They were on alert. All the pictures, negatives, and stories that I had done that year were confiscated. 100%...gone. I did not have any atrocity pictures or what we now call war porn. I had some great pictures that are probably in somebody's garage in Omaha. But, it wasn't that long after My Lai, and the Army was sensitive about its public relations image. I wasn't bitter about it. I understood their perspective, and I knew the MP's that were just doing their job, even if they did not seem that bright. I had already decided that I still wanted to fly, and was going to find a way to get to Flight School.

When I finally got home and was walking through the airport in San Francisco, my only thoughts were a promise to myself to always be grateful for every day I have, and never be cynical. I have tried hard to keep that promise.

It took me a couple more years to finish college, and I was lucky to be the DMG of my ROTC class, and get a Regular Army Commission, and although I did not get back to Vietnam, my time in the 1st Infantry Division, and the 2nd Armored Division, was a great experience.

Years later, when I got off of Active Duty and walked into a V.A. Hospital for the first time, I had to turn around and walk out. I was shocked by my reaction. Every old man I saw had the eyes of an 18-year-old -- scared, lonely, but heroic. It was years before I could go back into a V.A. Hospital, despite being in the medical business.

Vietnam *changed* me. The experience of Military Service, from the *Gallic Wars* to the war in Iraq and Afghanistan, changes us all. It changed me for the better, *I hope*. I raised my 3-sons to serve, they are all Eagle Scouts, and they all attended **The Citadel**. Two served on active duty. One of them went through Iraq and Afghanistan, and both came home to start families and careers. I am so *thankful* for they all came home. I learned from my wife how much the ones you leave behind suffer while you are gone. That was *humbling*. I had no idea. My experiences and service are why I helped start **Cobb Salutes.org**, and why we offer *free* mental health screening to Veterans.

It is a pleasure to share my story with you and I look forward to reading yours. I was no hero, but I met some that were. That changes you. We never know what heroes live next door to us unless we ask.

Mark Maloney

Chief Executive Officer, Venops, Inc.

Hilbert Margol
WWII Dachau

WWII U.S. Army
Cell: 404-863-4692
email: Pappa79@aol.com

The Dachau concentration camp was liberated on April 29, 1945. Hilbert Margol and his brother Howard were there and documented the tragedy.

Pi Lam and Army enlistment

Hilbert "Hibby" Margol pledged Pi Lam at the University of Florida in 1942 with his twin brother, Howard. He said, "We had boyhood friends who entered the University of Florida just ahead of us. We followed them into joining the Delta Chapter of Pi Lambda Phi."

He joined an ROTC unit and after just a few months was called upon by his country to serve in WWII. Margol quipped, *"The Army decided there were too many healthy young men in college."*

He and his brother Howard enlisted together and wanted to fight alongside each other but they were initially separated due to U.S. policy driven by the tragedy of the *Sullivan brothers.* After his *"Two Star"* mother wrote several letters to President Roosevelt, the brothers were reunited.

WWII and Dachau

The Margol brothers' unit, (the 42nd Infantry "Rainbow" Division), was activated and went into Combat in France in January 1945. They fought across Europe serving in the Alsace, Ardennes, and Rhineland campaigns, until their unit found their way to Dachau, Germany, a northern suburb of Munich in Bavaria, in April 1945.

THEY APPROACHED THE TOWN, DUG IN, AND SET UP THEIR HOWITZERS, but the brothers noticed an unusual strong odor. Their gun sergeant gave them permission to go through the woods to determine the source.

They came upon the Dachau concentration camp.

Near the gates of Dachau, Margol and his brother stumbled across a line of boxcars that were full of prisoners' bodies, and they took photographs of the shocking sight. Margol said, *"We had a Brownie box camera that we had liberated somewhere along the way. But we only had one roll of film, so*

we were very judicious in taking pictures." The two photos of the boxcars were later donated to U.S. Holocaust Memorial Museum.

Though he doesn't consider himself a "liberator," after his unit and other American forces reached the camp, over 30,000 prisoners were freed.

Before, and even after seeing Dachau, Margol remembers not understanding the full extent of the concentration camps in Germany. It was only after Dachau, when his unit was transporting liberated Jews to Austria, that he was reminded of the strong faith that gave them the strength to survive.

Coming Home and passing on his knowledge

Hilbert and Howard survived the war and returned home. He reflected on his good fortune saying, *"we returned to the University of Florida and rejoined the fraternity."*

Hilbert enjoyed his days in Pi Lam and continued to stay in touch, *"after we graduated, the fraternity brothers continued our association with each other, especially my fraternity brothers in the Jacksonville, Florida area."*

After college, Margol and his brother started a business selling furniture in Atlanta. They were identical twins and used it as a marketing tool, "My twin brother and I started making TV advertisements." Our theme was, "Mama got two for the price of one, and so can you!"

Later in life, Margol who is Jewish, decided that his experience should be known to future generations.

He has given numerous interviews to newspapers, TV stations, historical organizations, and museums. He said, *"I hope and pray that my offspring and the offspring of other witnesses outlive the offspring of deniers, and that's what history*

P.S.~ When Hibby visited our local Veterans-For-Lunch-Bunch group on July 18, 2023, T.D. Jorgensen learned that Hibby was a part of a parade and U.S. Army ceremony at the Zeppelintribune Grandstane, (*which is where Adolf Hitler made his fiery speeches to the million Nazi masses from that platform*) which the U.S. Army later called, *"Soldiers' Field."*

Hibby also said his unit took over the Nazi garrison in Fürth/Bayem *(a suburb of Nürnberg, where the post-WWII War Tribunal took place at the Palace of Justice)*, which the U.S. Army later re-named, "William 0. Darby Kaserne," *named after the 1st-Commander of the U.S. Army Ranger Battalion*). Fürth is the birthplace of Heinrich Kissinger, better known to Americans as former Secretary of State of Richard M. Nixon -- Henry Kissinger. Interesting small world, yes? And, almost simultaneously, my wife Yvonne's father (*1Lt. Paul W. Aman and his 7th U.S. Army unit*) was entering Niirnberg's city limits to begin the Battle of Niirnberg from April 16-20, 1945, while Bibby and his unit entered and liberated Dachau, a northern suburb of Munich in Bayern (Bavaria).

Dates and additional historical WWII info (*in last 3-paragraphs, herein*) supplied by T.D. Jorgensen, who attended Nürnberg American High School, and acknowledged that our fellow alumni played our football games and held our Track & Field Meets at the humongous field that Hitler used to address his Nazi troops from that platform at the *Zeppelintribune Grandstane*

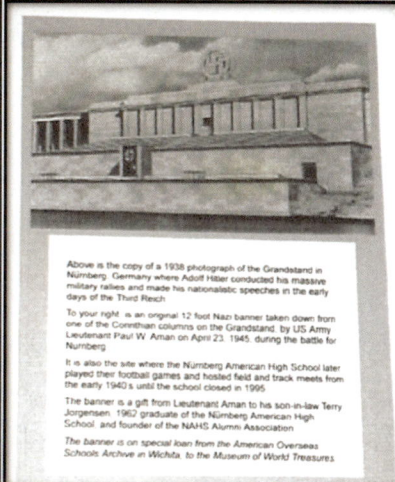

Above is the copy of a 1938 photograph of the Grandstand in Nürnberg, Germany where Adolf Hitler conducted his massive military rallies and made his nationalistic speeches in the early days of the Third Reich.

To your right, is an original 12 foot Nazi banner taken down from one of the Corinthian columns on the Grandstand, by US Army Lieutenant Paul W. Aman on April 23, 1945, during the battle for Nurnberg.

It is also the site where the Nürnberg American High School later played their football games and hosted field and track meets from the early 1940's until the school closed in 1995.

The banner is a gift from Lieutenant Aman to his son-in-law Terry Jorgensen, 1962 graduate of the Nürnberg American High School, and founder of the NAHS Alumni Association.

The banner is on special loan from the American Overseas Schools Archive in Wichita, to the Museum of World Treasures.

Hilbert Margol — Army

BEN MARTIN

USA/USAF/USN
678-570-0101
TraderBen@Yahoo.com

MY MILITARY EXPERIENCES

In 1964, after a great deal of consternation, I joined the Army and became a Nike Track Radar specialist. My C.O. was Jack Lucas.

A.I.T. was at Redstone Arsenal, skunk capitol of the South. I learned how to catch a skunk without getting squirted.

One hot sticky Saturday night, I was jerked to my feet, while still sleeping, handed a skunk by the tail and left to fend for myself. Passing the live skunk from sleeping man to sleeping man until all were awake. Now what? We had troops from 7 different countries on the base.

There must be a way to prank somebody. Someone produced a German A.F. Garrison Cap stolen from the mess hall. The result was a trip to the German Mountain Troops barracks with skunk in hand. At 1:00 AM no one was awake. We placed the A.F. cap on the steps, opened the screen door and launched the skunk into the barracks. Within a minute there was a great commotion. A howling mob descended on the German A.F. barracks and the fight was on.

In South Korea my ride from Kimpo Air Base to Camp Humphreys was a bus with bars on the windows. I should have known. At a railway crossing, I saw a steam engine on the tracks. What a sight. While waiting for the train to pass, I saw a woman washing her hair in a ditch puddle, and a man not six feet away pissing in the same puddle. I couldn't imagine.

After 13-months in Korea, I was reassigned as an Instructor at the *Ordnance Guided Missile School* at Redstone Arsenal.

In 1976, I found a *"Title 32"* job with the Utah Air guard. I had a 90-man shop and a multi-continent Electronics Installation operation. I used my status as Cadre to take dates to Hawaii aboard KC-135 tankers.

In 1980, the U.S. Navy called to me. *"Fly Navy"* sounded good to me. My first deployment with VA-305 was for carrier qualifications in the Gulf. I never saw anything like it. Young guys would work till they couldn't stand, curled-up in a coil of cables for a nap and then go back to work. I took 11 of them to a strip bar. We wore out the strippers after an hour or so, and they began buying us drinks. You fill in the blanks.

The girls came out to the flight line to wave us off.

At England Air Force Base in 1982, a USAF Deputy Commander for Maintenance walked into my shop and said, *"I want you"*. So, I was back in *Air Force Blue* as an avionics technician in the 917th Maintenance at Barksdale AFB. While working at England AFB, I became a real *live, raise-your-right-hand* Deputy Sheriff in Rapides Parish, LA. I knew it was time to leave when my next-door neighbor started calling me Bubba.

In 1984, I entered a Naval Intelligence School. I was assigned to a *Fleet Intelligence Rapid Support Team*. Last deployment was to the Pentagon Alert Desk. I liked being able to find out anything about anything, but retired from the U.S. Navy in 1994.

MIKE McCABE
USAF
770-855-9729
MikeMcCabe43@Yahoo.com

My Military Experience

I was born in the small town of Forestville. Ohio, just east of Cincinnati, Ohio. It was the 21st day of June 1943, the longest day of the year, especially for my mom.

At that time, I had one older sister, but I was destined to be the oldest boy of six, more to come after me. As the oldest boy, I had to break the way for my younger brothers. All my errors steeled my folks to the point that the follow-ons were compared to me; nothing was a surprise to them. I really made them look good! I wasn't a delinquent, but I had more than my share of frowned upon experiences and I kept my Irish Catholic parents on edge for several years.

I spent my high school after-hours time working at a local drug store, jerking sodas and delivering prescriptions. I still remember my starting wage was **50¢**/ hour. Academically, I wasn't stupid, but I just didn't have the drive to achieve. I was much happier to be working on cars or hunting the small game found around my area. Remembering when I was struggling to pass Latin, my teacher told me, *"McCabe, I'll pass you, if you promise NOT to take Latin II"*. It didn't take long to make that decision! I did squeak through, and managed to graduate. (*A bachelor's degree in Engineering Technology came eighteen years later*).

The year before graduation, my girlfriend's brother went into the U.S. Air Force and that put the desire in me to enter the following year. I followed a typical recruit's path, beginning with Basic Training in San Antonio, Texas, and a follow-up assignment to technical school at Chanute Air Force Base, Illinois, to train as an *Aerospace Ground Equipment Repairman*.

At that time, it was one of the longest tech schools in the service, and we were familiarized with all types of flight line *Yellow Iron*. Most of my class got assignments overseas, with the majority to Japan, and a few to France. I went to France, assigned to Detachment-2, 2nd-Mobil Communications Squadron, Evereux Fauville Air Base, France, and later to Dreux A.B. As fate would have it, the *MOB* had not a spec of yellow equipment. It was all blue, truck mounted, diesel driven equipment, which wasn't taught in tech school at all. Not a big setback for me but kind of comical. It was a great assignment being assigned to a mobile outfit and I got to see a large part of the Middle East, and much of Europe, not to mention when we were not traveling, we were located only 60-miles west of Paris. Many long-lasting memories were gathered on that tour.

Regardless of having such a great 1st -tour, I told myself I should give civilian life a try. So, I took a discharge and landed a job as the assistant to the Chief Engineer (*Ole Ed*) at Mercy Hospital in Cincinnati, Ohio. Ole Ed kept me humping in the boiler room scraping and painting miles of boiler room pipe! Occasionally, Ed would turn me out to change air conditioner filters and light bulbs in the hospital rooms and that was a welcomed part of the job, after spending most of my time in the boiler room. It didn't get its name by accident!

So, after 5-months, I went back in the Air Force for what would be 16-more years. Those years were spent with permanent assignments to Lockbourne AFB, (Columbus, Ohio), Ramstien A.B., Germany, Ankara, Turkey, McChord AFB, (*Washington State -- where our son was born*), CCK A.B., Taiwan, Seymour Johnson AFB, North Carolina, Udorn A.B., Thailand, Altus AFB, Oklahoma, and finally, Scott AFB, Illinois.

That assignment to Seymour Johnson AFB resulted in two 90-day back-to-back TDYs to Ubon A.B., Thailand, to support the bombing of North Vietnam. I suppose most have heard the adage, **"Don't volunteer for anything"?** Well, I never believed it and volunteered for many temporary assignments. I don't recall regretting one of them. Most memorable was a 6-month TDY to Fort Smith, Arkansas. I was part of a maintenance team supporting three C-130's that were crammed full of electronics. These aircraft flew daily sorties, flying orbits over western Arkansas and Eastern Oklahoma. Their mission was to track fighter aircraft flying out of England AFB, Louisiana, as they electronically bombed targets within the C-130 orbits. It was a great TDY.

We were living on the economy, living in a very nice motel, and we had one room set up as *"Tex's Tavern"*. That was our watering hole with draft beer available for those that wished to imbibe. That tavern was a highlight, but best of all . . . I met my wife there in Fort Smith. We were married just before I shipped out for Germany. She caught up with me 2-months later, and we enjoyed many weekends enjoying the many sites of Germany.

We only had about a year there when I got orders for Turkey. That was an experience to remember. It was a small unit, about 30-strong, located across from the Ankara International Airport, just off the taxi way. We had three aircraft to support a C-118, C-54 and a T-29. It was what you would call a good assignment, if you didn't mind not having a commissary, with only a small B.X.

Soot in the winter was omnipresent from the Turkish heating with coal and a perpetual cloud hung over the city. We did have a 3-story NCO Club, that was the center of our social world and where we made many enduring friends. In all, it was a great way to spend the early marriage years. A marriage that will be **56** years' young this coming January 2023.

I received many awards, decorations, and commendations over my 20-year military career, but the real commendations are far more deserved by my wife. While I was off dancing around the world, she handled the hard work of keeping our home together. Through many moves to unfamiliar places, she carried us through. Most importantly, she raised our son in his early years, and helped to shape a young man of whom we are very proud. That young man went forward to earn a Chemical Engineering Degree from Georgia Institute of Technology, and a Law Degree from the University of Georgia. He's now, a retired Patent Attorney and father to two, wonderful grandkids.

Voluntary, Temporary, Duty Assignments: New Delhi, India, Dezful, Iran, Dendolder, The Netherlands, and Tan Son Nhut A.B., RVN.

At Tan Son Nhut Air Base, Saigon, Vietnam, Circa 1971.

Dezful, Iran Supporting Talking Bird Team, 1963.

Talking Bird Team (*along with 2-Iranian Air Force Officers*), Dezful, Iran, 1963.

GEORGE MURPHY

USAF LTC-Retired
RF-4 Pilot
Cell: 470-506-5300
Sambran007@Bellsouth.net

My Military Experience

I Flew reconnaissance in the RF-4 Phantom out of Udorn, Thailand, Sept. 68 - Sept 69, and completed crew transition training at Bergstrom AFB, Texas, and paired up with a B-52 Nav Bombardier; a real wizard on a radar scope.

My instructor had just returned from a 100-mission tour, and his "*not in the book*" training was key in preventing rookie mistakes on early combat missions. Most missions were low altitude / high speed, so my Nav and I made an agreement -- he dodges the rocks and I dodge the flak.

With the holidays coming up, the Nav and I decided volunteering to fly night missions was the best way to get through them. We became one of two crews, "**The Night Owls.**"

One memory I'll always hold was a night mission with a full moon on a jet black Laotian landscape turning every body of water, river, lake and stream to a bright silver. Awesome sight!

Another benefit was the perfect view you had of all the fireworks coming up at you. Nights allowed you to discover the true meaning of *lonesome* -- being the only friendly aircraft over enemy territory. All other air missions were day only. Did put you at the top of the enemies' "*item of interest*" chart.

The night mission we would never forget was an "*in the rocks, down the valleys*" one. Saw a missile light up and head our way. Pulled an 8G descending, evasive maneuver, dumping chaff loaded in our flap and speed brake bays. One of those" *not in the book*" items, which can save your butt. Regular chaff was dispensed from a system, which exploded too far behind the aircraft to fool enemy tracking radars.

Dumping chaff from speed brake and flap bays allowed you to disappear in a cloud of silver for a few precious seconds. During the maneuver one of my system malfunction lights blinked on. As I rolled out, it went out, and since I was busy at the time, I never checked which one it was. All my systems seemed fully functional.. The RF-4 radar system is slaved to read directly in front of the aircraft. The 8Gs caused the radar to reslave 20-30+ degrees off-line, while still presenting a radar reading of straight ahead. We were actually flying through the mountains, instead of the valleys. Only realized something was wrong as we climbed out and found ourselves heading for Cambodia instead of northern Thailand.

Wound up at the bar at 4 AM, trying to drink everything in sight to stop shaking. Nav and I both knew there was someone else in our cockpit that night, since we were unknowingly flying through solid mountains. Both of us remembered that WW-2 book "**God is my co-pilot**" There was definitely a *Higher Power* riding with us on that mission.

~ The End ~

George S. Murphy LTC USAF (*Retired*)

GEORGE NELSON

USMC – Captain

Tel: 770-924-6524

NAG_enterprise@bellsouth.net

One of My Unusual USMC Experiences
Military Story by George Nelson

HOW THE USMC INTRODUCED ME TO SOMETHING EXCITING, INTERESTING, & SPECIAL:

At first, I was a little reluctant to participate in this Viet Nam War story project, because I didn't want to relive the war. However, as I thought about it, there was one thing where the United States Marine Corps played a significant role in something that, from time to time, would be a part of my life for almost 24 years. As far as I know, only a few of my veteran friends know what this exciting, engaging, and unique item is.

If the term *"Horse Racing"* sounds boring to you, then read no further. It was something else the Marine Corps helped nurture into me during my five years of service, and before I was given a disability retirement. Read on, if you know a little about the horse racing game, have ever attended a thoroughbred racetrack, or watched the Kentucky Derby at Churchill Downs on television.

My first exposure to *horse betting* was at the end of December 1961. Two of my college friends and I drove down to Florida during our La Crosse State College Christmas break. Unfortunately, it was the coldest Christmas week in the history of Florida, and we had to find some alternate entertainment other than the beaches. What we found was *Flaggers Dog Track,* and *Hialeah Horse Racing Track*. As it turned out, we spent the daytime hours with the horses, and nights with the dogs. Fortunately, we met several people during the nightly *Happy Hours* at the place we were staying, and they gave us tips on the betting game, as they were there to spend their vacation at the racing facilities.

Although, I remember we made a few bucks at a couple of the racing programs, I'm sure we all lost money by the time we were ready to go back home; I know I did. One thing to remember was … *betting was only legal in a limited number of states*, with Nevada being the most open with its gambling casinos. The only other way to make a legal bet was in those states that had horse or dog betting, and if you wanted to do that, you had to go to the track to make your bets, or find someone to take, and make, your bets for you illegally. These people were called *"Bookies,"* and if you did get lucky and make some profit, the Bookies payoff was always less than the track payoff, and that's how they made most of their money.

Nothing else concerning horse betting happened until a year later. At this point, I had graduated from college, accepted my commission as a 2nd Lieutenant in the United States Marine Corps, and was arriving at Camp Pendleton, located in California, in my brand-new, 1962 black Ford Fairlane 500, with an all-red leather interior. It was one good-looking automobile.

When I checked into the base, no vacant Bachelor Officer's Quarters were available, so I headed to San Clemente, just 10 miles from Camp Pendleton. There, I met up with two other 2nd Lieutenant friends from Basic School -- **Phil Devarenne and Bob Donohue** -- and we went out and were able to rent a house on the cliffs just north of San Clemente Beach on the shores of the Pacific Ocean. We were able to rent it for **$150!** (*per month*), which meant we had a priceless living location for a steal.

The beach house was fully furnished with all essentials, plus a four-foot cactus plant that we could use as a Christmas tree, several radios, and a 19-inch TV; what a deal!

It's funny how fate unknowingly comes into your life when least expected. After we had what little stuff we had moved into the house, I finally turned on one of the radios. It was 6:00 PM, and the program coming on the air was called *"**Turf Craft**,"* whose slogan was, *"The organization with the winning information brings you race results."* At first, I didn't think much of it other than I knew there was a *Santa Anita Racetrack*, but when the announcer started to call the first race of the day, I thought I would give it a listen. It became more interesting when the announcer stated the race results, *"The winner, XXXXX, paid $Y.YY and was today's $100 Turf Craft Wonder Winner service-play-of-the-day."*

To make a long story short, I listened to the whole program as my horse racing interest from the Florida trip a year earlier came to life again. My new roommate Bob and I didn't need to report for duty until the following week, so guess what we did? You got it! We drove the 60 miles to Santa Anita over the next week, before we reported for duty at Camp Pendleton.

All this time, we kept meeting different people in San Clemente and at the racetrack willing to help educate us on the actual horse racing game. It was amazing how *big* the game was on the West Coast back then. The West Coast had first-class horse racing all year between Santa Anita, Hollywood Park, and Delmar. All of these racetracks were built to hold a large capacity crowd, with Santa Anita being the largest at a capacity of over **60,000**. All the tracks were also in excellent condition. It was not unusual to see movie and television stars like Jimmy Durante, Micky Rooney, James Arness, Art Carney, Lee Marvin, and Henry Kulky.

As it turned out, Henry Kulky lived right up the street from us. We became good friends, and he often came to our house when one of his 84 movies or television performances was going to be on the tube. He liked to tell us about all the actors and flaws in the shows. Going to his condo for Sunday dinner was always a big deal, because he was a great cook, and prepared all the meals. The last time I saw him was just before I left for Okinawa on my way to Viet Nam. Unfortunately, I would never see him again. When I returned to the States 13 months later, I discovered that Henry had died of a heart attack while reviewing a new television show script on February 12, 1965. He was 53 years old and had always been a good friend with a great sense of humor. I still miss him.

Because of my new position at Camp Pendleton as an Executive Officer of one of the Marine Infantry Training Regiment's Companies, I could adjust my work schedule to have most

Henry Kulakowich, *a.k.a.*, Henry Kulky.

Wednesday afternoons and Saturdays off. This scheduling allowed me to get serious about the horse racing game.

It didn't take long to find out where the 8:00 PM deliver of the following day's Racing Forms was. The form's primary sale location was a drug store in midtown San Clemente, which had a nice bar across the street.

During the five racing days per week, the bar was always filled in the early evening hours with racing fans waiting for delivery of the next day's *Racing Forms* to the drugstore. Once I got involved with the group, I met many people affiliated with the racing game.

In a short time, I learned more about horse racing than you could shake a stick at, especially when it came to betting, handicapping, and how the insiders controlled the sport. Two primary practices were, (**1**). *never to be afraid of high odds*, and to, (**2**). *play your system with win-only bets*. The trick was, and always has been, to beat the odds if you are going to win. After all, the public and their short-priced favorites *lose* every day!

You also need to realize that you will be tearing up many more losing tickets, than cashing in winning ones. And always play with discipline, discipline, **discipline**. I have always believed that you can't beat the races, but you can beat the race. What that means is … to be *selective* in the races you play. **Avoid** *maiden or 2-year-old races*, races with big purses like *High-Grade Allowance* or *Handicap races*, and *Stakes races*. These races are the most honest, resulting in a smaller win price. My system was designed for a race that could be tampered with, usually resulting in higher win prices. I listened to the `Turf Craft Show` whenever possible and started reading everything I could about *how to play the horses*.

I started using other people's ideas on *how to play the races*, but a few months later, I began to develop my own system. I created several betting systems that *failed*, but finally … made something that had some merit. I opted to ignore the standard items used by most systems like weight, finish position in last race, days since last race, win record, speed rating, *etc*. My system went against many of these golden measurements of horse racing that only produced **30%** winners with very low payoffs. My approach had fewer *winners*, but *much higher profits*.

As my system improved, I started increasing the bets, and by April 1963, all my bets were $50, win only, and that has been my standard bet ever since.

I used to average 4-5 plays per day; some were good, and some were bad. My longest winning streak was seven in a row, with the winning odds being between **4-to-1** *and* **13-to-1**. My longest losing streak was 14 races. My biggest winning odds were **112-to-1** *and* **100-to-1**. I also had several others that paid over **50-to-1**. The overall win percentage was about **16%** and the overall win price was just over **8-to-1**, which meant the average profit per win was *just under* **30%** of the money spent to get that win.

After accumulating 12 months of racing forms and racing statistics, it was time to head for Viet Nam. This presented a problem, because I didn't want to discard all the racing information I had accumulated. After all, I was hoping to return home someday and put some of the information back to work. What was I going to do with all this stuff? The answer was ... *my cousin* **Shirley Hamilton**, who lived with her husband in San Diego, CA. Although I never told them I had horse racing stuff in over half of the five storage boxes, they said it would be okay to store them in the overhead of their garage. I then went through a major sorting job before I showed up on their doorstep with the boxes.

I had marked three of the boxes with large lettering reading "**RF**." When Shirley's husband saw the letters, he said, "*What do the letters mean, **RAT FINK**?*" I responded, "*Close enough,*" and left it at that. As far as I know, no one ever knew what was in those boxes. Thank goodness, because being a pony player was not the most respectable profession.

When I returned to the States, the Marine Corps was good to me, again. This time, they stationed me 20 minutes from Arlington Park Race Trak in Arlington Heights, IL. I became the Adjutant for the **C**ommanding **G**eneral (*Art Adams*) of the 4th **Marine Air Wing**. I was there until July 1967, when my disability retirement was approved, and my new wife, *Barbara*, and I built a new house in Arlington Heights. We lived there for 11 of the next 12 years, and I was now only 15 minutes from the track!

4th Marine Air Wing

Semper Fi

George A. Nelson, Captain, USMC
~ **Member, The Georgia Military Veterans Hall of Fame** ~
~ ***The End*** ~

SANTA ANITA HORSE RACING PARK.

Para-Mutual Betting Results Scoreboard

During that time, I was working for **IBM**, and when they transferred me to White Plains, NY, I started a new phase in my horse racing career. I stopped betting, and became a local, small-time Bookie. Now that was fun and very profitable. But all the horse racing stuff ended in 1986, when my family and I moved to Roswell, GA, and we still live in the northern suburbs of Atlanta, today.

There is much more to horse racing, and I know I have not gone into much detail explaining the game, but if it wasn't for my time in the Marine Corps and at Camp Pendleton, this important part of my life would have never been discovered.

My Military Experiences

On August 5, 1990 (*as a reservist*), I set myself up for my two week annual tour at **SAC** (*Strategic Air Command*) Headquarters as an understudy to the one star Commander of all SAC Command Posts. For two days, my boss would walk-in, in the morning, tell me to handle everything on his desk, and walk out with no explanation. Because of the initial *high classification*, he & few majors, were working in the back room for the initial planning.

Wednesday, he walked-in and asked me how long I could stay? I, of course, told him, "As long as need be, Sir." (*That, ended up being five weeks!*). Then, he told me that I, and five local active-duty Colonels were going to form a Battle Staff. You can guess who got the night shift – **Me**, the Reservist!!! We started planning to send SAC assets, *i.e.,* B-52's, KC-135's, *etc.* to the sand box (*i.e.,* Operation Desert Shield).

Friday night about 2100-hrs., a note came down from the four-Star, who wanted to know how many B-52's & KC-135's we could put on Diego Garcia ???

Not having the computers & Apps, *etc.*, to do all that magic stuff back then, we were at a loss on how to answer his question! To make a long story short ... we took an airport diagram of Diego Garcia, made a copy of that airport diagram about the size of the top of a desk, and then made "*paper airplanes*" **to scale**, and practiced what we call an "*Elephant Walk*"-- that's moving these big airplanes around so that if number three or four in the line of 10 airplanes had a mechanical problem, you were able to move them out of the way and still launch the rest of the airplanes, because if you didn't figure out how to pull number three or four out of line and get the ones behind it launched, that could mean ***not as many bombs on target***, and probably causing a bunch of guys on the ground to be overrun and die **!!!** So, yes ... I made General by doing my job for over a quarter of a century, being in the right place at the right time, and answering the tricky question . . . WITH "***PAPER*** "airplanes**!** Go figure, eh? 😊😊

Reserve A-10, B-1, B-2, B-52, F-15 and F-16 units in the Central United States.

General Pfister entered the Air Force through Officer Training School at Lackland AFB, Texas, in March 1964, and completed pilot training at Craig AFB, Ala., in May 1965. He then flew KC-135s with the 919th Air Refueling Squadron, including 16 months in Southeast Asia. As a Reserve officer, he has served in the unit program as well as individual mobilization augmentee at three numbered Air Forces, two major Commands and at the Air Staff level. His command experience includes Strategic Air Command's Desert Shield and Desert Storm Battle Staff. His joint experience includes U.S. Atlantic Command and Strategic Command's "Looking Glass" Battle Staff.

In his civilian occupation, he was a Senior Captain with a Delta Air Lines

EDUCATION

1963 Bachelor of Science degree in psychology, University of Houston 1979 Air Command and Staff College

1981 Industrial College of the Armed Forces, Washington, D.C 1983 State Department Senior Seminar,

Washington, D.C.

ASSIGNMENTS

1. April 1964 - May 1965, student, undergraduate pilot training, Craig AFB, AL
2. July 1965 - September 1965, student, KC-135 training, Castle AFB, CA
3. October 1965 - May 1969, 919th Air Refueling Squadron, Turner AFB, GA, and McCoy AFB, FL
4. September 1969 - August 1970, 433rd Airlift Wing, Kelly AFB, Texas
5. September 1970 - August 1974, Air Operations Officer, Eastern Air Force Reserve Region, Dobbins AFB, GA.
6. September 1974 - August 1976, Air Operations Officer, Central Air Force Reserve Region, Ellington and Bergstrom AFB's, Texas
7. August 1976 – Oct. 1981, Air Operations Officer, Headquarters Military Airlift Command, Scott AFB, IL
8. November 1981 - August 1984, mobilization augmentee, Airlift and Rescue Division, Directorate of Operations, Headquarters U.S. Air Force, Washington, D.C.
9. August 1984 - January 1988, Mobilization Assistant, Pacific and East Asia Division, Directorate of Plans, Headquarters U.S. Air Force, Washington, D.C
10. January 1988 - August 1991, mobilization assistant to the Director, Command Control, Headquarters Strategic Air Command, Offutt AFB, NE.
11. August 1991 - present, mobilization assistant to the Commander, 8th Air Force, Barksdale AFB, LA

FLIGHT INFORMATION:
Rating: **Command Pilot** **Flight hours:** More than **3,000** military; **19,000** civilian
Military aircraft flown: B-1B, B-52, C-119, C-124, C-130, EC-135, F-15, F-16, HH-43, KC-10, KC-135, RB-50, T-29, T-33, T-37, T-38 and Navy E6B
Civilian aircraft flown: A-310, B-727, 737, 747, 757, 767, CV-880, DC-8, DC-9 and check airman on L-1011 and MD-11

MAJOR AWARDS AND DECORATIONS:
Defense Meritorious Service Medal
Air Medal with two Oak Leaf Clusters
National Defense Service Medal
Vietnam Service Medal
Republic of Vietnam Campaign Medal

EFFECTIVE DATES OF PROMOTION:
Second Lieutenant March 30, 1964
First Lieutenant Sept. 30, 1965
Captain Sept. 30, 1967
Major April 17, 1974
Lieutenant Colonel Sept. 22, 1980
Colonel Aug. 1, 1984
Brigadier General July 31, 1991
Major General Feb. 29, 1996
(*Current as of January 1999*)

F-16

F-15

B-52

B-1

Delta L-1011

PETE PILLAR

U.S. Army
Transportation Corps
404-771-5733
PPillar@att.net

As a student at Wofford College, I was enrolled in **ROTC**, and served as Captain of the **ROTC**'s Rifle Team (*a competitive firearm shooting-skill affair*). The **NRA** (*National Rifle Association*) sponsored a collegiate Rifle Match of all ROTC teams in 1967, and Wofford placed ... **27**th. ☹ Our Team was hampered with *Inferior Equipment*, and what equipment we did have, was not enough to equip each Rifle Team member with a suitable *Rifle!* ☹

After I graduated from Wofford College in August of 1967, I was commissioned a 2nd Lieutenant and was off to Fort Eustis, Virginia, to attend the Transportation Corps' Officer Basic Course **(O.B.C.)**. The curriculum revolved around the study of Trains, Planes, Boats, and Trucks, and how they served our U.S. Army's needs, *coming-and-going*. Following the O.B.C., I was assigned to Fort Benning, Georgia, at the *Center Troop Command*. While at Ft. Benning, I was sent TDY to New York City to attend a course on, "***Improving Safety In The U.S. Army***." My memory is sketchy as to what we learned there, but do remember receiving post-graduate level credit from New York University.

My #2 most-memorable event while back at Ft. Benning, was a **James Brown** Concert I attended in Columbus, Georgia. The audience went . . . ***CRAZY!*** They clearly **LOVED** `The Godfather of Soul,` and his distinctive brand of Soul Music.

In late Spring 1968, I received my Orders to Vietnam, and promptly got married before I departed the U.S.A. (*it SEEMED like the thing to do, at the time*). Upon arrival in Vietnam, I learned I would be assigned to `B` Company, 9th Supply & Transport (**S&T**) Battalion, 9th Infantry Division, in Dong Tam. `B` Company was a Light, Medium Truck Company, equipped with 2½ Ton Trucks and 5-Ton Tractors & Trailers. The S & T Battalion supported a *Re-Arm & Re-Fuel site*, where I believe 2.75" Rockets, 7.62-Caliber Linked Ammunition, 40-MM-Linked, and fuel were handled by the aircrew members. I saw every Rotary Wing Aircraft in-country, including the CH-54 Flying Cranes, [*from the underside*😊😊]

My Platoon Sergeant and I developed a very interesting working relationship. He did **not** want to leave the Division Base Camp, *EVER!* ... and, I was fine with running all the Convoys myself. Travel was either up & back to Long Binh outside of Saigon, or throughout the Mekong Delta region of IV-Corps. One of the ironic problems we had was not getting tires for trucks, or if tires *were* available, you couldn't get tubes for the tires. So, it was not uncommon to view our patched tire tubes looking like quilts.

In 1969, **Bob Hope** brought his **U.S.O. Show** to our base camp at Dong Tam, and *THAT* was a **BIG DEAL** back then! Hope was joined by **Ann-Margret, Rosey Grier, Penny Plummer** (The newly-crowned, *'Miss World'*), **Honey Ltd.** (*a 4-beautiful ladies' musical group*), **Les Brown and his Band of Renown**, *et. al.* I had a new Jeep and, therefore, was one of several Escort Officers directed to provide transportation for Bob Hope's Entourage. I ended up with two young women from the 4-Ladies' band, *"Honey Ltd,"* and was up-close-and-personal with Ann-Margret.

My 1-year tour in Vietnam began to close out with Neil Armstrong on the Moon, and rumors that the 9th Infantry Division would begin to draw-down Stateside. When I got to Vietnam a year earlier, there were no speed limits, and no paved roads. As I was leaving, the M.P.'s were using Radar Guns to catch speeders. Go figure, eh? If we did nothing else to modernize Vietnam, we can always say, *"We gave them Speed Limits."* By now, the Communists have done away with them, too, right?

The beautiful & talented Ann-Margret, along with The Lovely *Honey Ltd.*, during Bob Hope's U.S.O. Show stop-over at Dong Tam Base Camp, Vietnam.

(TOP): Lt. Pete Pillar, back from RVN. (BELOW): Pete (on Left) enjoying a cold adult beverage with his Sergeant.

Bob Hope Entourage arrives in Vietnam in 1969 to resume their U.S.O. Show for the Troops

1969 Bob Hope U.S.O. Show w/ Margret, Rosey Grier, et. al.

My Secret Army Life

Once a Upon a Time in a far-off sector of the United States, a young lad merely 17-years of age, who hailed from the Commonwealth of Massachusetts in a City founded in 1640 known as Gloucester, and who decided that he **had** to escape from the island of little or no future, and so joined the United States Army.

The narrative begins:

I was in the United States Army Security Agency for 4 years; it was a *Secret* Organization. That's all you need to know! If you are reading this as a free person.... *You Are Welcome*!

The real narrative:

While in High School, the Army Recruiter came and gave a wonderful presentation on how young men & women could advance in occupational training and enjoy a wonderful future. I took the initial tests that the Recruiter furnished, and finished with very high scores, according to the Sergeant. I fell for it and decided to investigate joining the Army Intelligence Branch on a 3-year enlistment. After a short interview, I was convinced to pursue a 4-year enlistment to get into the U.S. Army Security Agency, a super-secret branch that he could neither get, nor provide, any further information about. The Land of Spooks and Spies was too intriguing to pass up. After all … it was only one more year.

Basic Training at Ft. Dix, New Jersey, was my introduction to the "real" Army until my 6th week, when I was called down to the Army Security Office to be informed that I was granted a Top-Secret Clearance and I would be assigned to Fort Devens in Ayer, Massachusetts, for New Language Training. At Ft. Devens, I was trained in Morse Code and Radio Intelligence Intercept. After qualifying at 18-word groups per minutes, I informed my OIC (Officer-in-Charge) that I could not envision listening to Morse Code for 4-years and would like to be cross-trained into something I would be able to use in civilian life after my enlistment. My request was granted, and I attend Military Police Training at Ft. Gordon, Georgia. It was February and the snow in Massachusetts was knee deep so that sounded great to me as I aspired to become a State Trooper in the future. Also, I was told there was no snow in Georgia So, off to Georgia taking 13-hours of flight time, because of the snowstorms on the east coast, all the way to Ohio. We landed in Augusta, GA, with about 1-inch of snow on the ground. Great improvement.

After about 4-weeks in M.P. School, they washed me out because I was NOT 19-years of age, which was their bare minimum at the time. So, ASA sent me to Comm Center School, and then on to Crypto Training. I was finally in my element of an easy life in the Army. That was a breeze. Then, it was off to Germany in May of 1964. I was assigned to the 319th USASA Bn, where I spent about two fun-filled years chasing every blue-eyed blond and consumed more than my share of a local Hercules Bier. Initially, I worked in S-1 in support of the "Allied Military Mission", S-2, and the Com Center. I volunteered for every FTX that Group Hdqts. participated in, just for the experience, and hopefully, rank advancement. I volunteered for Vietnam and was turned down, because I had scored very high on my Pro-Pay Worldwide Test. I thought that the Army in their wisdom, would reject the transfer request because of the critical standing of my test. Four months later, I received orders to report to Davis Station, 509th RR (USASA) GROUP, Saigon, Republic of Vietnam. Ten days' notice to clear Germany, and head to Vietnam. Yikes!! This was NOT in my plans at all. I had to dump my girlfriends, my apartment in the city of Kassel, my Mercedes, and more hurtful of all, my beloved Bier! Thus begins the conversion of the Prodigal Son named Bruce.

Within an hour of arriving in Saigon, we got mortared! Double Yikes!! My stay in Saigon was short as they "had no open slots" for my MOS. So, rather than send me back to the States or Germany, they sent me to Battalion Hdqts. in Nha Trang. It was an R&R center atmosphere. However, they had the same issue and sent me to the 1st Air Cavalry in An Khe, in the Central Highlands of Vietnam. Not quite the garden spot I would have picked. But it was a great unit where the "Esprit de Corps" was extremely high. I was promoted to Sergeant /E-5 and Comm Center Trick Chief. That year found me as NCOIC of the Special Units assigned to LZ English, LZ Hammond, and LZ Betty, primarily working ARDF ground and associated comm stuff, which included a brief stay in the Field Hospital back at An Khe. To top the adventures off, a small group of about 12 of us were pulled out of the field to prepare to fly to Israel in late April/early May 1967, for support of the war buildup in the Middle East.

Luckily for us, the war only lasted for 6-days, and we were to dress down and relax. My enlistment time was nearing an end. A reenlistment offer of E-6, Bronze Star, and Purple Heart was dangled in front of me, all of which I declined in order to go home to that island city of Gloucester, Massachusetts, where I could attend college, get married, and have children.

I worked for Anaconda Wire & Cable, Anixter Brothers, and American Wire & Cable before moving to Georgia.

I was ordained a Permanent Deacon for the Archdiocese of North Georgia and assigned as Scout Chaplain for all the Boy & Girl Scouts of the Archdiocese for 10 years. Currently, I've been assigned to Transfiguration Catholic Church for the past 38 years.

The luncheon group was started with Rick McDowell (now deceased), Jack Kowall, Mike Lichter (now deceased), and me. It was great to be able to have lunch with about 20 guys or so each Monday, before turning it over to T.D. Jorgensen, with whom attending Veterans has increased to about 35 - 40 Veterans each Monday, and the total registered membership has grown to 193.

That is all the B.S. I could conjure up on this cold October morning! 😊

~ The End, *So Far* ~

Cell: 678-697-9958
OneIrishman40@Yahoo.com

MY MILITARY EXPERIENCES

On or about 1965, when I took over the NAVAIDS shop as supervisor at Vandenberg Air Force Base, there was a 2nd-class Airman named Veresck. I noticed that whenever anything went wrong, they were always blaming Veresck for it. Anything and everything is Veresck's fault.

When I asked about him, I found out that he had messed up once before I got there. The supervisors at that time did not want him to move beyond it. They will never let him forget about it, even though it had been a long time, and it was just a mistake.

Then it became my time to do the A.P.R., based on the work he had performed, so I gave him 8 and 9 out of a possible 10 score.

The Endorsing Officer lowered it down to 3, which is a huge difference from what I gave him. Because of this discrepancy, I had been called to report to the Wing Commander to explain the difference. I explained to them what I learned, and that he messed up one time, and they are not letting him forget about it.

After the Endorsing Officer met with the Wing Commander, he had to explain about the low rating he had given to Airman Viresck compare to the high rating that I gave. I do not know what transpired next in that closed-door meeting between the Wing Commander and the Endorsing Officer, because what I learned was that Viresck was promoted on the next promotion round.

Also, while I was talking to the Wing Commander, I mentioned to him about their encouragement to us about using a bicycle as a form of transportation. The problem is that the storm drain cover bars were parallel to the road, which a bicycle tire could go into, and might bring harm us or cause an accident. As I left his office, I saw civil engineers putting steel straps on the storm drain to prevent bicycle tires from going in.

On or about 1965-1966, while stationed at Camp New Amsterdam, I was walking on a dirt path, I saw what appeared to be a large pipe. I saw people walking on that dirt path and just kicking it.

I told E.O.D. about it and they went out there and examined it. They found out that what appeared to be a large pipe was actually an unexploded bomb from World War II.

When I was in Vietnam, 1967-1968, I was an Air Policeman, whose main duty was building guard towers and security control rooms. Since I was the one in-charge, what we had to do was to drive around during the daytime to find the things that we needed, then go back at night and get them. Because we were resourceful, we were able to build the necessary guard tower and security control room that basically protected our base.

On or about 1976, I was stationed at Dobbins Air Force Base. We had few Airmen living in the barracks. No mess hall, unless it was a duty weekend. We had no transportation. I decided to talk to Congressman McDonalds about it. As a result of that meeting, a small portion of the mess hall was opened to the active-duty people living in the barracks.

These were some of my military experiences during my U.S.A.F. career.

JIM ROGERS
Captain, USAR, (1966 - 1975)
Army Aviator
Flight Class 68-6
Vietnam '68 to '69
(UH-1C, AH-1G and OH-6A)
Maintenance Officer
D Co., 101st Avn., Bn 101st Airborne Div.
678-494-9760   JRogers04@ATT.net

My Military Experience

My military service began in March 1966. I knew that the Draft was coming so I got myself qualified for the Army Warrant Officer Candidate Flight Program (WOC, for short). Prior to entering, I received my Draft Notice, so I decided to go in on March 16, 1966. Before being inducted, I had to take a P.I. (Physical Inspection). Unfortunately, I had been working around heavy machinery before entering, and my hearing was down, so I was disqualified from the program. Since my draft notice was coming up, I had no other choice but to go ahead and enter service on the 16th. I wanted to stay in Aviation, so I choose Aviation Maintenance as my Primary after Basic.

On the day of my Induction, I caught a bus from Columbus, Georgia, to Fort Polk, Louisiana, for eight weeks of being yelled at, crawling in the mud, and a lot of physical training. I went in at 147 lbs. and came out at 165 lbs., solid as a rock and a 28" waist. I shot Expert on the M-14 and did better than 400 on the P.T. Test. I actually enjoyed Basic Training and, in my 2nd-week was made the Platoon Guide, which I held for the remainder of the 6-weeks. When I completed Basic on May 18th, I caught a train in Leesville, LA, to my home station of Columbus, Georgia, where I enjoyed Leave for one week.

My next duty station was Fort Rucker, Alabama, for A.I.T. (Advance Infantry Training) in Aircraft Maintenance. In my first month, I was trained on the O-1 Bird Dog. Then, in my second month I was trained on the U-6 Beaver, and on my third month I was trained on the OV-1 Mohawk. During my final week, the Company Commander called me in and asked if I wanted to go to OCS (Officer Candidate School), which I jump on immediately. They only had the three combat arms available, Armor, Artillery, and Infantry. I chose Armor. Two weeks later, I was heading for Fort Knox, Ky.

When I first reported to my new Class and Company assignment, our Class was told that they had made a mistake and that out Class wouldn't start until December, so our whole class was put out in some of the Basic and A.I.T. Units until our class began. On Dec. 7, 1966, our Class began for O.C.S., Class #16-67, Company H-2. After 6 months of being yelled at again, and doing a hundred thousand pushups, I was Commissioned a Second Lieutenant on May 21, 1967. During our last weeks of training, the Company Commander asked our Class if anyone wanted to go to Fight School, which I jumped at, and this time I fully qualified. There were eight others in my Platoon that also qualified.

Since my Flight Class wouldn't begin until September, I played S-3 in a Battalion Headquarters for three months. After taking a couple of weeks of Leave at home in Columbus, GA, I headed out in my brand new 1967 GTO to Fort Wolters, Texas, wherever that was? There wasn't much of an Interstate Highway at that time, so most of the road was 2-lane. I met up with a guy in Montgomery, Alabama, heading in the same direction in his '67 Malibu Super Sport, and we raced through the rest of Alabama, Mississippi, and Louisiana, and I lost him somewhere around Shreveport, LA. When I arrived at Fort Wolters and signed-in at the Officer Student Company, I ran into one of the guys that I went to O.C.S. with, so we found a house in Mineral Wells to live in while in Flight School.

For the next couple of days as we got settled in at our new place, and our Class 68-6 formed, and we received our Flight Gear, and met with our I.P.'s (Instructor Pilots). I was assigned for my first phase of training with Captain Jimmy Stewart on the TH-55. The first 3-4 days were spent learning how to hover that vertical take-off Messerschmidt at the three-foot level, and then we were off; learning how to take off and land was a breeze after that hovering exercise. While I was in my 2nd-Phase of Training on the TH-55 with CW2 Ricky Nelson, Captain Stewart was killed while flying another student and flew up into some high-power lines, and one of the blades from the helicopter hit him in the back of the head and killed him; his student survived. In January, we completed our Primary Flight Training and were heading to Hunter Army Airfield in Savannah, GA, for Advanced Flight Training in the UH-1 Huey.

The Advance Phase of our training was on the UH-1D or H. I can't remember who my fight instructors were in this phase of our training, but they must have been good, because I came out fully qualified as an Aviator, and received my Wings on May 21, 1968. On May 24th, I was promoted to First Lieutenant, got married, and received Orders for A.M.O.C. (Aircraft Maintenance Officers Course) at Fort Eustis, VA. I'm not sure why I received Orders for A.M.O.C., but think it was because of my earlier training at Fort Rucker. After three months, I graduated, and took a couple weeks Leave and then headed to Vietnam.

I arrived in Saigon, Vietnam, on October 11, 1968, and after a short stay caught a C-130, and headed to I-Corps, landing in Phu Bai. Someone picked me up at the airfield and took me to Camp Eagle to report into Delta Company, 101st Aviation Battalion, in the 101st Airborne Division. I reported to the Company Commander Major Ronald C. Perry, and after a short introduction and meeting with the other unit personnel, I was assigned as the Company Maintenance Officer. The unit had 16 UH-1C gunships, and only 8-flyable with two hanger queens. The helicopters were scattered all over the place and most of the maintenance was being done out in the open. Within a month I had all of our gunships flyable except the two hanger queens -- my first big accomplishment. By December, our Unit moved to a new location in Phu Bi at a large PSP pad for helicopters with PSP bunkers and two large maintenance tents. The area had already been built, and had great places for all of us to live-in. After Camp Eagle, this was Heaven. By January, we had the U.S.N. Seabees build an Officer's Club for us along with a large refrigerator, and a Horseshoe-shaped bar. By the end of February, we were boxing up our Huey Charlie models, and getting in new AH-1G Cobras. I was one the first pilots to go to Vung Tau for Cobra transition, and after two weeks, I was back at my Unit, test flying the new Cobra to get them mission ready.

In May, our Company lost its first and only pilot during my tour. John M. Rucker, who had two weeks before DEROS'ing back to the USA, and probably 1,000 hours of Fight Time. He took off from our area and right outside of our perimeter were a bunch of rolling knolls with a large creek running through them. The engine had quit in the Cobra he was flying, and when he went to set it down one of the skids hit the top of a knoll and turned the aircraft upside down into the creek submersing the canopy of the aircraft. John was in the back seat and his door fell against the knoll making it impossible for him to get out. David, who was in the front seat, was able to get out of the aircraft, but was unable to break the canopy to get John out so he drowned. The really sad part, besides him dying, was that a week before this happened, John had received a "Dear John letter," from his wife and he was planning to return to the States, to try and work things out with his wife. I'm sure that this must have been on his mind. I will never understand why our C.O. sent him out on this last Mission.

In the next couple of months, our unit was asked to go down and support the Americal Division at Chu Lai, since they were getting beat up so bad in their area by the VC and NVA. We were told that there was an area between DaNang and Chu Lai that had a large enemy force, and when flying down there to either fly at 10,000 feet over that area, or along the coast. One day while we were supporting the Americal Division, one of our Cobras sitting in a bunker took a direct hit from a mortar. Our Commander called back up to our Unit and asked me to bring another Cobra down to replace the damaged one. Since it was just a ferry flight, I decided to go by myself. As I was going through the Hy Mann Pass, I radioed DaNang Control to let them know that I was flying through their airspace from the north to the south at 10,000 feet and flashed my light to let them know that it was me. As I cleared their airspace, I called again to let them know that I was clear and descending down to the coastline, which I followed until I reached the Americal Div.

My Commander arranged with the Americal to have someone take me back to my unit in Phu Bai. We were in a Huey going back and I was sitting in the back seat of the aircraft, and since it was going to be a short flight, I decided that I didn't need to wear my helmet or buckle up. As we are cruising along the coast … all of a sudden, the pilot decides to go tree top level over none other than the enemy territory. As I jumped out of my seat to tell him to get the hell out of this area … and before I could reach him, all Hell broke loose with rounds flying everywhere around us. At least he was smart enough to pull pitch to climb, and turned right, to go back to the coast. When we landed in DaNang, and after I chewed his ass out, up one side and down the other for almost getting us killed, he explained that he thought that we had cleared the enemy area and was going to take a short cut over to DaNang.

I told him by not thinking at the right times can get you killed in this country. We went around and counted the bullet holes in the aircraft, there were 32 of them, and as amazing as it may sound, 2 of them went through the seat I was setting in, so in a way by jumping out of the seat earlier, I, literally, saved my own ass. I caught another ride home, and when we arrived, I told our X.O. what had happened and that I had been nicked in the leg from one of the bullets. He wanted to put me in for a **Purple Heart,** and I told him I can just see how this was going to read, "For Meritorious service and in the face of the enemy Captain Jimmy Rogers is awarded the *Purple Hear*t, while sitting in the back of a helicopter, and while jumping up to warn the pilot that he was heading into hostile territory, and by doing so, was nicked in the leg while under fire, and literally saved his own ass." I told him to save the Purple Hearts for those that really earn them.

On October 11, 1969, my tour had ended and as I was leaving my Unit, the Monsoon was setting in and had already flooded our area. Again, I caught a C-130 back down to Cam Ranh Bay to catch my flight back to the Land of Round Door Knobs. Before I left, I got a hot steam bath and a massage to clean out all the red dirt in my pores. My Orders were to report back to Fort Wolters, TX

On an added note: In January or February 1970, the `Stars and Stripes,` recognized our Unit D-Co., 101st Avn. Bn., and was written up for having the best aircraft availability in the country for 1969, 94.6%. Even though my name wasn't mentioned, I know that this was my second big accomplishment, and was glad that our Unit got the recognition it deserved.

While I was on General Staff, in the Admin Division under General Starry in 1974, the Officer/NCO Clubs, Post Exchange, all schools on post, the golf courses, CFC, and Community Centers, all came under our Division. During this time, we opened a new Post Exchange at Fort Knox and had **Barbi Benton**, *(the popular centerfold at the time for `Playboy` magazine that year)* at our opening ceremony, and guess who was her escort? Well, good guess!   None other than yours truly for the whole day. If you don't remember her, you can find her today, online. She was one good-looking woman, but her body was even more enticing, if you know what I mean. She was the kind of woman your wife wouldn't approve of you staring at.One final tidbit I would like to share with you . . . while I was stationed at Fort Knox, I was qualified in the OH-58A helicopter, and during my last assignment as the Commander of an Armor A.I.T. unit, I was asked to fly some photographer for the U.S. Army to take airborne, to videotape for a commercial of Army tanks in-action in the field, which was my Company. At one point, I had my helicopter almost completely on its side in a 90-degree banking turn. I think that this video was eventually on national TV and used for a recruiting ad commercial for the Army Armor Corps.

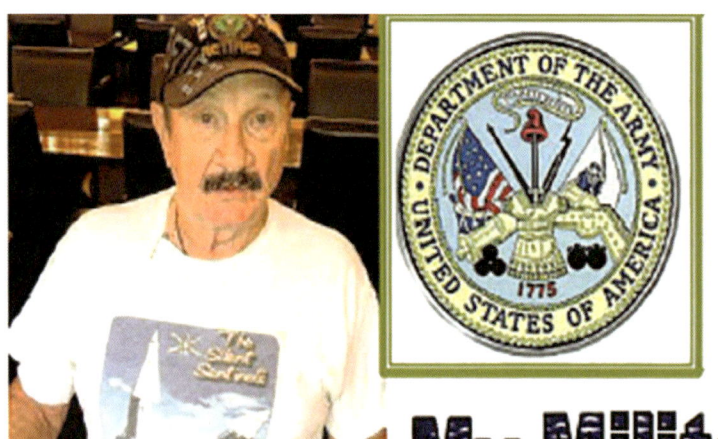

ROBIN SMITH
U.S. ARMY
Warrant Officer 2 (Retired)
Cell: 770-843-1110
RSmithCW2@aol.com

My Military Experiences

My short, abridged version of my 20-years active duty in a defensive weapons field.

I joined the Army National Guard in Macon, Georgia, my hometown, in November 1958 at age 17 1/2, so I could shoot on their smallbore rifle team. I took my 6-months active-duty after graduation from high school starting in July, 1959. I took Basic Training at Fort Jackson, South Carolina, and then stayed there to take training to be an Army Truck Driver. My last 5-weeks at Ft. Jackson had me driving a Staff Car for the post Inspector General, and I seemed to do everything right. I got off of active-duty in 5-months and 13-days, and went home to Macon, GA, where I again attended weekly National Guard meetings. Because I had missed the first 3-months of the college year, I had a part-time job until September 1960, and then started at Georgia Institute of Technology (a.k.a., Georgia Tech), planning to be an Engineer.

However, I had a hot-rod Chevrolet and a girlfriend in Atlanta, so I was making low grades at Tech. So, in August of 1961, I went down to the Central Recruiting Station in Atlanta to see about going on active-duty for a few years. I was absolutely positive that I didn't want to be a U.S. Marine, and I also left out the U.S. Navy, because I liked girls, a lot; and there were no women on ships in those days, so I didn't want to take a chance on being out to sea all the time. That left the U.S. Air Force, and I had heard of a program that someone with very high scores on all the standard tests, plus at least some college, could enlist for, and upon graduation, would have a Commission as a 2nd Lieutenant. The Air Force Recruiter gave me the bad news: "You are about 2-weeks late!" Two weeks ago, I could have gotten you into that program, but now the requirements have changed. I then asked, "If I give up my National Guard rank of SP-4 and come in as an E-2, how long would it take me to get back to E-4?" His answer, "Probably 3-years or so, after all, it is Peacetime now, so promotions are slow." So, I went to the Army Recruiter and asked the same questions. "You will get PFC back in 90 days, if you don't screw up. Probably get E-4 back within twelve months." So, I held up my right hand and told him, "Sarge, sign me up for the duration!" He then answered, "But son, it is peacetime." To which I answered, "Yes, that is what I am signing up for the duration of!"

I went on active-duty on 3 August, 1961, as an E-2, with over 2-years of service, which gave me a little more money that an E-1 under-2 years would get paid. That afternoon, I was in-charge of a bus, loaded with 32 new Recruits, who were all going to Fort Jackson. Once we arrived there, we had to take all the Standard Tests, which was my second time in two years, so I did really well on all the tests except radio-code, which I flunked on purpose. That afternoon, the raw Recruits were issued one uniform with what we called a KP Cap. There were two other Prior Servicemen in our group, and the three of us were issued only a different cap than the raw recruits. The following day, the other two guys were told they had to do Basic Training over again, but I was told that I didn't have to do that, because I finished Basic at Fort Jackson, less than 2-years ago, So, over the next several days, I marched the group around for physicals, shots, and all the tests. Then I was issued new uniforms and given Orders to report to my first Army unit, on an Air Force Base! That didn't just happen; I had signed up for a fairly-new and exciting field of Nike-Hercules Air Defense Missiles, while my mother, father and later, my brother, worked for the Air Force as D.A. Civilians there. So, I signed up to be a Nike-Hercules Missileman.

On the morning of 08/10/1961, I was standing in the hallway, waiting to process in at my new unit. The only Khaki uniform I had that wasn't all wrinkled up from being in a duffel bag was my National Guard one, from which I removed the SP-4 stripes. I still wore a 48th Armored Division patch on my left shoulder, and my Armor brass on my collar as I stood there. Then, something funny happened. A young 2nd Lieutenant, who had probably just graduated from college ROTC in June, walked up to me, looked at my uniform, then reached up to grip my left lapel, which had the Armor brass on it. He looked me directly in the face and asked, "Soldier, do you know that you are wearing the wrong brass?" Hey, I saw that he was a 2nd Lieutenant, but I just couldn't help myself, so I answered his silly question! "Yes Sir, I am aware of that, but I have only been in the Army for one week, so what do you expect?" Instantly, I knew that was the wrong answer, but it was too late to change my statement. He gave me a scowl and asked, "Soldier, are you sassing me?" (By the way, the Lieutenant in question just happened to be an extremely dark African-American, so that was a double NO-NO in 1961!) "No, Sir! I would never do that, I have my orders right here and am trying to process in today, so I should have the correct brass to wear in an hour or so." I opened up my stack of papers, and showed him the date of my enlistment, 3 August, and he looked at me sort of apologetically, and while shaking his head he said, "Well, I will just be damned! You actually have been in the Army for only one week!"

That afternoon, I learned that I would be working in the Battalion Command Post, because of my really high grades on all the tests, and would have some of the best working conditions and hours of anyone in the Battalion. Our van was air-conditioned and no bugs entered it. I also learned that the 2nd Lieutenant, who had inspected my brass was to be my crew chief, so I would be around him constantly whenever I was on-duty. Then, I learned that our control facility was

16-miles East of Robins AFB, where our HQ buildings were. The Senior NCO informed me that I had to get a Military Drivers License, because, as the lowest ranking man on my crew, I would be driving our Chevrolet Carry-all back and forth. I reached in my wallet and showed him the Military License I had gotten when I fished school at Fort Jackson, and noted that it had no expiration date. So, from then on, I drove the carry-all back and forth, each shift change. On 13 August 1961, the East Germans began to build the "Berlin Wall," which almost resulted in the outbreak of WWIII, even though I had only been in the Army 10-days when that happened. Remember that I signed up for Peacetime.

Now, I will skip forward to late September 1962. I had made SP-4 back in June that year, so in only 10-months. I had been given orders transferring me to France, as a Light Truck Driver, and that was the Army MOS Code I had given up my National Guard SP-4 rank for. In the meantime, my old high-school girlfriend and her mother were both living in the Washington, D.C. area, and I went by to visit them. I explained my dilemma to my girlfriend, and she told me to tell that to her mother, since she had married an Air Force Major, and had met quite a few Officers. Her mother then told me to come to work with them the next day, in-uniform, with all my records in hand, and they would give me a map of the Pentagon, which was called "The Potomac Puzzle Palace," by the people who worked there. We were just going over her instruction together, when her boss walked in with his entourage of about a dozen Officers. He took one look at me and asked her, "Judy, is this the boyfriend you have been telling me about? I see that you both work for me." He then shook my hand and walked into his inner office. The man who shook my hand? None other than the SECDEF himself, Robert S. McNamara. I took all my records and went down into the bowels of the Pentagon, in some basement, and found the Major I was supposed to see. He looked at my records and my Orders and said, "I am taking two copies of your orders, you can expect to have new ones sending you to Germany in 2-3 days, so just go on up to Fort Dix, NJ, and report in.

I did go to Fort Dix and arrived there just a few days before "Peacetime" almost ended with a bang! The Cuban Missile Crisis started while I was at Fort Dix, waiting to board a WWII Liberty Ship named "The Patch." I already had orders for a departure that actually fell about a week after everyone got all excited. I found out later that my girlfriend had to go home, pack a bag, and come back to her office, then stay there for the 13-days of the "Crisis." She and I still talk regularly on our phones. We both outlived our spouses.

So, I did not get the great **privilege** of going to Germany via the WWII Liberty Ship. Instead, they loaded six of us onto a plane in New York, and we flew non-stop, in First-Class no less, to Paris. We then had 24-hours to kill in Paris before we could load onto the Well-known "Orient Express" train in Paris, and take that to Stuttgart, Germany. In about 32-hours, I had decided that I had to learn German, and do it as quickly as possible. Thanks to some great advice from a little old lady who ran the Stars and Stripes bookstand, I had learned enough in the first 90 days to have other soldiers asking me to translate for them. Almost every time that happened, I learned some new German words. And that came in handy when the local outdoor swimming pool opened in May 1963, the first time I went there I met 2-German girls. In October 1963, I was at the right place to see a car go off the road and down an embankment. I was the only one who saw it happen, so I rescued the German couple in the car, but later heard no more about that.

In 1964, I married one of those girls, who just happened to be the daughter of the Burgermeister, (Mayor) of the small town where our Missile Battery was stationed. Luckily, her father had been a soldier in WWII, but he only served on the Eastern Front, against the Russians, so he bore no ill will to an American soldier marrying his only daughter. I spent 10-years in that same location, during 2-tours in Germany. During my 2nd-tour, I was plying my trade as a radar and computer mechanic, and then as a Warrant Officer in-charge of 5-radars, and a lot of other assorted technology. So, I had enlisted for Peacetime, and in 20 years active-duty, never shot at anyone, even though as a Warrant in Nike, I had a license to kill with nuclear weapons. I had many adventures in Germany, and in 1963 I saved two lives. My wife and I met the German couple I had saved in 1963, at a Soccer game in 1975. They thanked me, and were very grateful, since it had been 12-years and one month since the accident happened. After my retirement in 1981, I worked at NATO for 5-years, teaching Nike Radars to students from 6-NATO countries still using Nike Hercules, because they didn't trust their large neighbor over to the East.

BOB SNIDER

U.S.A.F. Pilot
1972 – 1978
404-510-4740
SSnider770@aol.com

MY USAF EXPERIENCE

After college, the story of my experiences in the USAF starts in 1972 and ends in 1978.

My first assignment in the Air Force after pilot training was to fly copilot on the HC-130 rescue aircraft; call sign King 21, 56 ARRS (Air Rescue and Recovery Squadron) for a year at Karat RTAB, Thailand. Our mission was to conduct search and rescue on downed crew members fighting and bombing the Kymer Rouge in Cambodia. We would orbit for 12 hours over the largest lake in Cambodia (Tonie' Sap) which is 160 miles long and 62 miles wide, and listen to the combat that was ensuing. We also refueled the "Jolly Greens" H-53 helicopters that rescued the downed crew members.

After my tour in Thailand, I was assigned to fly C-141 cargo aircraft, 53 MAS "Backjacks" as Captain and Co-pilot out of Norton AFB in Southern California. During the fall of South Vietnam, it was our mission to help evacuate Saigon and Tan Son Nhut AB.

During "Operation Babylift" in early April 1975, we would land at Tan Son Nhut AB and bring mostly Amerasian babies that were fathered by GI's back to the States. The babies were brought onboard the aircraft in cardboard boxes and placed widthwise; side by side, with a tie down strap draped on the top of the boxes and cinched down. The rows were separated so the nurses onboard could tend to the babies needs during flight. We took the babies to Clark AB in the Philippines and then they were transported from Clark AB to Little Rock, AR. and new homes.

We were then tasked to evacuate as many refugees as possible out of Tan Son Nhut AB. In late April 1975, we flew directly over the runway at 10,000 ft and spiral down to a landing. We had 'Very" pistol flare guns mounted mid aircraft in the crew doors to act as an anti-SA7 (ground to air shoulder fired missile) deterrent to create a different heat signature for the SA7 to follow instead of our engine heat exhaust.

After engine shutdown, we would load as many refugees as possible through the aft ramp (approximately 250 refugees) and told them to sit down and hold on to the tie down straps for the fight to Clark AB. After takeoff from Saigon, we would spiral up to 10,000 ft. (the range of the SA7) and then fly directly to Clark AB.

After landing at Clark, the refugees, (eventually totaling over 100,000) were sent to camps on Guam and then proceeded to enter the USA at various locations. I enjoyed my time in the Air Force which took me from the vast Pacific to Europe, the Middle East, Area 51, and other exotic places.

~*The End*~

Nowadays, one of those tiny infants from that flight of Amer-Asian children was Dr. Jennifer Lieu-Chi Harkins, who is now a Physician, and Dr. Harkins had the opportunity to go back to Vietnam and be reunited with her birth parents and siblings. Here are some of those pictures of that trip, plus a couple of pix with Bob Snider, who flew Jennifer to the U.S.A., where she was adopted by loving parents, Becky & Jon Harkins.

Bob Snider with Dr. Jennifer *Lieu-Chi* Harkins.

Bob Snider with his son, and Dr. Jennifer *Lieu-Chi* Harkins, and adoptive mother Becky Harkin

Dr. Jennifer Lieu-Chi Harkins with her birth parents and siblings.

Dr. Jennifer **Lieu-Chi** Harkins with her birth parents, siblings, and adoptive father Jon Harkins.

My Real Vietnam Experience

Duc Tran
Son of ARVN Airborne
Cell: 678-595-5285
DTran4602@Yahoo.com

My story differs from other Vietnam Vets stories in that I am a South Vietnamese boat refugee who immigrated to America in the early 80s. After the fall of Saigon, my ARVN dad became a POW for 10 years. I never knew him, because I was 2 when he was taken away in 1975.

I was 9 when Mom woke us up in the middle of the night in Saigon. She just said we're visiting relatives. Little did I know that the previous day was my last day ever seeing my friends, teacher and relatives. We took a bus and arrived in a small staging house in a small town called Ba Ria, south of Saigon. We stayed there, along with 30 other strangers. I was confused because these were not my relatives. We stayed there because to the authorities, it has to look like people have been living there and not just come there for one day just to go to the boat.

On the 3rd night, we all left the house in the cover of darkness and hiked. It was my mom, 4 of us siblings and the rest of the people, all in one line. After passing through a cemetery, we came upon a swamp. This is where I lost both of my shoes and hiked the rest of the night barefoot through the jungles. My mom couldn't take care of all four of us, so she asked some strangers up front to care for my younger twin brothers, age 7. We jumped in a river one time and someone just grabbed my hair and pulled me above the water since I didn't know how to swim. After 8-hours of hiking with an occasional 5-minute rest to nap, we came upon the dock waiting for the boat to come. I didn't mention that there were supposed to be 79 people, but others heard, and it ended up with 140 at the dock.

When the boat came it was every man for himself. You only have a few minutes to get onboard before authorities spot you. Well, being small and young, our family was last. The boat started to depart when the captain and his two teenage sons jumped in the water, grabbed and threw us on board. I can't help but think how our lives would be so different if it wasn't for their actions. Once aboard, all 140 have to go to the storage below deck. It's a fishing boat so it wouldn't look good with 140 souls cramming on the deck. Thus, we all crammed in a storage room that smelled of rotten fish and kerosene while the temperature rose to 120 degrees and barely any oxygen. Because of this, and the boat-rocking, we all just threw up and pissed on each other.

Six hours later, we escaped out to sea and were allowed to come up for air. It was a sight to behold. Nothing but endless ocean in front of you. That's when I realized we had become a few of the hundreds of thousands of the *Boat People*. The first feeling that hit me was of thirst. We all were so dehydrated from the whole ordeal at that point. Yet, the boat only had one container of water since the captain rationed it for 79 people. We were allowed 4 teaspoons of water per day, in that heat and humidity of the South China Sea, and with no cover. On the 2nd night, I wasn't feeling well, so my mom asked to if she can come above deck to check on me. After several refusals, she made her way up and the deckhand punched her in the eye. She carried that black eye for months, but understood his actions because if he let her, everyone would ask the same. On the 3rd day, a beautiful Swedish freighter stopped in front of us. We were so happy and cried. We thought we would be rescued. Yet, after 15-minutes, it took off. My guess is that it wasn't allowed to pick us up. We understood, but just wished that they would have at least given us some water. Hunger wasn't the problem, it was thirst.

To make a long story short, we were at sea for 5-days before someone spotted land. It was a sight to behold. Since there is no instruments on board, the captain navigated by the stars. He just went south and came upon Indonesia. We were processed and went through 4-different islands and camps. These camps were built for WW2 prisoners so there were neither bathrooms, nor running water. We would hike 2-miles a day just to bathe in the rivers and bring back water for mom. On the last island, my mom was granted an interview with the U.S. delegation. All the previous refugees taught her that when asked, *"Why did you leave Vietnam,"* you should answer that you are looking for political freedom. Thus, she waited for that question. Yet, the tall man just looked at us up and down and asked her if he were to allow her to settle in the U.S., how could she possibly take care of 4-kids by herself. She paused for a few seconds, put her hands out and answered that she had brought us this far, she certainly can raise us in America. He was so impressed with her that he accepted us without any other questions. Exactly a year after leaving Saigon, President Reagan gave us five, one-way tickets to freedom to begin our new lives. After arriving in America, my mom went to school and took on 3-jobs to support us. She didn't want to be on welfare and burden a country that had welcomed us with open arms.

We were lucky that it was our first time escaping. Many others tried 13 times, but were either caught, or were swindled. Others died at sea, due to typhoons. One man told his story of being the only one left alive on his boat, because no one else could swim. He slowly witnessed 80 people drown in front of him. Some encountered Thai pirates and were raped and murdered. Some suffered mechanical problems and were stranded at sea for weeks. Many became cannibals, due to no fault of their own. Many women committed suicide at camps, because they were so ashamed for having been raped by pirates. Yet our family made it. This was not only due in part to Divine intervention, but also with help from the U.S. Our new country sent these men and women, who protected and sacrificed, so that we had the chance to escape. 58,000 men and women died for our freedom. Going through this, I've learned not to take things for granted, and to appreciate the Vietnam Vets so much. They stood tall, fought well, and gave us opportunities that thousands of others at the bottom of the South China Sea wanted so badly

Regarding my dad, he was released from POW camp in 1984--2years after our escape. He was afraid to go see my aunt, fearing that we all died on our journey. Luckily, my aunt gave mim good new. My mother sponsored him to emigrate to the US, and our family was united in 1989. This was my first time meeting my dad, and I was 16 years old. It was and is still strange because you lose all those years of growing up and bonding with your father. Regardless, I was happy to see him. He loves and was proud of fighting alongside American troops and even received a US Army Commendation Medal with "V" for Valor after the battle in 1971. He currently lives with mom in Tampa, and they both love America so much. .

The Boat People of Vietnam

GUS J. VASQUEZ

U.S. NAVY

Aviation VAW-111

G.V.V.A. Member

Cell: 404-643-2975

GJV@Engineer.com

My Military Experiences

My life's three years of military and its Naval path into the unknown, and living life one day at a time.

In my early life there were two good friends that inspired me to follow the aviation path. One was a beautiful, young friend in high school, whose father owned a Cessna 172 Skyhawk airplane. In a small town of early-Sixties south Texas, the only runways were the country roads that were slightly traveled and without powerlines. This friend was learning to fly at the time and was going for her solo flight at the young age of sixteen. I was so happy for her - as she had the good fortune and opportunity to learn to fly an airplane so early in life. Her name is Yvonne Yeager, she was a very smart, beautiful girl (it isn't just my opinion - she was voted the 'Most Beautiful girl' in her graduating class). I was extremely proud of her, and she inspired me to dream of being a pilot myself, someday.

My good friend somewhere in Montana

As time went on, my dad, unfortunately, passed away suddenly from a heart attack. I was seventeen at that time, and it rocked my world. I had no sense of direction, afterwards. As a last resort, I enlisted for three years in the U.S. Navy for the sole reason that the previous year, I had won an award at the school Science Fair that allowed me to participate at the Regional Science Fair in Corpus Christi, TX.

There, I won one of the higher awards that afforded me and 49 other winners (*two from each state*) an all-expenses-paid trip via C-47 military aircraft from Laughlin Air Force Base in Del Rio, TX, to Biggs Air Force Base in El Paso, TX. Onwards to San Diego, CA, where we spent the entire two weeks at a Naval Training base, and then on to General Dynamics Laboratory Corporation.

There we went on tour in San Diego and to different U.S. Naval installations and two naval ship cruises: one being the **USS Daniel Boone** (SSBN-629) submarine, and the other a guided-missile Destroyer, the **USS Henry B. Wilson** DDG-7. That experience left an impression on me and is the main reason I joined the Navy.

Once enlisted, the new recruits go through a battery of tests to determine in what field they excel. Mine was aviation electrical and electronics. Completing boot camp, I ended up at my duty station, U.S. Naval Air Station North Island, San Diego, CA (*Coronado*) at Air Wing Squadron VAW-11 Carrier Airborne Early Warning Squadron (*CARAEWRON 11*). There, the aircraft were the Grumman E-1B Tracer, and later replaced by the Grumman E-2A Hawkeye. After the completion of my schooling, I became Plane Captain while advancing to a higher pay grade. At that time, my goal was to complete my training to become an Air Crewmen. Over time, you get to know the pilots on a personal level; and during that time, I got to know a super-great pilot, **Lieutenant Larry Fisher**. I am honored to call him my friend (*and second to inspire me to one day fly*). We had good chemistry from day one.

Receiving our Orders for the Far East cruise (*Vietnam - Tonkin Gulf*) from 1966-67, the Squadron boarded the Aircraft Carrier (**CVA-31**) **USS Bon Homme Richard**, and we prepared ourselves for a long journey ahead. LT Fisher knew of my interest in flying, so he asked me to accompany him for a number of air missions. During the Vietnam War, things were lenient in the war zone, and he allowed me to sit at the right-side of the cockpit. Explaining things to me when he could during the flight, I was allowed to take control in flying without jeopardizing us and the crew. A great thrill of my life was also when he allowed me to remain in the cockpit during a flight deck landing.

On May 6, 1967, one of my friends and I were working the night of the usual 12-hours on and 12-hours off schedule. With nothing but red lights to preserve our night vision and facing extreme wind and noise, one must never be too casual to the unforgiving conditions encountered during those routines. But, having to be well-suited for the occasion by wearing hearing protection headset and goggles can be troublesome during nighttime. *Unfortunately*, my friend walked into a plane's propeller that night and lost his life. In a way, I am sort of glad it happened in the limited light. It was a horrific and gruesome accident; one that I will never forget (**his name – Larry Lindell - is on the Vietnam Veterans Memorial, as another stark reminder**). I always think about Larry Lindell and wonder what his life would have been like.

I still think about the operations day where I was guarding the propeller clearance for proximity to the ship's island, and a sailor walked in front of me, knowing he would end up like Larry Lindell. I *immediately* grabbed him, to stop him from learning Larry's fate. After redirecting him, I happened to look up at the cockpit and saw the co-pilot officer **Ensign Reagh** looking furious at me. Later, when I spoke with him, the reason he was so upset with me was for me not getting the sailor's *name* and *rank,* so he could be reported. Nonetheless, he did thank me for saving that man's life. Glad I was there to do my job, and help a shipmate get back to his family, and to a mother that loved him.

In memory of the 134 shipmates that lost their live on the USS Forrestal (CVA-59)

On July 29, 1967, during our time in the War Zone (*Tonkin Gulf – Vietnam*), we received messages from the **USS Forrestal (CVA-59)** informing us that a major mishap had happened to her. Our ship suspended operations and once our situation was secured, we headed full-speed ahead towards the Forrestal approximately 18 to 20 miles away. As our distance closed, we could see the Forrestal was listing and on fire with black smoke billowing out. The surrounding area was swarming with floating, aircraft dropped fuel tanks, and with ships trying to assist in whatever way they were able.

On the scene were the **USS Oriskany (CVA-34)**, the **USS George K. Mac Kenzie (DD-836)**, the **USS Henry W. Tucker (DD-875)** and the **USS Rupertus (DD-851).** Air traffic was well congested with helicopters from both our ship and the Oriskany, searching and rescuing sailors in the surrounding water. We also had working parties, assembly lines gathering 5-gallon containers with firefighting foam to transport to the Forrestal in the firefighting effort. Some wounded sailors were also transported to Sick Bay on our ship and the Oriskany.

Our ship escorted the USS Forrestal (CVA-59) on 31 July to the Naval Air Station Cubi Point in the Philippines to undertake repairs sufficient to allow the ship to return to the States. Because of the ship's fire, all shipmates from the Forrestal were allowed to go out on Liberty in their dungarees.

The aircraft carrier USS Forrestal was under plenty of scrutiny, due to the controversy of the Admiral's son, Lieutenant Commander and A-4 Skyhawk pilot John McCain having a reputation that preceded him. At the time the fire broke out and the explosions commenced, John McCain was on deck and manning his plane. Later, the main culprit was announced that it was a Zuni rocket missile misfire.

We have all heard the old clichè, *"It's a small world."* How true it is, for in Kennesaw, GA, back in the early 70s that I met Navy veteran **Bill Clapp,** and learned, surprisingly, that he had served on the USS Forrestal during that dreadful day, July 29, 1967.

After my enlistment was completed and it came time for my Honorable Discharge (*separation*), I had my little book of addresses to stay in contact with all of my military buddies. Because of my military training and schooling, I had a job waiting for me at Lockheed-Martin Aerospace Corporation in Marietta, GA. During the move to Georgia, my 1964 Chevy II was, unfortunately, broken into and I lost everything (*even my dirty clothes*). Among the belongings stolen was a valued possession, my *Address Book*. And to this day, I am saddened without it. Perhaps my buddies thought I had been killed, or had just forgotten them; far from it. While their addresses were to remain lost, their names and friendships remain fond memories.

Because of Yvonne Yeager's and Lieutenant Larry Fisher's inspiration, I am now a pilot. I owe my aviation path to these two good friends that shared moments in my life. While I have no idea where they are now, I often think about them. And as God as my witness, I have tried to find them, but to no avail.

I have prayed about this, hoping somehow, that they would one day learn what actually happened to their friend from long ago.

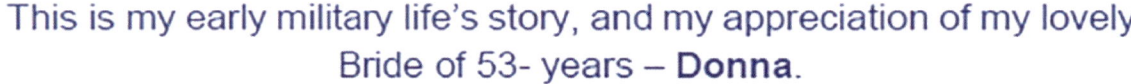

This is my early military life's story, and my appreciation of my lovely Bride of 53- years – **Donna**.

Picture of my bride Donna of 53 years ... and counting

RUSSELL VAUDREY
U.S. Army Air Corps
404-660-5338
RCVaudrey@aol.com

My Military Experiences

Stock Photo (NOT russell's Crew)

WWII U.S. Army Air Corps Veteran Russell Vaudery

*I interviewed 101 year (young) **Russell Vaudery** over the phone this afternoon after listening to his `Witness to War` documentary, earlier last year. I'm humbled and honored to share his amazing story of WWII **U.S. Army Air Corps** military service.*
~ Hal Burke ~

"It's something I never expected to do of course," Russell commented on celebrating his 101th birthday. *"I never smoked and tried to eat properly and exercise."*

Born on 10 July 1922 in Glendo, WY, (*100 miles North of Cheyenne*), Russell was the fourth of 6-boys in his family. According to Russell, his grandfather was a soldier in Napoleon's Army in France before his ancestors migrated to Michigan, and then on to Wyoming. Life was rough on the ranch, but Russell eventually made his way to college, and met his future wife of 77-years -- **Shirley (Komegay)**. Sadly, Shirley passed away in 2021 at the age of 98.

Shirley worked for United Airlines in Cheyenne, WY, and Russell was also employed at United as an aviation mechanic. Pearl Harbor was attacked on December 7th, 1941, and Russell remembers playing cards when he heard the news. Ten months later, Russell enlisted in the U.S. Army Air Corps on 6 October 1942 at age 20. Russell's quest for knowledge and experience earned him an MOS as Aviation Crew Chief, because of his previous training at United Airlines.

A routine April 1945, DC-47 flight from the Biak Island, northwest of New Guinea, unfortunately, became a crash-landing site into palm trees off the runway, because the pilot, who normally flew B-24's, wasn't familiar with the operations of taking off in a C-47 cargo plane. C-47's had a Conventional gear, unlike the B-24's Tri-cycle gear. The pilot was unable to get enough airlift halfway down the runaway, and quickly realized he was in trouble, so tried to abort the takeoff, which resulted in crashing into palm trees that were lined-up along the runaway, after being cut down and only partially-removed, while building the airfield. Russell and five crew members escaped the wreckage and realized that the co-pilot was still in the wreckage. Russell and a crew member named *"Red"* ran back to the cargo plane, as flames began to consume the C-47. They pulled the unconscious co- pilot out through the top hatch, and when they were 100 feet from the burning plane, it exploded!

During WWII, Russell served as a Flight Engineer, Side & Tail gunner in the 5th Air Force on a B-24 Liberator in the Pacific Campaign. *"We were all brothers, and helped one another,"* recalled Russell of his military service. Russell's pursuit of knowledge had him constantly reading the B-24 Liberator's Operator Manual, and was soon promoted to the rank of Master Sergeant.

Russell and Shirley celebrating their Wedding Day, 5 Nov 1943.

A few months later, Russell was refueling a B-24 Liberator on Mindanao Island in The Philippines, when the air raid siren was activated, warning of an approaching Japanese aircraft attack. Russell was standing on the B-24 wing, which was 18' off the ground, and he grabbed one of the propellers to lower himself to the ground. As Russell ran to the bomb shelter, a bomb dropped by the attacking Japanese aircraft that hit the tail section of the B-24 *next* to the Liberator he was refueling, and the explosion blew off the tail section.

Russell believes it was an anti-personnel bomb that exploded, because he had over 20 shrapnel wounds on the back of his left leg. The largest piece of shrapnel removed was 3/4". His wounds were cleaned & bandaged, and Russell reported back to full duty.

Russel & Shirley on the occasion of their 75th Wedding Anniversary.

Russell believes it was an anti-personnel bomb that exploded, because he had over 20 shrapnel wounds on the back of his left leg. The largest piece of shrapnel removed was 3/4". His wounds were cleaned & bandaged, and Russell reported back to full duty.

Sadly, Russell was never awarded **The Order of The *Purple Heart*** for his wounds.

Russell recalls listening to "Tokyo Rose's" propaganda and threats on the radio, and laughingly said, "They listened to her ramblings, because she played great USA Big Band music!" He also humorously recalled that one site on their bombing raids was declared,

"Off Limits" -- a brewery!

Russell volunteered for many dangerous flights, and during an April 1945 bombing run on a Japanese airfield on the Panay Island of the Philippines, the Liberator was hit by enemy anti- aircraft guns, which knocked out the left-outboard engine and damaged the left-inboard engine. The pilot kept the B-24 airborne, but a violent monsoon developed, and the Liberator crashed into the dense jungle in April 1945, killing seven of the ten crew members.

The crash broke the Liberator in-half, and fortunately, Russell and two crew members were able to climb out of the wreckage and escape. Russell and one crew member were uninjured, but the other crew member had a broken collar bone. Unknown to the survivors, the plane crash was witnessed by a Coast-Watcher, and he sent Filipino Guerrillas to rescue Russell and his crew members.

Finally, after 3-days, the Filipino Guerrillas found the survivors, and for the next 3-weeks they Escaped & Evaded (E&E'd) the Japanese troops searching for them.

"We were not going to be captured, because we knew about Japanese troop atrocities on POW's," Russell stated.

"They came so close to us hiding in the jungle that one time, I could've reached out and touched a Japanese soldier searching for us!"

When they finally reached the coast, Russell and the two crew members were each put into a separate dugout canoe and covered with bananas and fruit. For the next 5-hours, the Filipino rescuers paddled and were observed and passed over by Japanese planes, but fortunately, ignored.

They finally reached a rendezvous point for a U.S. Navy PBY to pick up Russell and his fellow survivors. The PBY was escorted by P-38's and P-51's. Russell loss 20# during his 3-weeks in the jungle.

After recovering from his jungle crash and ordeal, Russell went back to working on aircraft and actually flew over Nagasaki, after the 2nd Atomic Bomb was dropped on the city. In fact, WWII had just ended, but there were still pockets of Japanese resistance, and Russell's newly- issued Liberator was fired upon, once again.

The next day, 10-Liberators flew over and bombed the area of resistance.

Finally, Russell's WWII experiences brought him to Ie Shima (Okinawa) in the South China Sea, where the famous War Correspondent Ernie Pyle was killed.

During Russell's time on the island, he witnessed the Japanese Diplomatic Delegation arriving for their journey to meet General Douglas MacArthur in the Philippines to negotiate Japan's Unconditional Surrender (which was signed in Tokyo Bay aboard the USS Missouri on September 2nd, 1945). Vaudrey and his fellow Americans there, also survived two back-to-back typhoons in October 1945, with 180-mph recorded winds!

Russell's Distinguished and Honorable military service ended on 26 November 1945. During Russell's honorable service, he was awarded several medals including **5**-Bronze Stars and **1**-Silver Star; although, no Purple Heart.

Interesting, yet disappointing. Yes?

****

Interestingly, the Japanese soldiers fighting in the Philippines didn't surrender until 2 September 1945. Some hunkered down in caves in the jungle and didn't come out for decades.

****

Upon returning home from WWII, Russell held several sales jobs in the Bay area of California for 23- years, and 33-years ago relocated to Woodstock, Georgia. Russell and Shirley had **2**-children, and were Blessed with **3**-grandchildren, and **7**-great-grand-children.

God Bless *"The Greatest Generation!"*

Russell, at his 100th Birthday Celebration in Woodstock, Georgia, 7/10/22.

The Mayor of Woodstock, delivers the City Proclamation, honoring Russell Vaudrey on the occasion of his 100th Birthday, 7/10/2022.

Editor's Note: Russell Vaudrey's incredible story of survival & heroism was compiled and written by Vietnam Era Sailor **Hal Burke**, by listening to Vaudrey tell his story over several days. We **thank Hal** for his time and great story filed.

Russell's adventures should be made into a WWII true story, action-packed movie.

May you always be blessed with Fair Winds & Following Seas

Hal Burke
Founder & CEO
Victory & Valor Memories, LLC.
604 Greenleaf Court
Canton, GA 30114
708-387-7779
hal@victoryandvalormemories.com www.victoryandvalormemories.com

MILES WILLIS
U.S. Navy
770-883-8609
Miles.Willis@Bellsouth.net

My Military Experience

Seldom have I originated a plan for my life but have tried to make well of the opportunities God placed before me for that is how my life started. I was born in January 1927 to a couple who grew up on farms in South Georgia (*GA*), and neither had a high school education. My Father was born in January 1900, and served in the U.S. Army during World War I. I have pictures of him in uniform but know little more, because he died in 1931 when I was four years old, and my sister was only 8-months old. Fortunately, we were Blessed with a strong and loving Mother who devoted her life to her children. After doing domestic work and working in the Cotton Mill in Dalton, Georgia, for over 2-years and despite his being 19-years older, she married John W. Evans, the man who moved us from South Georgia, and who she had worked for originally. He had three sons by his first wife who had died of Tuberculosis.

As the Great Depression faded, my Stepfather was recalled to his job with the Nashville, Chattanooga, & St. Louis Railroad (**NC&STL**), and when he had enough work that he could afford to rent a house, we moved to Smyrna, GA, in December 1936 to be near his work. By that time, the oldest Son (*Harold*) was 17-years old and convinced his Dad to sign for him to join the U.S. Army. Son #2, *Kenneth*, was a High School Freshman, and he accepted an invitation intended for Harold, where he attended **Martha Berry School** in Rome, GA, and worked his way through high school. When he graduated in 1940, he joined the U.S. Coast Guard. Son #3 (*Harry*) and I attended Smyrna High School and after Harry graduated in 1942, he joined the U.S. Marine Corps. In my Senior year, Navy Personnel came to our school giving the Navy V-12 Exam and all Junior and Senior boys were encouraged to take it. The three of us who made a passing grade and were 17-years of age were encouraged to join. I was sworn in April 1944 and called to Active-Duty on July 1, 1944. In October 1944 in their Publication, his employer the NC&STL Railway published a Salute to *"Mr. J.W. Evans, employee in Atlanta, because of his four fine sons, who are all in-service of their Country."*

By the early part of World War II, *Harold* was promoted to Warrant Officer and elected to make the Army his Career. He served two years in England during the War, followed by post-war service in the Philippines and in the occupation of Japan. *Kenneth*, the Coast Guardsman

was in the Invasion of North Africa for a year, and then was at Staten Island, New York. *Harry*, the U.S. Marine, was in the Invasion of and Battle for Okinawa.

I only lasted one Quarter in V-12, making A's and B's in all subjects, except Physics Lab (**F**) and History (**D**). About 50 of us were sent to Great Lakes for Boot Camp, after which I was sent to Gulfport, Mississippi for training on the maintenance and operation of a diesel engine, of the type that powered a LCVP. That was followed by Amphibious training at Little Creek, Virginia. On May 7, 1945, I was transferred to LSM-306 as a Fireman 1st Class and we sailed the following morning for the Panama Canal. After traveling the Canal at night, we moved up the Coast to Long Beach, California, where we remained for three weeks while the Ship was being prepared for combat duty. Following a stop in San Francisco to pick up cargo and some passengers, we left in late June 1945 for Pearl Harbor, assuming we would be in the Invasion Fleet for Japan. For defense, the LSM had three 50-Caliber Guns; one each mounted on the Starboard, Port and Stern super-structure deck. Over the Bow Doors was mounted a twin 20-MM Cannon, that required two men for operation. My General Quarters position was Port Side Operator, responsible for elevation and firing.

After off-loading the cargo and personnel at Pearl Harbor and our loading ammunition and supplies, we sailed for Guam, and then Saipan in the Marianas Islands. We sat at anchor for more than six weeks off Saipan, during which time we had a ring side seat watching the B-29's take-off for their bombing runs over Japan and their returns. Also, we had a view of a huge fleet of Amphibious Ships we assumed for the Invasion Fleet. We cheered reports of the Atom bombs and had a celebration on news of **Japan's Surrender on August 15, 1945**.

The following week, we were sent to the Philippine Islands, where we transported Army personnel within and out to other assignments. During the War, the ship was manned by 50 Officers and men and following Japan's surrender, the Crew was reduced to 38 Officers and men. I was promoted to MoMM 3rd Class, and was Throttleman on the Port Engine, a 16-cylinder GM Diesel, and one of two that powered the ship. When moving an Army unit, we traveled with several other ships as they were required for that volume of men and equipment. In the first week of September 1945, we moved an Army unit to Okinawa, where after hitchhiking the Island, I found my step-brother (Harry) and we spent the weekend together. We then moved another Army unit to Sasebo, Japan, arriving on October 1, 1945. Being an Amphibious Ship, we were assigned anchorage in the back of the harbor in shallow water, but this gave us an opportunity to explore some of the adjoining area. We found in a very steep hill that joined the harbor, a series of caves that housed a complete machine shop, with the last cave containing a large stock of large, live shells of the type that probably were used on large guns. We also had an opportunity to visit an inland village, where with the help of two boys we encountered, we were able to meet a number of friendly citizens.

On returning to the Philippines, we continued moving Army personnel and equipment. One assignment involved 11 trips from Lingayen Gulf on the East of Luzon to Aparri on the North, and return. The alternative for the Army was to drive on unpaved mountain roads through an area occupied by Japanese soldiers who were living off the land and probably didn't know the War had ended.In mid-April 1946, we sailed for home with stops in Guam and Pearl Harbor, and arrived in Port Hueneme, California, on May 8, 1946. I was discharged on June 20, 1946 and arrived home following day to join Harold (Army) and Harry (Marine). Kenneth (Coast Guard) came the next week -- the first time the family was all together since February 1937 -- over nine years. My Military Service was a great experience -- a teenager, who had not been out of Georgia, I traveled many U.S. States, as well as Pearl Harbor, and a number of Pacific Islands, all within the safety of the U.S. Navy. However, I felt the impact of the War when I served as a Pallbearer for three, good friends -- two Army, and one Marine -- who Gave All for our Country!

WE SALUTE

Mr. J. W. Evans, employe in Atlanta because of his four fine sons who are now in the service of their country. Corp. Harry W. (upper left) is a Radar expert in the Marines. Miles (lower left) is in a Navy V-12 Unit. Keneeth L. (upper right) with 12 months combat duty in North Africa is now in Coast Guard. Harold (upper left opposite page) is in a Medical outfit somewhere in England.

EDWARD A. WOODS, JR.
Atlanta, GA.
09-17-1942
Navy Seabees, NMCB 10
Petty Officer 2nd Class Builder
Cell: 678-350-6023
EdWoods55@Comcast.net

Vietnam 1966-1967

MY SEABEE EXPERIENCE

I flew from Atlanta to New York to Providence, Rhode Island (RI). This was the first time I had ever flown. My first duty station was 'A' School in Davisville, RI. This was a three-month school in my rate, which was Builder. This is where I learned to be a builder. There, I met a lot of different people, some with whom I would serve in Vietnam, and with whom I am still connected.

When I finished 'A' School, I was assigned to Naval Mobile Construction Battalion 10 (NMCB 10). This battalion was based at Port Hueneme, California, located just outside Oxnard in Ventura County, just north of Los Angles. MCB 10 had just recently returned from its first tour of Vietnam. MCB 10 was the first Seabee Battalion to go to Vietnam, landing there in May 1965 and returning home in January 1966. The Battalion went to Vietnam a total of five times earning 13 Campaign Stars, two Meritorious Unit Commendations, two Navy Unit Commendations for exemplary performance at Da Nang, Quang Tri, Diễn giả phòng, and Chu Lai. The Battalion had a detail at Khe Sanh that also received the Presidential Unit Citation.

While at home on Leave, after "A" School, I bought a 1966 red Volkswagen. In May, we rented a U-Haul trailer, attached it to our Volkswagen, and off to California we went. When we got to Oxnard, we rented a small two room apartment. It had a living room, kitchen and dining room combination and a bedroom-bath room combination. It worked for us.

MCB 10 left for Vietnam on May 11, 1966. It took eight days and a total of six C-141's to move the entire Battalion. We had just arrived in California, and I was scheduled to leave with them. Then, they realized I had not received any combat or rifle training. I stayed back for another month with some other guys. After being taught how to use the M-14 weapon, I was off to Vietnam. We were issued the M-16 at some time during our tour in Vietnam. We flew from Port Hueneme, to San Francisco, Hawaii, Wake Island, Guam, and on to Da Nang in a 4-engine Navy prop plane; possibly a P-3? We flew into Da Nang at night over a firefight. This was the first of many that we would see. We left the Air Base and went to our Base, Camp Hoover, in what I would call a Cattle Car. It's a trailer that is commonly used today to transport cows and hogs to slaughter. It was dark and very hot. Hoover was named after the first Seabee killed in Vietnam. It was located about two miles from the Air Base. I was first assigned to guard duty. My assigned place was a little guard stand at the southwest corner of our Base Camp. This was a place where I could see the entire Da Nang Air Base. There were fighter jets taking off and landing 24-hours a day, every day of the week. I had my own personal AM / FM radio. I would listen to Armed Forces Radio. I could also listen to the Da Nang Air Base Tower. I could hear the Tower, but I could not hear the pilots. One day they had to foam the runway. A jet was coming in without his nose gear. He made an almost perfect landing in the foam. All survived!

During this time, I made friends with a guy running the Base Radio. One night he was able to patch me through to Carol at her Bank. Patching means bouncing radio signals from one radio tower to another. We were not able to talk long. He told me he would have to break it off if we got hit. Just my luck, we were hit in about three minutes. This would be the only time I would talk to her until January of the following year. This was long before the Internet and Cell Phones. After about a month of guard duty, I was assigned to Charlie Company. I was promoted to Builder Petty Officer Third Class (E-4) on August 16, 1966. Charlie Company was made up of Builders and Steelworkers. Other Companies were made up of other rates. I started going out with Charlie Company doing various building jobs for the Marines. We would leave about 0600 and return about 1800. While traveling from Base Camp to the outpost we were constantly harassed by Viet Cong small arms fire. Mostly we would go out to the Marine outpost and do what had to be done. We built their sleeping quarters, showers, heads (toilets/latrines), dining halls, and whatever else needed to be done. We also built a Morgue, bridges, airstrips, and repaired those that had already been built, and blown-up. We built a water treatment plant that produced a million gallons of water a day for the Marines in the Da Nang area. We built the 5,000-seat Amphitheater on Freedom Hill, where Bob Hope would perform later that year. We built revetments at the Da Nang Air Base to protect the Marine aircraft. We built a library at the 3rd Marine Amphibious Force Recreation Center, and a POW camp. We built the Base Camp for the 8th Marine Artillery Division. We also spent a lot of time at 1st Marine Scout and Sentry Dog Camps. While at the Scout Dog Camp we were shot at several times. We shot back. We could only see where the rifle fire was coming from. After a short firefight, we would go back to work not knowing what, if any, injuries we had sustained. We did all this in the 115° heat, until the wet monsoon rains began. We worked 6½ days/week under constant enemy harassment. I saw a lot, and did a lot. At no time did I ever think I would be shot at, or that I would have to shoot at someone else.

No matter where you were in Vietnam, you could always hear small arms fire, rocket fire, mortar fire, and larger artillery fire. At night, flares were always going off with their little parachutes, so they would stay up a while, and just float down, later. Helicopters were always flying; 24 hours a day. There was no letting up; always moving men, both dead and alive, supplies, and providing fire power.

Unlike the guys that lived in the 'field,' we had dry sleeping quarters, and except when we were out all day at an outpost, we had three good meals a day. I ate a of lot things, and sometimes I had no idea what it was. Over there, we referred to it as `Mystery Meat` day when we weren't quite sure what it was. The drink was always 'Kool Aid'. Every day the Kool Aid was a different flavor. We did have coffee as well, but in that temperature, not many of the younger men drank it. When we were in the field during a meal, we would eat 'C' Rations. Some were good, others were awful. My favorite was Beanie Weenies. Often as a late-night snack, we would eat a can of 'C' Rations. As Enlisted Men, we could not get Hard Liquor. However, Marine Corps Officers could get it. But, they could not get wood, and they always wanted wood for personal reasons. A swap seemed inevitable. They got wood, and we got Seagram's Seven. To this day, I will not drink Seagram's Seven. We could go to the 'E.M.' (Enlisted Men's) Club at night for a beer or two, and a movie. There was a different movie every night.

On an occasional Sunday, we would pack and go to the beach about an hour away. Yes, there really is a China Beach. The beach was wide and beautiful. Upside? There was plenty of beer. Downside? No women to stare at. 🙁

We had entertainers and athletes come visit us: The Hondells, Martha Raye, Chris Noel, Stan Musial, and Brooks Robinson. At the Freedom Hill Amphitheater, we were able to see, Arthur Godfrey, Dr. Billy Graham, and of course Bob Hope with his U.S.O. Christmas Show. In 1966, The Bob Hope Show included Phyllis Diller, Joey Heatherton, Anita Bryant, Carroll Baker, and Vic Damone.

For outstanding construction feats, MCB 10 was awarded the Navy Unit Commendation; the first for a MCB unit in Vietnam. MCB 10 was also picked as the "Best of type of the Pacific Fleet" for the year 1967. I am proud to have served with such a fine and well-awarded unit.

NMCB 10 started leaving Vietnam January 27, 1967, to return home. As we were leaving, another Battalion was replacing us. It took about two weeks to complete the exchange. We landed at Mugu Naval Air Station in California. Mugu is on the coast, south of and not far from Oxnard. Carol met me there. I would return to Vietnam in September 1967. One of my buddies, Larry Ray Riddle, from my reserve unit in Atlanta was in the Battalion that replaced us. He was killed in March 1967. MCB 10 was in Vietnam for nine months and had no combat related deaths. Larry's Battalion replaced us, and in less than two months they had three deaths. THIS WAR MADE NO SENSE! He and two other Seabees were killed by a road mine on a road that I had traveled many times. Young men died for no reason. The politicians would not let us fight to win. During the entire war the U.S. did not lose a single battle or fight. It was a search and destroy war. Land was not gained. I saw death and I smelled death. It is NOT romantic! I still have issues with Huey helicopters. They have a uniquely different sound. To me, Huey's meant either new fresh Marines or Soldiers were coming in or filled body bags were leaving. I will never forget seeing young men (most were younger than me) in body bags.

During home deployment we trained to build bridges over land. After building it, we had to drive over it to prove its worthiness. We went to classes, and built more huts. We also spent two weeks at Camp Pendleton for more combat training. We also had weekend training at a place called Conejo Grade (a.k.a., Camarillo Grade, a 7% steep grade). Conejo Grade is a mountain range near Thousand Oaks, California. Home duty was good. We were often permitted to leave the base early. I would go home and spend time at the pool and wait for Carol to come home.

In 1967, we were the 'Pacific Alert Battalion' meaning we had to be prepared at a moment's notice to be deployed. In August 1967, MCB 10 was deployed to Okinawa (a Japanese Island). We were stationed at Camp Kinser, a Marine Corps Camp on the west side of the island. This was a typical mount out. It could take as many as ten C-141 planes to move a Battalion from home base to its final destination. We stayed at Kinser for about five weeks waiting on assignment to Vietnam. We did a lot of work at the Marine Corps Base, like repairs, upgrades, etc., as well as spending a lot of nights on 'BC' (Bring Cash) Street. Okinawa was full of service personal (Marines, Solders, Seabees, and Airmen) waiting on deployment to Vietnam. The whole island catered to the military. When we left Okinawa, we boarded C-130's for the trip to Vietnam. Interestingly, this plane was built in Marietta, Georgia.

On August 29, 1967, we left Okinawa for South Vietnam. We landed at Gia Le Combat Base. From there we were airlifted to Dong Ha. Men from MCB 10 were spread all over the I-Corps area -- Quang Tri, Camp Carroll, Qua Viet, Phu Bai, Cam Lo and Khe Sanh. Charlie Company (my company) was assigned to Detail Golf and was sent to Camp Carroll. This was the first time a Battalion was so widely dispersed over such a large area.

When we landed, my sense of smell brought back memories of my first tour. The aroma was almost overwhelming. This was a combat zone in a third world country. There was the smell of death associated with gun powder, napalm, Agent Orange, and human excrement. A Porta-Potty would be a luxury to the Vietnamese in these areas.

Camp Carroll was the Command Post of the 3rd Marine Regiment and was located on a ridge just south of the DMZ (De-Militarized Zone). The Marines and Seabees had the outer perimeter. The Army had an artillery base in the center. Looking at the picture of the Camp, the Seabee Base Camp area is seen *below.*

The Army had 175mm Artillery, which could fire a projectile about 33,000 meters or 21 miles. The Marines had smaller Artillery -- 105mm and 155mm. We were tasked with building 300 huts, three galleys capable of handling 1,250 men, five clubs (Enlisted and Officer), twelve heads, and three shower facilities. There was constant Artillery firing, either in support of a nearby base, or into North Vietnam. We were working 12-hour days, seven days a week. During the Fall … it constantly rained. No matter what the conditions were, rain or shine, the work had to be done. *The war never stopped.* This was not like the Da Nang tour, where we got Sunday afternoons off. The area around Carroll was *very* hostile. We seldom left the Base. There were occasions when we left to go to other Fire Bases, such as The Rock Pile or Khe Sanh, to do one day jobs.

I did have to drive to Quang Tri one day in a pickup with a shotgun rider. I cannot remember why I was sent. We got back just before dark. There were incidents in my Vietnam experience when I was afraid, however, driving to Quang Tri was my most frightening moment. Often it was raining, especially during Monsoon Season, and the roads were mud-covered and narrow, and hard to drive on.

We could see North Vietnam and the South China Sea from Camp. It was during this time, Con Thien, a Marine Corps Combat Base, about three miles away and very visible to us at Carroll, was being blasted 24 hours a day. Often at night, we could see the Navy ships shooting from the South China Sea in support of Con Thien, or to a target in North Vietnam, or the DMZ. We could also see B-52 Arc-Light raids in the DMZ. This is the most awesome display of American fire power anyone could possibly see! One night, there was a B-52 raid between us and Con Thien. Not only did it wake us up, but the whole hut was shaking. Between what the Army and the Marines had, there was always someone firing into North Vietnam. On occasion, we were attacked, but nothing like Con Thien. Often the Fire Base west of us, *Khe Sanh*, would fire Artillery in support of Con Thien. Sometimes a short round would fall on us. When short rounds, or mortar fire was coming in, we would run to the mortar trenches to seek more safe shelter. Often, there was water in them, but they were much safer than being outside. During this time, I was offered a promotion to 2nd Class Petty Officer. The only catch was that I would have to stay on active duty for an additional year, *meaning* I would have to stay in Vietnam as well. Knowing that I would get the promotion as soon as I got back to my reserve unit I kindly said *"No!"*

In January 1968, Detail Golf was sent to Khe Sanh for the duration of the tour; about four months. This was a Fire Base west of Camp Carroll that would remain under siege for the next two months, the longest and bloodiest siege in Vietnam. Once you were at Khe Sanh, you were not expected to leave for at least two months. Khe Sanh was supplied by air. Most of the time the planes could not land due to enemy artillery and the supplies had to be slid out with parachutes. I was blessed, because some of my friends did not make it out of Khe Sanh alive. Khe Sanh was under siege for 67 days and was not declared safe until late March 1968.

On December 6th, our Camp was hit by three mortar rounds. Damage was minimal, but a couple of unfinished huts were damaged. The VC (Viet Cong) come in fast, set off a few mortar rounds and quickly leave (didi mao), however, mostly for harassment purposes. Over 1,400 men were killed on their last day in country. When it's close to your time to leave all kinds of thoughts go through your head. I left Camp Carroll on December 9, 1967. I had to stay at a Marine Corps exit Camp for a couple more days, finally flying out of Da Nang on Dec. 13th. One month later, the north would launch their Tet Offense. That meant that the North Vietnamese would start the biggest offensive push into South Vietnam of the war. I was very lucky, because I left Vietnam in December and on January 31st, 1968, 245 men were killed there in the worst day of the war!

There has been a lot of talk and discussion about drug use in Vietnam. I made two tours that consumed the better part of two years. At no point did I see any drug use. I'm not saying it wasn't there, I am saying I didn't see it. I understand towards the later part of the war, drug use was far more prevalent.

On my last trip home, I was one of the last to board the commercial (Continental Air Lines) aircraft, called a 'Freedom Bird,' therefore, I flew in the first-class section. Regardless of rank, all men were boarded from rear to front of the plane. We flew into Norton Air Force Base, where Carol met me. She took me straight to the motel so that I could quickly get out of that uniform, and she had Champagne waiting, as well. She already had everything packed and was ready to leave for Atlanta. When I landed it was snowing.

I exited active-duty at the Naval Air Station (NAS-Atlanta) in Marietta, Georgia, on 23 December 1967. I returned to my Reserve Unit in January 1968, where I was promoted to Petty Officer 2nd Class on March 5, 1968. I stayed in the Reserve Unit for two additional years, attending monthly meetings, and doing a two week tour in Gulfport, Mississippi, in 1969. At that time, I learned Carol was pregnant with Scarlett, who was born September 5, 1969. On January 8, 1970, I completed my military requirements, and was honorably discharged. I am proud of my service to our country and will never regret my serving in our U.S. Navy's Seabees.

Carol was packed, and ready, to leave for Atlanta, after I got back from Vietnam. I only needed to change out of my uniform back at the motel, drink a little bit of that Champagne, and start driving home.

RICHARD WRIGHT

U.S. Army
770-883-2614
PoohBear@GreySteele.com

I was working in the shipyard and had just turned 17. My girlfriend and I went to see "Jumping Jacks," a movie starring Dean Martin and Jerry Lewis. It was all about the fun and adventure of being a Paratrooper. On Monday morning, I quit my job at the shipyard and went to the Army recruiting office. I told the recruiter I wanted to be a Paratrooper.

This was 1952, and The Korean War was in full swing. He said, "I think we have an opening." About a week later, I was on a train for Richmond, Va., where I took my physical and was sworn in. From there, I went to Ft. Meade, MD., where I was processed and tested. From there, I went to Camp Breckenridge, Ky., for basic training.

I was working in the shipyard and had just turned 17. My girlfriend and I went to see "Jumping Jacks," a movie starring Dean Martin and Jerry Lewis. It was all about the fun and adventure of being a Paratrooper. On Monday morning, I quit my job at the shipyard and went to the Army recruiting office. I told the recruiter I wanted to be a Paratrooper.

This was 1952, and The Korean War was in full swing. He said, "I think we have an opening." About a week later, I was on a train for Richmond, Va., where I took my physical and was sworn in. From there, I went to Ft. Meade, MD., where I was processed and tested. From there, I went to Camp Breckenridge, Ky., for basic training.

At that time, the 101st was not an Airborne unit. We wore the Screaming Eagle patch without the airborne tab. The camp was still the same buildings from World War II. Not in the best of conditions. At least they had a PX where you could get your beer at 15 cents.

After basic, I went to Ft. Benning, Ga., for jump school. Upon completion of jump school, I volunteered for Korea. I assumed I would be assigned to the 187th Airborne Regimental Combat Team, the only Airborne unit in Korea.

When I arrived in Korea, the 187th was only in need of medics and commo men. It seems a lot of jump school graduates were volunteering for combat looking for adventure. We were, after all, "ten feet tall and bulletproof." There were three of us who had gone through basic and jump school together. One was assigned to the 7th Infantry Division, one to the 40th Infantry Division,

and I was assigned to the 2nd Infantry Division. They weren't interested in the buddy system. I was assigned to the machine gun platoon of M Co. 3rd Battalion, 9th Infantry, where I spent the next 13 months. After rotating home, I was assigned to the 11th Airborne Division at Fort Campbell, Ky., until I was discharged in 1955.

When my 3-years hitch was up, I decided I did not want to make the Army my career. I was in the 11th Airborne Division at Ft. Campbell, Ky. I was in the Service Company of the 188th Infantry (Airborne). After being moved from being an Infantryman to working the supply side of things didn't exactly set my world on fire.

The 11th was preparing for Operation Gyroscope and would spend the next three years in Germany. Operation Gyroscope was a project started by the United States military after World War II that was active from 1947 to 1956. The plan was to ship soldiers out of the U.S. state of California instead of New York. Although there were exceptions since the 11th Airborne Division was transferred from Fort Campbell, Kentucky to Augsburg and Munich, Germany in 1956 out of New York to Bremerhaven by troopships as part of Operation Gyroscope. I only had a few months left and didn't want to sign up for three more years. They brought in a typist and a sewing machine, asking who wanted to go, and they assigned those to positions. A guy could be an E-5 if he chose to stay, he could become a master sergeant. I decided that was not for me.

After the Army, I used my GI bill to go to school. While in school, I had a part-time job with a bank and ended up making banking my career. The bank I worked for wanted all officers to have an MBA or Law degree. They paid for me to go to law school.

I spent 13 months with the 2nd Infantry Division in Korea and was on and off the front lines. One time they had the riflemen pull back except for those of us that had machineguns in bunkers. They dropped artillery and mortar rounds on our positions to repel the Chinese attack. The brass links piled so high I had to keep brushing them back to make room. I had the World War II M1917A1 Caliber .30 Heavy Machine Gun and fired about 10,000 rounds that night. I had to change the barrels twice due to the heat.

At night I wouldn't fire the machine gun so as not to mark myself as a target. If I heard anything or we were probed, I threw hand grenades. I had plenty of what we called the pineapple grenades. The Mk 2 was gradually phased out of service as the M26-series (M26/M61/M57) grenade was introduced during the Korean War. Due to the tremendous quantity manufactured during World War II, the Mk 2 was still in limited issue with the US Army. We threw them every night we had contact. It was too dangerous with the tracers giving away your position to fire the machine gun.

In Korea, you have freezing cold or heat. For me, though, the rain was the worst. Everything you had was wet and no way to get dry.

After the truce was signed, we pulled back and started rebuilding bunkers and laying barb wire until sometime in November. At that time, we went into Corp reserve, where I spent the remainder of my time.

In early July of 1953, we were on the front line in support of a rifle company.

One night, we were hit by a Chinese battalion, and the rifle company was ordered to pull back, leaving the machine guns in bunkers. They then called in artillery and mortar fire on the position. The combination of four machine guns and the artillery stopped the Chinese, and the line was not breached.

The quad .50 had the huge searchlights on the hill behind us. They did light up the Chinese but lit us up too. Very scary being blinded and knowing the enemy could see you. I remember the motto of the searchlight outfit behind us, "You find em, we blind em."

The Chinese would often follow a patrol into the wire opening and through the mine fields and once they entered, they would come through the same opening later at night to attack us. We were on 100% alert every night.

Around this time, a close air support aircraft, I think, it was an F-4U Corsair crashed near our position. The quad 50 units behind us on a higher hill kept continuous covering fire until a tank was sent out to pick him up.

I've been so lucky so many times in Korea. One time a .50 caliber round hit a sandbag next to me.

By far Ft. Campbell, Ky. was my favorite. It was 50 miles from Nashville, and my buddy and I would go a couple of times a month to go to The Grand Ole Opry. There was a bar around the corner from the Ryman called Mom's Place (it is now Tootsie's Orchid Lounge). Mom took a liking to me, and my buddy, Tom Cavender, and always had free tickets for us to the Opry. Mom's husband had lost a leg in WWI. He had been a machine gunner, and when she learned that I had been a machine gunner, she started referring to us as "her boys".

There was an upstairs room connected to the Ryman where the pickers and singers would drink in between their acts. On several occasions, Mom sent us up to sit and drink with them. When they all went back on stage for the midnight finale, they took us with them one night. We got to sing on The Grand Ole Opry.

My least favorite was being in Korea. The cold, the heat, and most of all, the mud that seemed to suck the life out of you. Once The Truce was signed, we pulled back and rebuilt the bunkers and dug more trenches. Always filling and stacking sandbags. The Engineers were placing out anti-tank and anti-personnel mines. That was the beginning of what is now known as the DMZ.

The last jump I made before being discharged was one of my most memorable. When we drew our chutes for the jump, the guy behind me asked to exchange chutes. He had drawn a nylon harness, and I had cotton. We exchanged. After exiting the C-119 aircraft and checking my chute, I saw a jumper whose chute hadn't opened and was unsuccessfully attempting to deploy his reserve.

While watching this, I was not paying attention to where I was and ended up on top of another man's chute. His chute stole the air from mine, and it collapsed. I was able to get untangled, and my chute regained air. I landed without any further problems. When I got to the check-in point, I learned that the man I had exchanged chutes with was the one who's chute failed to open. That was just one of many times in my life when I know the man upstairs was looking out for me.

What stands out is that it was on a cold December Saturday morning upon graduating from airborne training on the parade field. The pride of accomplishing something that would stay with me forever. We had four weeks of hell to go through. You never walked, always running. If we did stop, it was for doing push-ups.

The first week lots of falling, left, right, back, and front. Of course, you never walked anywhere and always doing push-ups. The swing landing trainer, or what we called it "suspended agony," was the worse thing ever invented. It hurt more hanging there than in the real jump. The second week was the 34-foot tower. We had many that just refused to finish it. In the third week, we had to do four jumps from the 250-foot tower. Last week we had five jumps, with the final one on that Friday night.

I could never understand that I would be getting $50 a month to jump out of airplanes and only $45 a month for combat pay. The math for me at the time just didn't make sense. No wonder I ended up working in the banking industry for the rest of my life.

My Combat Infantryman's Badge. It reminds me of the rough times I spent in combat in Korea. At that time there were three ways to qualify for the CIB; 1) Killed in action, 2) Wounded in action, and 3) 30 days under enemy fire. I think there have been some changes and 30 days under enemy fire has been replaced with any engagement with an enemy.

The second would be my parachutist wings. Being a paratrooper was, after all, the reason I joined the army. I think the Good Conduct medal was probably the hardest for me to earn. I dodged a bullet several times when I got into fights trying to prove that a trooper could whip any ten straight legs.

My closest friend was Tom Cavender. He got out a couple of months after I did, and he spent some time in Portsmouth with me and my wife. We kept in touch for several years, but as we lived about 200 miles apart, we slowly lost touch.

While in basic, we use to hang by the window ledge of the second floor and drop to the ground. We were stupid for doing this. We had no idea how to make a parachute landing fall, something we would learn in Jump School. We felt that we were 10 feet tall and bulletproof. Lucky no one was hurt.

The night the truce in the Korean war went into effect at 10 pm, we had accumulated a huge amount of ammunition we didn't want to haul back. We began shooting all of it off. This one guy wrapped a machine gun belt of ammunition around a rifle grenade. The belt broke loose and wounded him. I guess he was the last casualty of the war. Lucky YouTube was not invented yet. It certainly was not funny then, but it is now.

When I got out of the Army, I used the GI Bill to go to school. I had a part time job working for a bank and ended up making banking my career. Later, I went to law school and earned a law degree. I ended my career in the banking industry in August of 1981. I was going through my second divorce and was fully vested in the pension and profit-sharing plan. I decided to make a massive change. I converted everything I had in the pension fund into stock in the bank and resigned. I gave my soon to be ex-wife power of attorney to sell our house and went to the airport where I bought a one-way ticket to Fairbanks, AK.

I lived in Fairbanks for fifteen months and experienced a lot of different and unusual activities. Among others, I went into the salvage business with a former Political science professor from Seattle. We operated a warehouse in Fairbanks as well as an operation at Prudhoe Bay on The North Slope. I also helped form and operate a fueling company for private aircraft at Fairbanks airport. I did various legal and accounting work for several small businesses. I traveled over most of the state and had a wonderful time.

I had to cut it short when my daughter had some serious health problems, culminating in her death in 1989. I sold my interest in the companies I was involved in and returned to the lower 48 to spend time with her. I'm now retired and living in Georgia.

Currently, I do not belong to any military associations.

I suppose I got more out of the Army than it got out of me. I got the GI Bill to go to school and to buy my first house. I don't miss the service, but I realize it helped me grow and mature. I was 17 when I went in and 20 when I got out. Had I not gone into the Army, I probably would not have had the quality of life that I've had.

The military gave me the strength to persevere through anything thick or thin. So many times, my life had been spared by the grace of God. I miss the brothers I served with and cannot find. Hopefully, someone I served with will show up some day.

I don't think I am one to give anyone advice about the Army. For one thing, today's Army is nothing like the one I served in in the 50s. We were still using equipment from WWII and also eating C-rations from the 40s. Today's soldier is better trained and equipped than we were.

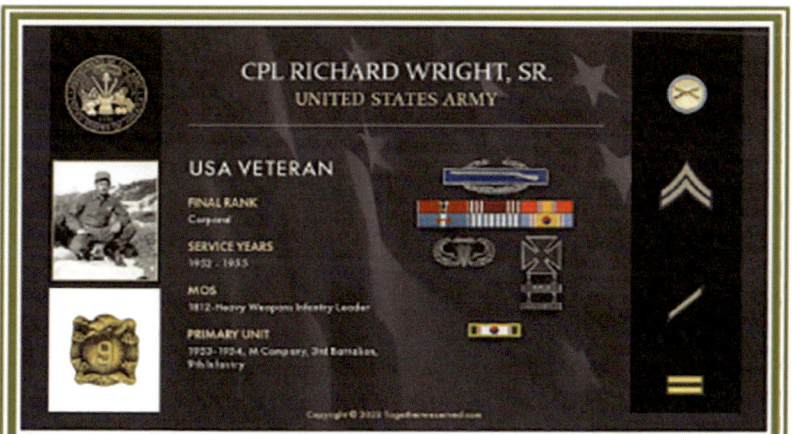

A couple of years ago I started writing my life story to pass on to my son and grandson. Doing that helped me bring my memories out. I have used that to help put down what I have for TWS.

~ The End ~

ACKNOWLEDGEMENTS:

The Veterans-For-Lunch-Bunch group is proud to acknowledge our **Publisher, Frank Eastland** of **Publish Authority**, who is renowned within the military Veteran community for delivering high-quality books in all formats that make for great reading for those who enjoy adventurous and heroics by our country's finest – our military armed forces. Also, we extend kind acknowledgments to **Teresa Evans** of **Publish Authority** for her skilled and dedicated assistance in the publication of this volume.

The **Editor** of our **Veterans-For-Lunch-Bunch** Book is a former U.S. Army Dual-Rated Aviator, Instrument Flight Examiner, and Test Pilot—**Terrence D. ("T.D.") Jorgensen** of Marietta, Georgia. Jorgensen pays homage to his high school Advisor and Mentor, **Dr. Robert A. McQuitty,** who helped to guide Jorgensen while he attended and worked on the Nürnberg American High School newspaper (the *"Trichter,"* which means in English, *"The Funnel"*) as the Sports Editor to begin with, but was elevated by Dr. McQuitty to be the Editor-in-Chief in Jorgensen's senior year when they received the coveted *1st* **Place Rating** by the Columbia Scholastic Press Association for mimeographed newspapers.

Jorgensen's labor of love on this very special book herein is, perhaps, his finest work of edited and enhanced war zone adventures by great American Armed Forces while serving in the European Theater and the Pacific Theater during WWII and in southeast Asia (*primarily during the Vietnam War Campaign*).

I would also like to acknowledge U.S. Navy Sailor-Veteran **Hal Burke**, who personally met with and extracted stories from a few of our beloved Greatest Generation Veterans who are of the envied Centennial age category and not of the computer generation. Great work Hal, and I thank you so very much for your contributions to our combined book of stories.

Finally, I wish to especially thank Counselor and Attorney-at-Law Mr. Duc Tran, for his personal vetting of potential Publishers we might use, and for his extremely-generous donation to the Book publishing project for our Veterans-For-Lunch-Bunch group. We couldn't have done it without you, Duc.

Terrence D. ("T.D.") Jorgensen, Editor

www.ingramcontent.com/pod-product-compliance
Lightning Source LLC
Chambersburg PA
CBRC091207010526
44107CB00021B/1258